BLACKS IN THE NEW WORLD
August Meier, SERIES EDITOR

Books in the Series:

Before the Ghetto: Black Detroit in the Nineteenth Century
DAVID M. KATZMAN
Black Business in the New South: A Social History of the North Carolina Mutual Life Insurance Company
WALTER B. WEARE
The Search for a Black Nationality: Black Colonization and Emigration, 1787–1863
FLOYD J. MILLER
Black Americans and the White Man's Burden, 1898–1903
WILLARD B. GATEWOOD, JR.
Slavery and the Numbers Game: A Critique of Time on the Cross
HERBERT G. GUTMAN
A Ghetto Takes Shape: Black Cleveland, 1870–1930
KENNETH L. KUSMER
Freedmen, Philanthropy, and Fraud: A History of the Freedman's Savings Bank
CARL R. OSTHAUS
The Democratic Party and the Negro: Northern and National Politics, 1868–92
LAWRENCE GROSSMAN
Black Ohio and the Color Line, 1860–1915
DAVID A. GERBER
Along the Color Line: Explorations in the Black Experience
AUGUST MEIER AND ELLIOTT RUDWICK
Black over White: Negro Political Leadership in South Carolina during Reconstruction
THOMAS HOLT
Keeping the Faith: A. Philip Randolph, Milton P. Webster, and the Brotherhood of Sleeping Car Porters, 1925-37
WILLIAM H. HARRIS
Black Georgia in the Progressive Era, 1900-1920
JOHN DITTMER
Abolitionism: The Brazilian Antislavery Struggle
JOAQUIM NABUCO, TRANSLATED AND EDITED BY ROBERT CONRAD

ABOLITIONISM

ABOLITIONISM
The Brazilian Antislavery Struggle

JOAQUIM NABUCO

TRANSLATED AND EDITED BY ROBERT CONRAD

UNIVERSITY OF ILLINOIS PRESS: *Urbana, Chicago, London*

LIBRARY OF CONGRESS CATALOGING IN PUBLICATION DATA

Nabuco, Joaquim, 1849-1910.
    Abolitionism.

    (Blacks in the New World)
    Translation of O abolicionismo.
    Bibliography: p.
    1. Slavery in Brazil. 2. Slavery in Brazil — Anti-
slavery movements. 3. Blacks — Brazil. I. Title.
II. Series.
HT1128.N213   326'.0981   77-7943
ISBN 0-252-00601-1

TRANSLATOR'S PREFACE

THIS TRANSLATION was made from the 1883 edition of *O abolicionismo* published in London by Abraham Kingdon and Co. However, in the spelling of proper names and some untranslated Portuguese terms, the translator has followed the 1949 edition published in São Paulo by the Instituto Progresso Editorial.

Because this English-language edition is intended to retain to the greatest degree possible the spirit and character of the original, the translator has refrained from altering either Nabuco's text or his original notes. All italicized and parenthetical elements within both text and original notes are Nabuco's. Where Nabuco placed an author's name within the text and cited his work without complete bibliographic information in the footnote, the translator followed a rule of direct translation without amplification in an attempt to avoid hopeless entanglement of original and translator's notes. However, to increase clarity of both text and notes and to put the reader in closer touch with Nabuco's world, notes designated "Translator's note," to distinguish them from Nabuco's original notes, have been added; and occasionally brief explanations have been inserted by the translator within brackets in both text and notes.

In the English-language citations throughout this work, in every case Nabuco translated from original English-language sources into Portuguese. In creating this edition, the translator has, whenever possible, gone back to the original source for the citation rather than retranslate from Portuguese into English. Some of these sources, especially within the text, were included by Nabuco in his notes. Other sources which the translator located and used are designated as translator's notes. In a few instances, however, when the original sources could not be located, it was necessary for the translator to retranslate from Portuguese into English. Such instances are so indicated.

Throughout this book Nabuco often makes reference to the Brazilian currency of his time. Currency units used in Brazil during the nineteenth century were the *milréis* (written 1$000) and the *conto*. A *conto* was equivalent to 1,000 *milréis* (written 1:000$000). Since this currency is generally unfamiliar to the modern reader, approximate U.S. currency values have been added in brackets whenever useful. In 1850 a *conto* was worth $580, and in the 1870s and 1880s approximately $550. See Stanley J. Stein, *Vassouras: A Brazilian Coffee County, 1850-1900* (Cambridge: Harvard University Press, 1957), p. 293.

For the reader interested in further study, a bibliographical essay emphasizing modern scholarly works on Nabuco and Brazilian slavery is appended.

As this edition nears completion, the translator would like to acknowledge the assistance of others who helped to bring this task to fruition. He expresses his thanks to Glenn Reitze, a friend, for having first aroused his interest in the task of translating. To John V. Lombardi, Robert Chrismer, August Meier, Robert A. White, Erdmute Wenzel White, Robin Anderson, and Ursula Conrad he expresses his gratitude for their helpful comments and suggestions, which undoubtedly improved this translation and the introduction. And he acknowledges with gratitude the assistance of Rita Zelewsky in smoothing over rough spots in the final manuscript.

Chicago, August 19, 1976   —*Robert Conrad*

CONTENTS

O abolicionismo has been made available to readers of English for several reasons. First, this is the most important book by any author to emerge from the last phase of the Brazilian antislavery struggle, and it is therefore a significant historical document which will be useful to English-speaking students of slavery and race relations. Second, it is an outstanding example of the protest literature which has sprung from the Iberian New World since Europeans first arrived there and began their seemingly endless exploitation of non-European peoples. Third, it not only outlines the problems which opponents of Brazilian slavery faced in the late nineteenth century, but also places that struggle within the context of Brazilian society. This book, in fact, is a portrait of that society, a personal and patriotic assessment of a nation at a critical moment in its history. Finally, despite the prominent place of its author in Brazilian letters, none of his major works has appeared in English. Thus this volume can serve as an introduction to the writings of one of Latin America's outstanding nineteenth-century thinkers.

The author of plays and poetry in his youth, Joaquim Nabuco might well have become a dramatist and poet of stature if he had not been confronted during the course of his life by tasks which seemed more important to him than creative literature. Like so many of his contemporaries in Latin America, he was distracted from purely literary pursuits by his involvement in politics, journalism, and government service. His interests were broad, and he was capable of undertakings as diverse as literary criticism —*Camões e os Lusiadas (Camões and the Lusiades)*—or a massive defense of Brazil's claim to territory in the Amazon basin—*O direito do Brasil (The Rights of Brazil)*—and works which deal with the problems, politics, and life of the Brazilian people. In this last group are his best works, those that unquestionably made him one of the major writers of nineteenth-century Latin America. Among them are his autobiographical *Minha formação (My Education)*, a historical account of his father's political career entitled *Um estadista do Império (A Statesman of the Empire)*, and this antislavery classic.[1]

Born in the northeastern province of Pernambuco in 1849, Nabuco was the descendant of eminent politicians and aristocratic Portuguese families who had made their home in Brazil since the sixteenth century, the wealthy owners of slaves and large plantations.[2] Though most members of his class were obviously rendered unsuitable by their origins for leadership in a radical social movement, it was undoubtedly this privileged background itself which awakened Nabuco's outstanding talents and qualities of leadership very early in his life. Trained in Brazil's best schools, the Colégio Pedro II in Rio de Janeiro and the law academies of Recife and São Paulo, he received an excellent legal and literary education, which was broadened and enriched by association with such talented companions as the future statesman and abolitionist Rui Barbosa and the great "poet of the slaves," Antônio de Castro Alves.[3]

Nabuco's father was a senator, a leader of the Liberal party, and, through his membership in the Council of State, a close associate and adviser of the Emperor Pedro II. Thus, in addition to intelligence and a high social position, Nabuco inherited outstanding political connections which practically assured him an eventual seat in the Brazilian Parliament, an honor which he in fact was granted by party leaders of Pernambuco in 1878, the year of his father's death. As a boy in his father's home in Rio de Janeiro he met most of the leading personalities of the day—the prominent politicians, writers, and reformers; therefore from his early youth he was no stranger to authority, power, and talent.[4]

The greatest single influence of his early life was Senator

---

1. For a discussion of Nabuco's literary career, see Carolina Nabuco, *The Life of Joaquim Nabuco*, trans. Ronald Hilton (Stanford, 1950), pp. 215-25. For a list of the major writings of Joaquim Nabuco, see the "Suggestions for Further Reading" at the end of this volume.

2. C. Nabuco, *Life of Joaquim Nabuco*, pp. 3-9.

3. Ibid., pp. 10-15.

4. Ibid., pp. 34-35; Joaquim Nabuco, *Minha formação* (São Paulo, 1947), pp. 13-15.

Nabuco himself, whose words and thoughts were dogma to the
young student at the Colégio Pedro II.[5] The senator's long advocacy of legislation to free the newborn children of slave
women, which finally passed into law on September 28, 1871,
undoubtedly helped the youthful Nabuco to remove any doubts
he may have had about the slavery issue.[6] In fact, while still little
more than a boy he had joined the abolitionist cause, translating
articles from the British *Anti-Slavery Reporter* for his father,
writing a brilliant book-length condemnation of slavery, "A
escravidão," and joining the staff of *A Reforma,* the organ of the
radical wing of the Liberal party which his father led.[7] While
still a student in Recife, Nabuco had made a dramatic public
appearance as an opponent of slavery by undertaking the legal
defense of a black man whose multiple murders, committed as
acts of vengeance and self-defense, had aroused the city. In his
defense Nabuco opposed what he called "two social crimes,"
slavery and capital punishment, and he saved the accused man
from the death penalty. At the same time, he demonstrated the
honesty, idealism, and great oratorical skill which would serve
him well in the abolitionist campaign of the 1880s.[8]

After graduation from law school and brief legal and journal-
istic experiences in Rio de Janeiro, he traveled to Europe and
North America, where he held minor diplomatic posts in London and Washington. Wherever he went, he studied and learned,
but his experiences in England and the United States were particularly important in the consolidation of his political and
social views. In his autobiography, he wrote that London was
for him "what Rome had been for the provincials of the time of
Hadrian or of Severus," the universal city, mistress of the earth.
The British political system and the sophistication, wealth, and
power of the Empire fascinated him, and he entered the Brazilian Parliament in 1878, he later admitted, "under the influence of English liberalism, . . . an English liberal with radical

5. Ibid.

6. For references to the older Nabuco's role in the passage of this law, see
Robert Conrad, *The Destruction of Brazilian Slavery, 1850-1888* (Berkeley, 1972),
pp. 78, 83-84, 93, 104. A full account is in J. Nabuco, *Um estadista do Império,*
4 vols. (São Paulo, 1949), 2:368-75; 3:21-72, 119-22, 135-53, 183-233.

7. J. Nabuco, *Minha formação,* p. 30: Conrad, *Brazilian Slavery,* p. 152. "A
escravidão," perhaps too outspoken for its time, was finally published in 1949 in
the *Revista do Instituto Histórico e Geográfico Brasileiro* 204 (July-September,
1949):3-1o6.

8. J. Nabuco, "A escravidão," pp. 40-42: C. Nabuco, *Life of Joaquim Nabuco,*
pp. 19-20.

affinities." [9] By that date the leaders of the British and American antislavery movements—Clarkson, Wilberforce, Channing, Garrison, and Harriet Beecher Stowe—had become his heroes. He was inspired by their example and by that of his father, and he looked upon himself as their follower and imitator. In 1884 he revealed his respect and admiration for such predecessors when he used the pen name "Garrison" for a series of antislavery articles published in the *Jornal do Comércio* of Rio de Janeiro in an obvious act of homage to the former president of the American Anti-Slavery Society and founder and editor of *The Liberator.*[10]

Under such influences Nabuco naturally drew insights and inspiration from events and experiences of his early childhood, which he spent among slaves on an isolated plantation in Pernambuco. The effects of that period upon him are best revealed in his own words:

> The first eight years of my life were . . . in a certain sense those of my formation, instinctive or moral, definitive. . . . I spent this initial period, so remote and yet more in my conscience now than any other, on a sugar plantation in Pernambuco, my native province. . . . The population of the small domain, entirely closed off, like all other fiefs of slavery, from any outside meddling, was composed of slaves, distributed through the compartments of the *senzala,* the great black pigeon pen set close to the residence house, and of tenants, linked to the proprietor by the advantage of the mud house which he allowed them to use or the small plot for farming which he granted them on his lands. In the center of the slaves' domain stood the residence of the master, facing the grinding mills, and behind on a rise of land stood the chapel under the invocation of St. Matthew.[11]

Slavery was best symbolized for him by one unforgettable childhood experience which had determined, he believed, the course of his life:

> I was seated one afternoon at the head of the outside stairway of the house when I saw rushing toward me an unknown young black man of about eighteen years of age, who embraced my feet begging me, for the love of God, to arrange his purchase by my

9. J. Nabuco, *Minha formação,* pp. 81, 155.
10. C. Nabuco, *Life of Joaquim Nabuco,* p. 109.
11. J. Nabuco, *Minha formação,* pp. 157-60.

godmother so that he might serve me. He had come from some-
where in the neighborhood seeking to change his master, because
his own, he told me, punished him, and he had fled at the risk
of his life. . . . This was the unexpected way that I discovered
the nature of the institution which until then I had lived with
familiarly, without suspecting the suffering which it concealed.[12]

A description of the same plantation as it was when Nabuco
returned to it as a young man reveals the decay of the ancient
way of life of northeastern Brazil and some of the personal
causes of Nabuco's decision to struggle in favor of the slaves:

Twelve years later I returned to visit the little chapel of St. Mat-
thew where my godmother, Dona Ana Rosa Falcão de Carvalho,
rests in the wall at the side of the altar, and through the little
abandoned sacristy I penetrated into the enclosure where the
slaves were buried. . . . Crosses, which perhaps no longer exist,
over heaps of stones hidden by the nettles, were almost all that
remained of the opulent *fábrica,* as the complement of slaves was
called. . . . Below on the plain the green patches of sugarcane
sparkled in the sun as before, but the sugar factory smoked and
whistled with a sharp burst of steam, announcing a new life. The
ox wheel had disappeared into the past. Free labor had generally
replaced the labor of the slaves. . . . Of the old house there
remained not a trace. The sacrifice of the poor blacks who had
incorporated their lives into the future of that property no longer
existed except perhaps in my own memory. Under my feet was
everything that remained of them. Alone I invoked all my memories, and called to them by their names. . . . And there, too, at
twenty years of age, I resolved to devote my life, if it was given to
me to do so, to [this] generous race. . . .[13]

These may be merely the romantic and nostalgic words of a
middle-aged aristocrat looking back at his youth, but they also
suggest some of the complex sentiments and personal sorrows
which inspired him to take the road to leadership in the abolitionist movement.

.   .   .

The Brazil of Nabuco's day, with its tremendous social problems, was the product of more than three centuries of contact
and collision between three races in a tropical environment. For

12. Ibid.
13. Ibid., pp. 165-66.

historical reasons, in the meeting of these three races—the Indian, African, and European—the latter was the dominant group. The indigenous tribes—Tupinambá, Guaraní, and others —encountered by Portuguese explorers and settlers along the continent's coasts and rivers had been quickly eliminated, absorbed, or swept aside in the sixteenth and seventeenth centuries; by the 1880s, the period of the abolitionist movement, the descendants of the first inhabitants survived mainly in the economically less important or more isolated regions of the country. In comparison with the Portuguese and Africans, the Indians were minor actors in the national drama, contributing nonetheless to the amalgam of cultural and racial ingredients which was and is Brazil.

In contrast, during almost the entire span of Brazilian history, black Africans and their descendants played a preponderant role in the nation's economic and cultural development. The Portuguese—explorers, conquerors, and settlers—were the first to arrive from across the Atlantic; but with the rapid decline of the Indian population and the growth of a plantation system in the sixteenth century, blacks began to be brought from the new Portuguese African colonies to replace the original inhabitants. From the very beginning, non-Europeans, both native and African, were enslaved to produce valuable exports and to create viable settlements. The affliction of slavery was, to use Nabuco's words, "as old as our country. . . . It was like a virus which we imbibed for many centuries into our blood. Our whole social existence is sustained by this crime." [14]

Slaves performed every conceivable kind of manual labor in Brazil. They cut down the brazilwood trees which gave the country its name, created the sugar plantations which by the second half of the sixteenth century were scattered along the Brazilian coast from São Paulo to Pernambuco and beyond. Their labor built the first colonial towns: São Vicente, Salvador da Bahia, Olinda, and Rio de Janeiro. The enslaved Africans gathered the diamonds and gold from the streams and mines of the interior captaincies of Minas Gerais, Goiás, and Mato Grosso in the eighteenth century, and their labor helped to construct the magnificent baroque churches and palaces of the interior mining towns. In the nineteenth century, enslaved workers chopped down the virgin forests of the provinces of Rio de

---

14. J. Nabuco, "A escravidão," p. 13.

Janeiro and São Paulo and replaced the natural growth with millions of coffee trees, creating an industry which became the basis of the wealth and commerce of an entire region. Slaves performed most of the physical labor in the cities. They were craftsmen, builders, sailors, fishermen, seamstresses, textile workers, servants, vendors, and day laborers. "The negro is not only the field labourer," wrote a British resident of Brazil in 1846, "but also the mechanic; not only hews the wood and draws the water, but by the skill of his hands contributes to fashion the luxuries of civilized life. The Brazilian employs him on all occasions, and in every possible way—from fulfilling the office of valet and cook, to serving the purposes of the horse; from forming the gaudy trinkets, and shaping the costume which is to clothe and decorate his person, to discharging the vilest of servile duties." [15]

When *O abolicionismo* was first published in 1883, there was little reason to believe that slavery would end in Brazil within five years. Hundreds of thousands were enslaved on the nation's plantations, as others like them had been for centuries. Some of the slaves knew of the antislavery movement which had grown up in many Brazilian towns and cities in previous years, but most of them were entirely out of touch with the small band of Brazilians, including Nabuco, who openly championed the abolition of slavery. Amid persistent rumors of liberation, the age-old system of servitude remained essentially unchanged, and for most slaves there was no certainty that freedom would ever come.

Because of the great economic and social importance of slavery during the nineteenth century, most influential Brazilians had been reluctant to see it end, despite foreign pressure and some heartfelt opposition at home. As a result, in 1880, when Spain abolished slavery in Cuba, Brazil was the last country in the Western Hemisphere where the institution was still legal. The ending of the African slave trade after 1850 and the passage of the Free Birth Law of September 28, 1871, which declared the freedom of all children born after that date, doomed slavery to eventual extinction, but complete abolition still seemed a distant prospect. Although the institution was rapidly declining in the sugar-producing provinces of the northeast (Nabuco's native region), the coffee plantations of the south-central provinces of Rio de Janeiro, Minas Gerais, and São Paulo were still well

15. Thomas Nelson, *Remarks on the Slavery and Slave Trade of the Brazils* (London, 1846), pp. 23-24.

stocked with slaves, many of whom had arrived there after a long journey from the northeast; and coffee planters were buying slaves from their neighbors with the intention of exploiting their labor for years to come.[16] With many Brazilians determined to make full use of their existing bondsmen, it is not surprising that Nabuco feared slavery capable of surviving into the twentieth century, and that he saw his struggle as an urgent duty.

To understand him better, we should see him, not only as a product of his family traditions and personal experiences, but also in the context of the long national struggle against slavery. Obviously, the first opponents of the system were the slaves themselves, whose reactions were even more violent and radical than those of their counterparts in the United States. Because of the hardships slaves encountered in Brazil, suicides were common, flight and rebellion were frequent, and *quilombos*—runaway slave settlements such as the famous Palmares of the seventeenth century—were a common feature of the Brazilian landscape until the last days of slavery. However, few slaves of Brazil were ever able to gain complete freedom through resistance and rebellion, because they lacked unity and weapons, and because the forces of authority were always able to eliminate isolated clusters of runaway blacks and to suppress plantation or urban rebellions. Yet, that slave resistance was a never-ending problem for the master class is clearly proved by nineteenth-century police reports and newspaper advertisements for runaway slaves.

The roots of abolitionism in Brazil can be traced back to the early years of the nineteenth century. Though most free persons always accepted slavery as natural, sanctioned by God, and even entirely indispensable to the economy of the nation, even before independence was granted, some exceptional Brazilians and Portuguese made known their distaste for the institution. In 1817, as Nabuco reveals in *O abolicionismo,* leaders of a short-lived liberal revolution in Pernambuco expressed antislavery sentiments; and in 1823, the year after independence was achieved, the authors of an abortive constitutional project called for "the slow emancipation of the blacks and their religious and industrial education." [17]

---

16. For a discussion of the slave trade between the provinces, see Conrad, *Brazilian Slavery,* pp. 47-69.

17. *Annaes do Parlamento Brasileiro. Assembléa Constituinte. 1823,* 6 vols. (Rio de Janeiro, 1876-84) , 5:23-24.

In that same year, José Bonifacio de Andrada e Silva, Minister of Empire in the first independent Brazilian government, prepared an extraordinary *Memoir* on slavery which strongly urged an end to the slave trade in four or five years and an eventual end to slavery itself. "It is time, and more than time, for us to cease carrying on a trade so barbarous and butcherlike," wrote this famous leader of the independence movement; "it is time also for us gradually to efface every vestige of slavery among us, in order that we may be able, in a few generations, to form an homogeneous nation, without which we shall never be truly free, respectable, and happy." [18]

José Bonifacio's views were far from unique. Although abolitionism in Brazil did not have the strength and persistence it had in the United States during the first half of the nineteenth century, antislavery sentiments were often heard in the Brazilian Senate and Chamber of Deputies, especially when the slave trade was a topic of debate, as it often was before 1850. In books and articles some Brazilians expressed deep concern for the slaves and the effects that slavery was having upon their country.[19] Poets, playwrights, and novelists sometimes made known their opposition even before the 1860s, when the great romantic poet Antônio de Castro Alves recited his popular collection of antislavery poems, *Os escravos*, before audiences in Bahia and São Paulo.[20] Between 1848 and 1852, when the African slave trade was finally suppressed, several newspapers of Rio de Janeiro carried on an active crusade against slave traffic; one notable example is the journal *O Philantropo*, which advocated an end to the trade and encouragement of European immigration to Brazil as a means of replacing slave workers.[21]

---

18. José Bonifacio d'Andrada e Silva, *Memoir Addressed to the General Constituent and Legislative Assembly of the Empire of Brazil, on Slavery*, trans. William Walton (London, 1826), p. 16.

19. Among the most important Brazilian antislavery works of the nineteenth century, in order of their appearance, are Frederico L. C. Burlamaque, *Analytica acerca do commercio d'escravos e acerca dos malles da escravidão domestica* (Rio de Janeiro, 1837); A. C. Tavares Bastos, *Cartas do solitario* (Rio de Janeiro, 1862); F. A. Brandão, *A escravatura no Brasil* (Brussels, 1865); Agostinho Marques Perdigão Malheiro, *A escravidão no Brasil. Ensaio historico-juridico-social*, 3 vols. (Rio de Janeiro, 1866-67); André Rebouças, *Agricultura nacional. Estudos economicos. Propaganda abolicionista e democratica* (Rio de Janeiro, 1883); L. Anselmo da Fonseca, *A escravidão, o clero e o abolicionismo* (Bahia, 1887).

20. A valuable account of the antislavery impulse in Brazilian literature is Raymond S. Sayers, *The Negro in Brazilian Literature* (New York, 1956).

21. Other newspapers that opposed slave traffic between 1848 and 1850 were *O Grito Nacional, O Monarchista*, and *Correio Mercantil* (all of Rio de Janeiro).

As Nabuco reveals in *O abolicionismo,* Brazilian governments had taken serious steps during the previous sixty years to eliminate human bondage, but each attempt had awakened effective opposition. In 1826, under pressure from Great Britain, Brazil had committed herself to a treaty to abolish the African slave trade within four years. This pledge was confirmed by passage of a national law on November 7, 1831, which declared the freedom of all slaves entering the country from that time on. These commitments, however, lacked the support of most powerful citizens and were flagrantly disregarded. For example, the law of 1831 was openly violated for twenty years, while at least half a million Africans were smuggled into the country, most to remain in unlawful bondage for the rest of their days.

On September 4, 1850, a law was passed by the Brazilian Parliament under strong British pressure, declaring the slave trade equivalent to piracy and establishing effective measures for its suppression. Yet nothing was done to free the Africans who had reached Brazil after passage of the 1831 law.[22] As Nabuco was writing this classic protest, hundreds of thousands of slaves were still held in illegal servitude, including grandchildren of Africans imported after November 7, 1831. In 1870 Nabuco wrote: "More than five hundred thousand Africans came into our country and into illegal captivity. These five hundred thousand people procreated, had families. Today their blood is mixed with the blood of our entire slave population; thus it can be said that slavery in our country is in large part against the law, illegal." [23]

Despite this disregard for the legal rights of hundreds of thousands of people, when slavery was unexpectedly abolished in the United States many Brazilians, led by Emperor Pedro II, began to support legislation to free newborn children of slave women. What Brazilian reformers envisioned in the aftermath of the American Civil War was a moderate measure intended to end slavery slowly without harming the nation's agricultural economy; but, like earlier attempts to restrict slavery, the free-birth reform met strong opposition. As a result, Brazil's disastrous war with Paraguay (1864-70) was allowed to justify a long delay in passage of a free-birth law.

Fought for by leaders of both monarchist parties, notably the

22. Leslie Bethell, *The Abolition of the Brazilian Slave Trade* (Cambridge, 1970), pp. 345-46.
23. J. Nabuco, "A escravidão," p. 83.

Conservative Prime Minister, Viscount Rio Branco, and Nabuco's Liberal father, the free-birth legislation, known as the Rio Branco Law, was sanctioned at last in 1871 after a hard legislative battle. It did not provide, however, for the immediate freedom of newborn children. Instead, upon reaching the age of eight, these so-called *ingênuos* (a legal term meaning "freeborn," as distinguished from "freedman" or *liberto*) were to be obligated to serve their mothers' masters without pay until they reached the age of twenty-one. In accordance with the law, more than one hundred children were turned over to the government's keeping in exchange for thirty-year bonds. But, as Nabuco points out in this book, by 1883 several hundred thousand *ingênuos* were living in the slave huts, doing the work that children could, acquiring the habits and attitudes of their enslaved parents.

Though abolitionists welcomed the law—particularly Nabuco, since his father had so long supported it—they knew it was at best a compromise, a way to do something without immediately changing much of anything. Yet, despite its inadequacies, the Rio Branco Law practically silenced the opponents of slavery for eight years.

In 1879, however, a new and more powerful antislavery movement began, this time led by Joaquim Nabuco himself, who with renewed urgency picked up where his father had left off. As a new member of the Brazilian Chamber of Deputies, Nabuco took the issue to Parliament in 1879 and 1880, introducing a bill into the Chamber in August of the latter year to end slavery within ten years. In 1880, frustrated by an overwhelming rejection of this legislation, he turned from parliamentary tactics and established the Brazilian Antislavery Society (Sociedade Brasileira contra a Escravidão) and the propagandist monthly bulletin, *O Abolicionista*. Simultaneously, editors throughout the nation, notably the great black journalist José do Patrocínio, began to express abolitionist views, and newly formed emancipationist clubs began to hold regular meetings in every part of the country to express an unprecedented opposition to slavery and to release a few fortunate bondsmen as a token of their larger purpose. Nabuco well expressed the outrage of his fellow abolitionists:

> The nation that in the present century shall tolerate this regime with indifference, as immoral as it is barbarous, will be a condemned nation. . . . Brazil can live without depending upon the

pitiless and iniquitous exploitation of man by man. . . . Slavery
has been for her only an impediment to progress; it is a tree
whose roots sterilize the physical and moral soil wherever they
extend.[24]

Both patriotic and moralistic feelings had motivated the new
wave of antislavery activity which briefly swept the country in
1879 and 1880. Many Brazilians appeared convinced at last that
slavery was an evil, backward institution, humiliating to a Christian country and inimical to the moral and social standards of
western civilization at the end of the nineteenth century. The
leaders of the movement made a strong appeal to their countrymen through speeches in Parliament and in the theaters, through
pamphlets, editorials, and articles; some even called upon the
slaveholding minority to sacrifice their interests to the higher
needs of the nation.

Nabuco, himself a member of the elite, who understood as
well as anyone the attitudes of his own class, took the lead in this
appeal to the slaveholders. "No members will be more joyously
welcomed among us," he wrote in 1880, "than those landed
proprietors who courageously and nobly desire to look the
emancipation question in the face, and who, in place of opposing it, lend themselves to aid and direct it." To those same
landed proprietors he gave a warning:

> the law can deal with you in two ways: either by protecting you,
> or by calling you to account. You may take your choice. . . . If
> you become an insuperable barrier to each emancipation scheme,
> and recoil in terror from every step in this direction; then the
> blame will be yours alone, when the law, after so many frustrated
> attempts, shall like Lincoln with those Southern landowners whom
> to the last he would have spared, [proceeds] against you as if you
> were a belligerent and rival Power.[25]

In most of Brazil such appeals to slaveholders had aroused
more anger than humanitarianism. Only in the northeastern
province of Ceará, where comparatively few slaves existed owing
to poverty and drought, were the abolitionists impressively successful during the first phase of the campaign. Flourishing liberation societies there freed many bondsmen, and in many cases

---

24. "Manifesto of the Brazilian Antislavery Society," in *Correspondence with
British Representatives and Agents Abroad, and Reports from Naval Officers,
Relative to the Slave Trade* (London, 1881), p. 29.

25. Ibid., p. 30.

masters agreed to free their slaves without compensation. The movement in Ceará, which was particularly fervent in 1881, declined by 1882; but as Nabuco was writing this book, abolitionists in Ceará were planning the systematic campaign which would all but end slavery in that province by March, 1884. In fact, in 1883 Nabuco had already dedicated *O abolicionismo* to Ceará in recognition of that province's special role in the antislavery struggle.

Elsewhere, however, the slave system maintained its grip, and the proslavery reaction was correspondingly effective. Faced with an angry response, the strong surge of abolitionism which had seemed so threatening to planter interests in 1880 diminished by 1881, and only a few stalwart leaders remained involved, notably André Rebouças and José do Patrocínio. In the parliamentary elections of November, 1881, Nabuco and other abolitionist candidates were defeated, and it appeared to friends of abolitionism that the movement had all but dissolved. Writing from London in late 1882, Nabuco expressed fear that his Antislavery Society, still held together by a few friends, might die out altogether.[26] As he worked on his book, the abolitionist movement seemed so weak, its forces so disorganized and scattered, that he referred to it as merely an expanding current of opinion, rather than as a political party. This is the setting in which *O abolicionismo* must be seen.

Although he was removed from the direct struggle within Brazil, the young exile had an urgent message for his countrymen, and this he delivered in his book—practically the only propaganda vehicle left to him in 1883. To make Brazilians understand and oppose the system of forced labor which still afflicted their country, and which had afflicted it for more than three centuries, he enumerated the endemic ills which the nation still suffered as a result of its colonial heritage. He not only analyzed slavery, the African slave traffic, the place of black people in Brazilian society, the slow development of emancipationism, and the aims, tactics, achievements, and prospects of the abolitionist movement; he also described the damaging and demoralizing effects of slavery, monoculture, and large landholdings upon Brazilian politics, government, law, agriculture, industry, commerce, religion, labor, education, and the national

---

26. J. Nabuco, *Cartas a amigos*, 2 vols. (São Paulo, 1949), 1:83-88.

character. He expressed a deep concern not only for the plight of the slaves, but for the entire Brazilian nation.

Few persons could have anticipated the sudden surge of antislavery activity which carried the struggle into city streets soon after publication of this book. Few could have imagined the ebullient antislavery campaign of 1884 in the provinces of Amazonas and Rio Grande do Sul, or the renewed parliamentary struggle which ended in 1885 with the liberation of slaves sixty-five and older. Certainly, few persons could have believed in 1883 that four years later the conflict would reach the plantations themselves, that tens of thousands of slaves, urged on by abolitionists, would abandon their masters' estates, all but destroying slavery in the key province of São Paulo and forcing Parliament to end slavery suddenly in 1888 as an emergency measure to restore the nation to order.[27] In 1883, as Nabuco was finishing this call to action, none of these events could have been realistically predicted. However, he himself outlined the elements of Brazilian society—slavery's weakness in spite of its appearance of invincibility, and the people's growing impatience —which were essential to the triumph of abolitionism only five years later.

Though Nabuco could not look into the future, *O abolicionismo* is a prophetic book. Its author knew that emancipation alone would not solve the nation's problems. He knew that the fight against slavery would not end when the last bondsman was freed. Abolition would take precedence over other reforms, but other social changes would also have to be fought for once this basic step was taken, including a broadening of educational opportunities, political participation, and land ownership. Slavery meant more than the relationship between master and human property. "Slavery" meant "the sum of the power, influence, capital, and patronage of all the masters; the feudalism established in the interior, the dependence in which commerce, religion, the poor, industry, Parliament, the Crown, the entire State, find themselves before the massed power of the aristocratic minority." Abolitionism, therefore, would not cease to exist when the slaves were freed, but would be a continuing struggle against the power of the landlord class and against all the harmful effects—"demoralization, inertia, servility, and irresponsibil-

---

27. For detailed accounts of these events, see Robert Brent Toplin, *The Abolition of Slavery in Brazil* (New York, 1972), and Conrad, *Brazilian Slavery.*

ity"—of three centuries of bondage. "The task of annulling these influences," he wrote, "is certainly beyond the ability of one generation, but as long as this work has not been concluded, abolitionism will have a reason to exist. . . . The struggle between abolitionism and slavery is of today," he warned, "but it will be greatly prolonged."

The power of the written word cannot be determined with any accuracy, but the reader may wish to remember that the words contained in this book, hastily assembled during a brief stay in London, made a significant contribution to the ending of slavery in its last stronghold in the Americas. For this reason alone it is a document worthy of our study and respect.

AMAZONAS

Manaus

Amazonas

PARÁ

Belém

São Luis

Fortaleza

MARANHÃO

CEARÁ

RIO GRANDE do NORTE

Natal

Teresina

PARAIBA

Paraiba

PIAUÍ

PERNAMBUCO

Olinda

Recife

Palmares

ALAGOAS

Maceió

SERGIPE

MATO GROSSO

BAHIA

São Francisco

Aracaju

Salvador da Bahia

BAHIA de TODOS os SANTOS

GOIÁS

Cuiabá

Goiás

MINAS GERAIS

Diamantina

Sabará

Mariana

Ouro Preto

Barbacena

São João d'El-Rei

Vitória

ESPIRITO SANTO

SÃO PAULO

RIO DE JANEIRO

Campos

Petrópolis

Niterói

Campinas

São Paulo

Rio de Janeiro

Santos

São Vicente

PARANÁ

Curitiba

SANTA CATARINA

Destêrro

RIO GRANDE do SUL

Porto Alegre

Pelotas

0 50 100   200   300   400   500 MILES

BRAZIL

ABOLITIONISM

To Ceará

Il fait jours dans votre âme ainsi que sur vos fronts,
La nôtre est une nuit où nous nous égarons.

—LAMARTINE, *Toussaint L'Ouverture*

THIS is the first of a series of works intended to propose to the active mass of Brazilian citizens a set of reforms which are truly vital for our country if we accept the view that the life of a nation is not only physical but endowed, as well, with a higher moral purpose. The authors of these works will attempt to base their proposals upon the most realistic foundations possible.

For many reasons, frankly implied on every page of the present book, the emancipation of the slaves and of the *ingênuos* and the need to eliminate slavery from the constitution of our people —in a word, abolitionism—must take precedence over every other reform. In fact, all others depend upon emancipation, since the elimination of slavery will mean nothing less than the establishment of a new groundwork upon which our country will rest.

The volumes to follow this will have as their topics: economic and financial reform, public education, governmental decentralization, religious equality, foreign relations, political representation, and European immigration. Whoever the authors of these works may be, they will all be inspired by the same purpose: that of lifting Brazil to the level of a more useful segment of humanity, of enabling her to compete with the other Latin American nations now progressing about her. These authors will be motivated by the desire to develop an unconstrained Brazilian commonwealth, liberal and progressive, peaceful and strong.[1]

---

1. *Translator's note:* Nabuco asked Sancho de Barros Pimentel, a former deputy from the northeastern province of Sergipe, to write one of the works on political reform; he hoped that Rui Barbosa, a brilliant intellectual from Bahia, would do the work on religious liberty and that Rodolfo Dantas, a prominent political leader, would author the work on education. See J. Nabuco, *Cartas a amigos,* 1:103-4.

Fortunately, there already exists in our country a national conscience—in a formative stage, it is true—which is bringing an element of human dignity into our national laws and for which slavery, though a heritage from the past, is a true mark of Cain upon our national image. This conscience, which is tempering our soul and must one day humanize it, is the result of a meeting of two dissimilar currents: repentance among the descendants of the master class, and an affinity of suffering among those who have inherited slavery.

Thus I do not doubt that the present volume will receive the applause of a rather large number of my fellow countrymen. It will be welcomed by those who feel the torment of slavery as though they were themselves its victims and who know its agonies as a part of a larger torment: that of Brazil, outraged and humiliated. It will be well received by those who are courageous enough to believe—and brave enough to accept the implications of their belief—that a nation, like a mother, which does not exist for its least fortunate children, does not exist for its luckier ones either. It will be welcomed by those Brazilians who understand that slavery—the systematic degradation of human nature for venal and selfish ends—is as harmful and humiliating to the more cultured and well-placed person who inflicts it upon others as it is for the degraded and oppressed who suffer it directly. Finally, this volume will be applauded by those who know slavery's ruinous cost, its past and present effects upon our country, and who foresee the results of its indefinite continuation.

Such persons should eagerly welcome this message from an absent friend, sent from abroad, from where one's love of country is greater than when at home; from where, deprived of familiar scenes, with the imagination always at work, with that longing for home which allowed Garrett to write so forcefully,[2] with Brazil seen as a single entity in which men and parties, friends and foes, are fused together on a surface brightened by the sun of the tropics, patriotism seems a more liberated thing, more generous and more tolerant.

As for myself, there will be more than enough satisfaction if the seed of freedom, law, and justice which these pages contain grows into a good crop in the fresh soil of a new generation; and

---

2. *Translator's note:* João Baptista de Almeida Garrett (1799-1854) was a liberal Portuguese poet and politician who was forced into exile on two occasions during the 1820s. Like Nabuco, he established himself in London.

if this book helps unite the Brazilian abolitionists into one legion, to hasten the time, if only by an hour, when we will see Independence consummated by Abolition, when Brazil will be raised to the dignity of a free country before America and the world, as in 1822 it was raised to the rank of a sovereign nation.

—Joaquim Nabuco

London, April 8, 1883

CHAPTER I

What Is Abolitionism? The Work of the Present and of the Future

> A country respected, not so much for the vastness of its territory, as for the unity of its sons; not so much for its written laws, as for a conviction of honesty and justice in its government; not so much for its institutions of one kind or another, as for a real demonstration that those institutions favor, or at least do not oppose, freedom and the development of the nation.
>
> —EVARISTO FERREIRA DA VEIGA [1]

NOT FOR LONG in Brazil has there been talk of abolitionism and an abolitionist party. The idea of suppressing slavery through the liberation of the existing slaves appeared only after it had been decided that slavery should be eliminated by surrendering to it the one and one-half million persons whom it possessed in 1871, allowing it to end with them.[2] It was during the legislative session of 1879-80 that there appeared for the first time in and out of Parliament a group of men who adopted the *emancipation of the slaves,* not the limitation of bondage to the present generations, as their political banner and as the first condition of their association with any party.

The history of the opposition which slavery had faced until that time can be summed up in a few words. In the period before independence and in the first years thereafter, there existed in the generation influenced by the liberal ideas of the turn of the century a certain uneasiness of mind in the face of its acceptance of the need to achieve national liberation while leaving a great part of the population in personal servitude. Political events, however, absorbed the attention of the people, and with the Revolution of April 7, 1831, there began a period of unrest

---

1. *Translator's note:* Evaristo da Veiga was the outstanding liberal editor of the Rio newspaper, *Aurora Fluminense,* and a prominent member of the Chamber of Deputies during the 1830s.

2. *Translator's note:* Nabuco refers here to the Rio Branco or Free Birth Law of September 28, 1871, which, though it declared the freedom of children born to slaves from that day forward, left about 1.5 million persons in slavery.

which lasted until the Majority.[3] It was only in the Second
Empire that the progress of public custom made possible the first
serious resistance to slavery. Before 1840 Brazil was prey to the
traffic in Africans; the state of the country was accurately symbolized by the slave market of Valongo Street.[4]

The first national opposition to slavery was advanced against
the traffic alone. Its purpose was to suppress slavery slowly, by
prohibiting the importation of bondsmen. In view of the shock-
ing mortality of that class, it was thought that, once the in-
exhaustible African source was eliminated, slavery would be
steadily diminished by death, despite the birth of slave children.

With the importation of Africans ended by the energy and
decision of Eusébio de Queirós [5] and the tenacious will of the
Emperor—who went so far as to announce in a message that he
preferred the loss of his crown to the continuation of the traffic—
and with the deportation of the slave traders and passage of the
law of September 4, 1850, there followed a period of profound
calm. This period of lassitude, or of satisfaction with work
accomplished—of absolute indifference, in any case, to the fate
of the slave population—lasted until after the Paraguayan War,
when slavery was again forced to retreat and to lose another
battle. Like the first challenge, this second opposition which
slavery faced was not an attack upon the camp of the foe to
rescue its prisoners. It was merely a limitation upon the territory
subject to the enemy's incursions and depredations.

In fact, the law of September 28, which was promulgated after
a period of constant political crisis which lasted from 1866 until
1871, respected the principle of the inviolability of the master's
power over his slave. This legislation did not dare to penetrate
into the rural *prisons,* as though they were sacred places, forbidden to the state itself. And again, like the attempt of a

---

3. *Translator's note:* Between April 7, 1831, the date of the abdication of the
Emperor Pedro I, and July 23, 1840, when Pedro II, contrary to the Constitution,
was invested with full imperial authority (an event referred to as the "Majority") ,
Brazil was under the rule of a series of regents. During this period the country
was disturbed by a number of serious regional revolts.

4. *Translator's note:* The Valongo was a winding street near the harbor on the
north edge of Rio de Janeiro where merchants specialized in the sale of newly
imported Africans, who were housed there in large warehouses. It was a section
of the city which particularly fascinated visiting foreigners.

5. Eusébio de Queirós, Justice Minister from 1848 until 1852, is the person
who has traditionally been given the greatest credit for abolition of the slave
trade. The law of September 4, 1850, which declared the slave trade piracy, is
known as the Queirós Law.

weakened organism to cast off the effects of the gangrene which
invades it, there followed another calming of opinion, another
epoch of indifference to the fate of the slave, during which
the government itself forgot to comply with the law it had
championed.

It was only eight years later that this apathy began to be
modified and there arose a third opposition to slavery. This time
the attack was not against slavery's expansion as represented
by the traffic, or against its expectations as represented by the
productivity of the slave woman. Instead, the attack was launched
directly against its substance, against the legality and legitimacy
of its *rights,* against the scandal of its existence in a civilized
country, and against its prospects of brutalizing the *ingênuo*
in the same slave hut where it brutalized the slave.

In 1850 it was hoped that slavery could be suppressed with the
ending of the traffic; in 1871 it was to be done by freeing
the infant still to be born, though only in fact when he reached
the age of twenty-one. Today what is desired is to abolish it
by freeing the slaves *en masse* and by rescuing the *ingênuos*
from the servitude of the law of September 28. It is this last
movement which is called abolitionism, and only it will resolve
the real problem of the slaves by the gift of freedom itself.
Public opinion of 1845 regarded the purchase of Africans, treach-
erously shipped from the shores of their continent and smuggled
illegally into Brazil, as legitimate and honest. The opinion
of 1875 condemned the transactions of the slave traders but
judged it legitimate and honest to register the victims of that
same traffic after thirty years of illegal captivity. Abolitionism
is the point of view which, in turn, must replace this last outlook
and for which all dealings in human beings are crimes which
differ only in their level of cruelty.

Abolitionism, however, is not only this. As a movement it is
not satisfied to be the advocate *ex officio* of that part of the
black race still enslaved. It does not limit its mission to achieving the redemption of the slaves and the *ingênuos* in the shortest
time possible. This work of ours—of reparation, of shame, of
repentance, however it may be termed, of the emancipation of
the existing slaves and their children—is only the immediate
task of abolitionism. Apart from this, there is even greater
work to be done, that of the future: that of blotting out all the
effects of a system which for three centuries has been a school
of demoralization and inertia, of servility and irresponsibility

for the master caste, which made of Brazil the Paraguay of slavery.[6]

Even if total emancipation were decreed tomorrow, the liquidation of that system would give way to an unending series of questions which could only be resolved in accordance with the vital interests of the country, by the same spirit of justice and humanity which gives life to abolitionism. After the last slaves have been wrested from the sinister power which represents for the black race the curse of color, it will still be necessary to eliminate, through vigorous and forthright education, the gradual stratification of three hundred years of slavery, of despotism, superstition, and ignorance. The natural process by which slavery fossilized in its own molds the exuberant lifeblood of our people lasted during the whole period of our development; and as long as the nation does not know that it is essential to adapt to freedom every part of its being which slavery usurped, the effects of servitude will continue to exist, even when there are no more slaves.

Thus abolitionism is a new concept in our political history, and, as a result of it, as will be seen, divisions in the present political parties will very probably develop. Until very recently it could be anticipated that slavery would end in Brazil as it did in the Roman Empire, that it would be allowed to disappear without convulsions or violence. The whole policy of our statesmen was, until now, inspired by the desire to see slavery dissolve imperceptibly in our country.

Abolitionism is a protest against that dismal outlook, against the expedient of waiting for death to solve a problem which involves not only justice and moral rectitude but also political vision. Furthermore, our system is much too corrupt to withstand the prolonged effect of slavery without damage. Each year of that system, which degrades the entire nation to the advantage of a few individuals, will be harmful. And if today, perhaps, the appearance of a new generation, educated in different principles, creates a new response and causes society to enter again into the retarded process of spontaneous development, in the future only a major operation will save us, at the cost

---

6. *Translator's note:* Paraguay suffered a bad reputation in Brazil, probably because of the war and the series of dictatorships which were imposed upon that country after independence.

of our national identity: the transfusion into our system of the pure and vigorous blood of a free race.[7]

Our character, our temperament, our whole physical, intellectual, and moral organization are profoundly afflicted by influences which during three hundred years were infused into Brazilian society. The task of annulling those influences is certainly, beyond the ability of one generation, but as long as this work has not been completed abolitionism will have a reason to exist.

Thus, like the word "abolitionism," the word "slavery" is used in this book in the broadest sense. It does not mean merely the relationship of the slave to the master. It means much more. It signifies the sum of the power, influence, capital, and patronage of all the masters; the feudalism established in the interior, the dependence in which commerce, religion, the poor, industry, Parliament, the Crown, the entire State find themselves before the amassed power of the aristocratic minority, in whose slave huts hundreds of thousands of human beings live brutalized and morally mutilated by the system to which they are subjected. Finally, it signifies the spirit, the living principle, which animates the entire institution, particularly at the moment in which it begins to fear a loss of its timeless power with which it is endowed, a spirit which in the whole history of slave countries has been the source of backwardness and ruin.

The struggle between abolitionism and slavery is of today but will be greatly prolonged, and the period which we are now entering must be characterized by that struggle. For slavery the poverty of its adversaries is no advantage; nor is its own wealth. Its immense power, which abolitionists understand perhaps better than does the slave system itself, is of no significance. The outcome of the drama cannot be in doubt. Contests of this kind are not decided by money, by social prestige, or—however abundant they may be—by a paid clientele. "Brazil would be

---

7. *Translator's note:* Like many of his contemporaries in Latin America, Nabuco believed that European immigration would help to solve the endemic problems of the region. Much influenced by current European and North American philosophy, Nabuco, unfortunately, was capable of statements which seem to reveal some racial bias. Hints of such attitudes are perhaps apparent in Chapter XIII of this book and were particularly noticeable in Nabuco's arguments against importing Chinese workers to replace the slaves. See Robert Conrad, "The Planter Class and the Debate over Chinese Immigration to Brazil, 1850-1893," *International Migration Review* 9, no. 1 (Spring 1975).

the last of the countries of the world," says the "Manifesto of the Brazilian Antislavery Society," "if, having slavery, it did not also have an abolitionist party. It would prove that its moral conscience has not yet developed." We must add today, now that that conscience has appeared, that Brazil would be the most disgraced country of the world if, having an abolitionist party, that party did not triumph. It would prove that slavery had completed its work and sealed the national destiny with the blood of millions of victims whom it transported into our territory. We would then have lost forever the hope of one day establishing the country of Evaristo's dream.

CHAPTER II

The Abolitionist Party

> There is no greater honor for a party than to suffer for upholding the principles which it deems just.
>
> —W. E. GLADSTONE [1]

THE MEANING normally given to the expression "abolitionist party" does not correspond to that which is ordinarily understood by the word "party." In this respect, some explanations are essential.

There can be no doubt that there now exists a nucleus of persons identified with the abolitionist movement who, because of their opinions, find it difficult to continue belonging to existing political parties. Under the banner of abolitionism, Liberals, Conservatives, and Republicans struggle today without any other commitment.[2] Their party allegiance is nominal, without subordination to partisan will, but subject only to a higher human conscience. Just as in the last legislature several Liberal representatives judged it their duty to vote for the abolitionist idea in preference to their party's position, in future sessions there will be Conservatives ready to do as much, and Republicans who will prefer to fight for the personal liberty of the slaves rather than the form of government they desire.

The mere subordination of the interest of any of the present parties to the emancipationist ideal is enough to prove that the abolitionist party, when it arises, will satisfy a more elevated, more all-embracing, and more humane ideal than that of any of the other organized parties, all of which are more or less maintained and favored by slavery. The current of opinion whose development we are witnessing, which is still not launched on the way to its ultimate form, cannot yet be called a *party*.

A party is not just a point of view, but a point of view organized to accomplish goals. At the moment abolitionism is agitation, and it is still too early to determine whether it will

---

1. *Translator's note:* The original English source for this quotation could not be located. The quotation as it appears here is a retranslation made from Nabuco's Portuguese translation.

2. *Translator's note:* The two major political parties of the Empire were the Conservative and Liberal parties. In 1870 a Republican party, which was dedicated less to democracy than to the establishment of a federative republic, was founded.

someday become a party. We see it spreading powerful discord within the existing parties and to some extent constituting a sect apart, composed of schismatics of all the other political groups. In the Liberal party, this current of opinion has at least managed to expose the false foundations of our Liberalism. As for the Conservatives, we must await their return to the power which has so demoralized the Liberals to learn what effect abolitionism will exercise upon them. A new dissidence like that of 1871 would be worth an army to our cause.[3]

Only the Republicans remain to be considered. Abolitionism affected this party in a profound way, and for no other party did it accomplish as much. It was the law of September 28, 1871, and the belief, intentionally spread among the planters, that the Emperor was the leader of the movement against slavery, which suddenly enlarged the Republican ranks with a levy of volunteers from the most unexpected source. The *Republic* understood the golden opportunity which had been handed to it and did not ignore it. The party (I speak not of the point of view but of the organization) profited greatly from the sympathies which it earned by its spirited defense of the interests of the great landholders, undertaken notably by Mr. Cristiano Otôni.[4] On the other hand, after much hesitation, abolitionism was naturally recognized by many Republicans as a greater, more urgent, more just obligation, a duty in every respect more important than that of changing the form of government with the aid of the owners of human beings. It was in the strong proslavery democracy of São Paulo that the contradiction of these two social tendencies was most clearly manifested.

Even supposing that the republic is the natural form which democracy takes, the duty to raise the slaves to the level of men comes before the establishment of the democratic political structure. Abolitionism in a country of slaves is for the *astute* Republican the republic of opportunity, the republic which seeks what it can get and what it needs most and which does not render itself sterile by seeking an order of things from which the country can derive true benefits only when it no longer contains *masters* and *slaves*. On the other hand, the theory that

---

3. *Translator's note:* The reference here is to the deep schism in the Conservative party which resulted when Prime Minister Rio Branco supported the Free Birth Law in 1871, and when many other Conservatives, particularly those of northern provinces, backed the law as well. For an account of the debate on the issue, see Conrad, *Brazilian Slavery*, pp. 90-115.

4. *Translator's note:* Otôni was an engineer and ex-naval officer who was appointed to the Senate in 1879 to represent the province of Espírito Santo.

it is the monarchy's responsibility to end slavery and that the Republican party has nothing to do with the issue, a theory invented in order to sidestep the question and to solve nothing, gave to many who enlisted in the ranks of the republic a clear and sinister understanding of the true meaning of the alliance contracted in 1871.[5]

It is indeed difficult today for a Liberal or Conservative, who is convinced of the cardinal principles of modern social development and of the innate right in a civilized state of each person to his freedom, to make himself a satisfied, conforming member of organizations which hold the view that a combination of democracy and slavery is acceptable to human nature. It should be even more difficult for a Republican to grant an individual the right to take part in his country's government while at the same time giving him the authority to keep other people in abject servitude for their entire lives simply because he bought them or inherited them. And yet constitutional Conservatives, Liberals who are offended by personal government, Republicans who look upon the monarchical regimes of Britain and Belgium as degrading, exercise within the confines of their plantations a greater power over hundreds of individuals who are deprived of the dignity of *person* than does the African chief in his domain. Unrestrained, untrustworthy, and irresponsible, they exercise their power without any written law to control them, and with no opinion to censure them. What more must be said to assure us that the temerity with which our political parties assume the great names they use is gross political deception?

It is for this reason that abolitionism draws away from such parties those persons who were once attracted to them because of their historical names, in accordance with their particular beliefs. All three parties base their political aspirations upon a social reality in which equality is granted no importance. Abolitionism, on the other hand, begins with the principle of equality. Before debating the best way for a *free* people to govern itself—and that is the issue which divides the others—it tries to make that people free, eliminating the immense gap which divides the two social castes.

---

5. *Translator's note:* The Republican party program agreed upon in 1872 at a convention in the town of Itú in São Paulo denied that the problem of slavery was a Republican responsibility. According to this program, if called upon to rule, the Republicans would institute a cautious policy on slavery which would take into account the interests involved, especially the interests of the provinces with the largest number of slaves. This refusal to commit itself to abolitionism resulted in the attraction of many proslavery planters into the ranks of the party.

In that sense, abolitionism should be the primary school of all the parties, the ABC's of our politics. But it is not. By a strange anachronism, there was a Republican party long before there was an abolitionist point of view, and there we have the main reason why our political system is a Babel in which no one can be understood. What will be the outcome, however, of the inevitable disintegration of the parties? Will the abolitionists, separated by the sincerity of their ideas from parties which have only personal interests and ambitions as their reason for existence and principles only as pretexts, slowly merge into a common party, united at first by the social condemnation which they suffer and later by the hope of victory? Will there be an abolitionist party organized with a full understanding of its present and future mission, that of presiding over the transformation of a slave state into a free nation, eradicating the heritage of slavery?

This at least is what happened in the United States, where the present Republican party, when it entered the political scene, had to suppress a rebellion, to emancipate four million slaves, and then to create a permanent new system of freedom and equality in the states which had aspired to form the greatest slave power in the world on the shores of the Gulf of Mexico. This development of a single abolitionist party may well occur in Brazil, but it is also possible that, instead of uniting into one party, because of the great internal disputes among Liberals, Conservatives, and Republicans, abolitionism will work within the parties so as to divide them whenever necessary, as was done in 1871 to allow passage of the Rio Branco Law. In this case, abolitionism would unite the progressive elements of each party in a disinterested and temporary union, in a political alliance limited to a specific purpose. Or it might break up the existing parties and reconstitute them in a new form without, however, creating a single united party.

The advent of abolitionism coincided with the establishment of direct elections.[6] And it has been strengthened by the force

6. *Translator's note:* When the abolitionist movement began to manifest itself strongly in 1879 and 1880, electoral reform was also being debated in the Brazilian General Assembly. The electoral reform law promulgated on January 9, 1881, provided for direct rather than indirect elections, created new electoral districts, and granted former slaves voting privileges equal to those of other citizens. The latter concession dramatizes Brazil's characteristically democratic racial tendencies, but its real importance was decreased by the income requirements of the electoral system which barred the vast majority of Brazilians from the polls regardless of racial origin.

of public opinion, which has been marshaled by the newspapers, now so inexpensive that they reach every class and are thus a significant factor in the democratization of the nation. All these factors must be considered if we wish to understand how the abolitionist movement will eventually be constituted.

Meanwhile, the term "abolitionist party" as used in this book will mean only the abolitionist movement, the current of opinion now developing from north to south. It is clear that the group of persons who have revealed their support for that movement are more than the embryo of a party. If, in fact, by some chance event an abolitionist cabinet were organized tomorrow, that solid abolitionist core would have an unexpected advantage, as great at least as that of the two official parties—if, that is, a political party amounts to nothing more than seekers after sinecures and political honors, candidates for paid employment, clients of ministers, and trainbearers to the government.

It is enough to remember that the more the government parties are fragmented, the greater are their retinues. Power among us, unfortunately, is the kingdom of spontaneous growth, and this is one of the unquestioned results of the servility which slavery left in its path. Any branch or twig, no matter how withered and dry, left for a night in the breath of that privileged atmosphere, appears the following morning covered with leaves. There is no denying the truth of the formula "Power is Power." It is our entire history. It is a phrase which sums up the experience of all our public personalities, which stands at the root of all their calculations. No independent belief even slightly at variance with that of the government can command the abundant clientele of the two parties which take turns distributing patronage and guarding the coffers of privilege. No such opinion can pass out jobs and favors and so find assembled about it and at its service all the dependent and needy segments of the population in a country left worm-eaten and destitute by slavery. This alone characterizes the difference between abolitionism and the two constitutional parties. The power of the latter is commensurate with the power of slavery as a private and public institution, whereas that of abolitionism is the power solely of forces now beginning to protest against such a monopoly—over land, capital, and labor— a monopoly which makes slavery a state within a state, a hundred times more powerful than the nation itself.

CHAPTER III

The Mandate of the Black Race

> If the native intelligence and buoyant indepen-
> dence of Britons cannot survive in the dank and
> baleful climate of personal slavery, could it be
> reasonably expected that the poor Africans, un-
> supported by any consciousness of personal dignity
> or civil rights, should not yield to the malignant
> influences to which they had so long been sub-
> jected, and be depressed even below the level of
> the human species?
>
> —WILLIAM WILBERFORCE [1]

THE ABOLITIONIST MANDATE is a twofold task uncon-
sciously accepted by those who undertake it, but in both respects
it is an undeniable responsibility. The abolitionist is the unpaid
advocate of the members of two social classes who otherwise
would have neither a way to claim their rights, nor even
an awareness of them. These classes are the slaves and the
ingênuos.[2] The reasons that this tacit support imposes upon us
an unforsakeable obligation are not purely—for some not even
mainly—motives of humanity, compassion, and generous defense
of the weak and oppressed.

In other countries the propaganda of emancipation was religious, preached from the pulpit, fervently supported by the
various churches and religious communities. Among us the
abolitionist movement unfortunately owes nothing to the state
church. On the contrary, the ownership of men and women by
the convents and by the entire secular clergy completely demoralized the religious feelings of masters and slaves. The slaves
saw nothing in the priest but a man who could buy them,
while the masters saw in him the last person who would think
to accuse them. Our clergy's desertion of the role which the

---

1. *Translator's note:* From *An Appeal to the Religion, Justice, and Humanity
of the Inhabitants of the British Empire, in Behalf of the Negro Slaves in the
West Indies* (London, 1823).

2. *Translator's note:* This term *(ingênuos)* has been left untranslated because
it defies accurate translation into a single English word. As stated in the translator's introduction, it was a legal term meaning "freeborn" as distinguished
from "freedman" or *liberto*. In Nabuco's period it referred specifically to the
children of slave women born after September 28, 1871, who were to attain their
complete freedom at the age of twenty-one.

Gospel assigned to it was as shameful as it could possibly have been. No one observed it taking the side of the slaves; no one saw it using religion to ease the burdens of their captivity, or to propose moral truths to the masters. No priest ever tried to stop a slave auction; none ever denounced the religious regimen of the slave quarters. The Catholic Church, despite its immense power in a country still greatly fanaticized by it, *never* raised its voice in Brazil in favor of emancipation.

If what gives strength to abolitionism is not mainly religious feeling, deformed by the clergy itself and so not the lever of progress which it should be, the abolitionist cause is also not generally inspired by a spirit of charity and philanthropy. In England the struggle against slavery was a religious and humanitarian movement, determined by feelings unrelated to politics, except to the extent that one can refer to the social morality of the Gospel as political. By contrast, abolitionism in Brazil is above all a *political* movement, with which, undoubtedly, the interests of the slaves and compassion for their fate powerfully concur, but which is born of a different purpose: the hope of reconstructing Brazil on the basis of free labor and of uniting the races in freedom.

Abolitionism did not possess in other countries the character of a basic political reform, because elsewhere the black race was not wanted as a permanent part of the population nor as a homogeneous element of society. The free black man would remain in the colonies; he would never be an electoral force in England or France itself. In the United States, events occurred with such speed and developed in such a way that Congress from one day to the next was forced to convert the former southern slaves into American citizens with the same rights as the rest, but this was one of the unforeseen results of the war. There the abolition of slavery did not have this broader meaning until the passage of the Fourteenth Amendment, and no one dreamed of seeing the black man obtain both his freedom and the vote at one and the same time.

In Brazil the question is not, as in the European colonies, a movement of generosity in favor of a class of people who are victims of an unjust oppression at a great distance from their shores. Nor is the black race for us an inferior race outside the community or isolated from it, whose well-being affects us like that of some native tribe mistreated by European invaders. For us the black race is an element of great national importance

closely associated by countless organic relationships to our
reality, an integral part of the Brazilian nation. Moreover,
emancipation does not mean an end only to the martyrdom of
the slave; it means as well the simultaneous elimination of the
two opposite types who in essence are the same: the *master* and
the *slave*.

It is this point of view, of basic importance to emancipation,
which causes us to defend the rights of the slaves and their
children, called *ingênuos* through a narrow use of the word
which well reveals the importance placed upon fictions so greatly
contrasting with reality. Of these rights the slaves and the
ingênuos can hardly be conscious; and if they are conscious of
them, they cannot make themselves heard because of the civil
death to which they are subjected. We accept this mandate as
political men with political motives, and thus we represent the
slaves and the *ingênuos* in the capacity of Brazilians who will
regard their own title to citizenship as imperfect as long as there
are Brazilians who remain slaves. Thus we represent them in
the interests of our country and on our own behalf.

Who can say that the black race does not have the right to
protest before the world and before history against the conduct
of Brazil? This right to accuse has been provisionally renounced;
the black man calls not upon the world, but only upon the
generosity of a country which slavery gave to him as a homeland.
Is it not time that Brazilians listened to that plea?

In the first place, the part of the national population which
is descended from the slaves is at least as large as the part
descended exclusively from the masters; this means that the
black race gave us a people. In the second place, everything
which has existed until today in the vast territory called Brazil
was constructed or cultivated by that race; this means that it
was the blacks who built our country. For three hundred years
the African has been the main instrument of occupation and
preservation of our territory by the European, and during that
long age their descendants mixed with our people. Where the
black man has not yet appeared, the country looks like that
seen by the first European explorers. All of man's struggle with
nature, the conquest of the soil for habitation and agriculture,
roads and buildings, sugar plantations and coffee groves, the
house of the master and the huts of the slaves, churches and
schools, customs houses and post offices, railroads and telegraph
lines, academies and hospitals—everything, absolutely everything
that exists in our land as a result of human toil, as well as the

use of labor and the accumulation of wealth, is none other than a gratuitous donation from the race that toils to the race that forces it to toil.

Through these countless sacrifices, through these sufferings, whose terrible links with the slow progress of the country make Brazilian history one of the most melancholy episodes in the settlement of America, the black race created a country for others which it might far more reasonably call its own. Mentally remove that race and its labor, and the greater part of Brazil will be little more than a deserted land; if much at all, a second Paraguay, Guaraní and Jesuitic.

Under these circumstances, has not the time arrived for us to renounce the exploitation of the last representatives of that unfortunate race? When Vasconcelos said that our civilization had come from the coast of Africa, he clearly but unintentionally revealed the crime which our country committed when it enslaved the very persons who civilized it.[3] We have seen the importance of this race in the formation of our people. Modern slavery rests upon a foundation different from that of the slavery of the ancient world: the color black. No one thinks of reducing white men to bondage; for this blacks alone are reserved. However, we are not exclusively a white people and so should not tolerate this curse of color. On the contrary, we should do everything possible to cast it off.

Speaking collectively, slavery never poisoned the mind of the slave toward the master—fortunately for us—nor did it arouse between the two races that two-way loathing which naturally exists between oppressor and oppressed. For this reason, the contact between the two races outside slavery was never bitter, and the man of color found every avenue open before him.[4] The debates in the last legislature and the liberal way the

---

3. *Translator's note:* Nabuco refers to Bernardo Pereira de Vasconcelos, a prominent Brazilian parliamentarian of the 1830s and cofounder of the Conservative party.

4. *Translator's note:* Modern scholarship has begun to contest this comfortable view. See, for example, Florestan Fernandes, *The Negro in Brazilian Society* (New York, 1969), and A. J. R. Russell-Wood, "Colonial Brazil," in David W. Cohen and Jack P. Greene, eds., *Neither Slave Nor Free: The Freedman of African Descent in the Slave Societies of the New World* (Baltimore, 1972), pp. 84-133. For recent statements on the question of race relations in Brazil by a sociologist and a historian, see Octavio Ianni, "Research on Race Relations in Brazil," in Magnus Mörner, ed., *Race and Class in Latin America* (New York, 1970), pp. 256-78; and Arthur F. Corwin, "Afro-Brazilians: Myths and Realities," in Robert Brent Toplin, ed., *Slavery and Race Relations in Latin America* (Westport, Conn., 1974), pp. 385-437.

Senate agreed to the political eligibility of the freedmen (that is, the extinction of the last vestige of inequality carried over from slavery) prove that in Brazil color is not, as in the United States, a social prejudice with such built-in obstinacy that little can be done for the person victimized by it, even by character, talent, and merit. This fortunate harmony in which the different elements of our nationality live is for us a benefit of the greatest importance.

It is said that, when Antônio Carlos was about to die, a man appeared at the house where the great orator was wasting away and asked to see him.[5] An order had been given not to allow any unknown person to enter the room of the dying man, and the friend responsible for enforcing this command was compelled to deny the visitor the favor of seeing the last of the Andradas before his death, a favor he was begging for with tears in his eyes. At last, observing the desperate insistence of the stranger, the friend guarding the door asked, "But why do you want so much to see Senhor Antônio Carlos?" "Why do I want to see him!" the man replied in an explosion of anguish. "Don't you see my color? If it were not for the Andradas, what would we be in Brazil? It was they who gave us a country!"

Yes, it was they who gave a country to the *free* men of color, but we in turn must grant that country to those not yet free. Only in this way can we say that Brazil is a nation too proud and generous to allow Africans and the Brazilian-born to be slaves solely because they belong to the race which made of Brazil what it is today.

---

5. *Translator's note:* Antônio Carlos Ribeiro de Andrada was the brother of the more famous José Bonifacio de Andrada e Silva, the "patriarch of Brazilian independence." The Andrada brothers were early advocates of the abolition of the slave trade and of the gradual emancipation of the slaves.

CHAPTER IV

The Nature of the Abolitionist Movement

> It is not by personal, direct action on the mind of the slave that we can do him good. Our concern is with the free. With the free we are to plead his cause. And this is peculiarly our duty, because we have bound ourselves to resist his own efforts for emancipation. We suffer him to do nothing for himself. The more, then, should be done for him.
>
> —WILLIAM E. CHANNING [1]

THESE WORDS of Channing reveal both the nature and the problems of an abolitionist campaign wherever the battle is waged. It is a struggle which, in Brazil as in every other country, confronts two serious difficulties. First of all, those whom we wish to save are hostages in the hands of our opponents. Second, the masters find themselves practically at the mercy of the slaves. For this reason, the abolitionists, who desire to conciliate all classes and not to incite one against another, who ask for emancipation not in the interest of the slave alone but for the good of the master himself and the entire society, cannot want to instill in the mind of the oppressed a hatred which he does not know. Much less do they desire to arouse passions which will not serve to advance a cause which is not limited to the rehabilitation of the black race, but is equivalent, as we have seen, to the complete reconstitution of the nation.

Abolitionist propaganda, then, is not directed toward the slaves. It would be cowardly, inept, and criminal, and political suicide as well, for the abolitionist party to incite to crime or rebellion men without any way to defend themselves who would have to be crushed at once by lynch law or public justice. It would be cowardly, because it would expose others to dangers which the instigator himself would not face; inept, because such efforts on behalf of the slave would all produce, as their sole result, an intensification of bondage. It would be criminal, because it would make the innocent suffer for the acts of the guilty —aside from the complicity which belongs to the person who persuades another to commit a crime. It would be political suicide, because the slaves, kept until now at the level of animals, with passions broken and bridled by fear, would seek limitless retribution; and in response the entire country, seeing the most powerful and influential class of the nation exposed to savage vengeance, would decide that the most urgent necessity is to save the society at all costs by means of a terrifying lesson. This would signal the death of the abolitionism of Wilberforce, Lamartine, and Garrison, which is ours, and the beginning of the abolitionism of Cataline or Spartacus or John Brown.

Slavery will not be suppressed in Brazil by a war of the servile class, much less by insurrections or local uprisings.[2] Nor should it be ended by civil war, as in the United States. It could disappear, perhaps, after a revolution, as occurred in France, this revolution being the work exclusively of the free population; but such a possibility does not enter into abolitionist plans. It is equally unlikely that such a reform will result from a sovereign decree of the Crown, as occurred in Russia, or by an act entirely the initiative and responsibility of the central government, such as Lincoln's proclamation in the United States.

Among us emancipation must be achieved by a law as capable as any other of meeting legislative standards. Thus it is in Parliament, not on the plantations or in runaway slave camps in the interior or in the streets and plazas of the cities, where the cause of freedom will be won or lost. In such a struggle, violence, crime, the awakening of sleeping animosities can harm only the side which enjoys the support of law, of justice, and of the power which comes from assisting the oppressed, and which enjoys the support of all humanity.

Slavery is a violent condition of restraint upon human nature, which from time to time must bring on a powerful explosion. We lack statistics on rural crimes but can comfortably assert that slavery constantly exposes the master and his agents to danger and continually tempts the slave to commit crimes of greater or lesser seriousness. Similarly, the number of slaves who escape bondage through suicide must approach the number who take

---

2. *Translator's note:* In fact, however, the runaway-slave movement of 1886 to 1888 greatly hastened the collapse of slavery, particularly in the recalcitrant province of São Paulo. For accounts of the mass flights of slaves from the plantations, see Toplin, *Abolition,* pp. 194-246; and Conrad, *Brazilian Slavery,* pp. 239-77.

revenge for the fate of their race upon their most frequent tormentors, usually their overseers. The life of the slave, literally under the whip from cradle to grave, is an endless provocation against the human spirit, to which all of us would prefer death a thousand times over. Who then can condemn the slave's suicide as cowardice or desertion? Exactly because criminality among the slaves results from the permanence of their condition, abolition aspires to shorten their suffering by granting hope to the victim.

In the last session of our Parliament, Mr. Ferreira Viana, in fashioning a condemnation of abolitionist propaganda, claimed that he who awakens unachievable hopes in the minds of the unfortunate slaves is *perverse*. This statement also condemns as perverse everyone who has aroused unachievable hopes in the minds of the oppressed during mankind's whole existence. Let the noted speaker glance again at the list of those he condemns. On it he will find the founders of every religion and—if these do not seem respectable to him—the outstanding figures of the Catholic faith, the martyrs of all ideas and of all crushed minorities, and the vanquished of the great causes. For him, a lay preacher of the Catholic faith, the perverse is not the one who oppresses, who violates the law, who prostitutes the Gospel, outrages the nation, and slanders humanity. Rather, it is he who says to the downtrodden, in this case the slave, "Do not lose hope. Your bondage will not last forever. Right must prevail over might. Human nature must redound to your favor, since its own essence is trampled upon in you. The nation must expand its moral frontiers until those frontiers encompass you." This he would find perverse, though he would not speak the name of André Rebouças, Joaquim Serra, Ferreira de Meneses, Luís Gama, or any of the other Brazilian abolitionists, or of Granville Sharpe, Buxton, Whittier, or Longfellow.

Even if the hope of freedom seemed illusory, it would not be perverse to bring a ray of light into the prison of the slave where night reigns endlessly, thus helping him to retain his humanity and survive. However, to us—thank God—that hope does not seem unachievable. And not only do we hearten the slave but we comfort ourselves as well, because on the day when he acquires his freedom—and on that day alone—we too will be granted an honor which we do not yet enjoy, the honor of Brazilian citizenship.

How in good faith can it be argued that those feelings are
socially dangerous which urge us to demand the establishment
of families among those for whom the law judges cohabitation
adequate? How can it be said that we expatriate ourselves
morally, whether at home or abroad, because we draw the frontiers of Brazilian nationality beyond the reach of our legislation,
which is written so as to encompass people who are neither
foreigners nor nationals and who before the law of nations have
no country? Before a court of law, if Christ and St. Francis of
Assisi were the judges, what crime would there be in identifying
our hopes with persons who, born Brazilian, are not part of the
community but *belong* to it like any other kind of property,
who are registered not in the electoral roles but in the inventory
of things upon which the state levies taxes?

The slaves, in general, do not know how to read and write, but
they do not need to spell the word "freedom" to know the harsh-
ness of their condition. Their consciences may be asleep, their
hearts resigned, their hopes dead. They may kiss with recognition the irons which bind their wrists. They may rejoice, in their
sad and touching desperation, before the high station, luxury,
and good fortune of their master. They may refuse the freedom
he offers them so as not to be separated from the house where
they were *crias* [children].[3] They might, when free, adopt the
name of their master or demean themselves like ascetics to live
in adoration of the deity of their own creation, ready to sacrifice
themselves to him completely. What does this prove except that
slavery in certain isolated and *domestic* cases creates a heroic
kind of disinterest and self-denial, and this not in the master,
but in the slave?

In conclusion, how can abolitionism, which in its vast unconscious part is not a social renewal but an outburst of sympathy
and concern for the fate of the slave, embitter the soul of the
bondsman when three hundred years of slavery have not done
so? Why must hope bring on calamities which hopelessness has
not recorded? Why today, when their cause has been placed before the tribunal of public opinion by advocates who identify
with it, who in order to defend them change the clothes of the
citizen for those of the helot, why under these conditions must

---

3. *Translator's note:* During the nineteenth century, *"cria"* referred to a slave
child as well as to a colt or filly.

the slaves compromise that defense, doing what they never did when throughout the entire country they found nothing but indifferent witnesses to their torment? [4]

That such should happen is obviously unlikely, and if a rebellion should occur it would not be the result of the spread of abolitionist ideas throughout the country. Rather, it would be because the slaves, shut up on the large estates, do not know that their plight concerns the whole nation, that their bondage has at last touched the hearts of the people, and that from the people there arises some hope—though still remote—of freedom. The more the work of abolitionism expands, the less reason there will be for a slave war, for uprisings, and for other insurrections.

Abolitionist propaganda is directed against an institution and not against people. We do not attack the slaveholders as individuals. We attack the power they exercise and the state of backwardness in which the institution they represent maintains the entire country. The following words of the "Manifesto of the Brazilian Antislavery Society" express the whole abolitionist point of view: "The future of the slaves depends in great measure upon their owners; our propaganda can only lead to creating sentiments of kindness and mutual interest between one and the other. Those who, as a result of that propaganda, subject their slaves to worse treatment are men who possess the innate qualities of barbarism and are without the qualities of just men." The latter case, I should add, would prove not the perversity of the propaganda, but the impotence of the law as a protector of the slaves and the unknown extremes of cruelty to which slavery can descend, like all power which is not checked by any other force and which lacks the wisdom to curb itself. In other words, abolitionism would have been justified to the fullest extent.

Setting aside the dangers of rebellion, for which we cannot possibly be responsible, the abolitionist campaign, in order to carry benefits to the slaves, will attempt only to prevent and decrease the crimes of which slavery was always a cause and which became so common—at a time when an abolitionist party did not exist and the ports of Brazil were open to traffic in

---

4. *Translator's note:* One of the most common proslavery arguments in the 1860s and again in the 1880s was that steps to free large numbers of slaves would probably result in massive slave uprisings. This is the argument that Nabuco is contesting in these paragraphs.

Africans—that they motivated the security law of June 10, 1835.[5]
It is not to the slaves that we speak. It is to the free. In regard
to the former, we will take as our motto the words of Sir Walter
Scott: "Do not awake the slave who sleeps. Perhaps he dreams
that he is free." [6]

---

5. *Translator's note:* Though Article 179 of the Brazilian Constitution of 1824
prohibited lashing, torture, branding, and all cruel punishment, the law of June
10, 1835, permitted whipping as a punishment for slaves who committed minor
physical assaults on masters or overseers and members of their families. The
same law provided the death penalty for slaves who committed more serious
attacks on such persons. Despite the constitutional provision regarding corporal
punishment, municipal ordinances of communities throughout Brazil also pre-
scribed whipping as punishment for minor offenses committed by slaves.

6. *Translator's note:* The original English source for this quotation could not
be located. The quotation as it appears here is a retranslation made from
Nabuco's Portuguese translation.

CHAPTER V

"The Cause Has Already Triumphed"

> Thirty years of slavery with its degradations, its corporal punishment, its sales of men, women, and children, like domestic animals and things, imposed upon one and one half million human creatures is a term too long for the friends of humanity to accept with resignation.
>
> —VICTOR SCHOELCHER [1]

"THE CAUSE you abolitionists advocate," we are told each day, not only by those who insult us, but also by those who sympathize with us, "is a cause which triumphed long ago in the public mind." So far as this proposition has any practical application, it means: "The country has already decided. You may relax. The slaves will all be freed. There is thus no need whatever for an abolitionist party to promote the interests of the forsaken ones whose cause the entire nation has adopted."

But those who make this claim have only one purpose: to disarm the defenders of the slaves in order to prevent slave prices from falling as a result of the lack of assurance that they can be held as property for as long as the law now promises the masters; to make certain that slavery disappears naturally, thanks to the increasing death rate among a population which cannot multiply. It is obvious that for those who argue in this way the *ingênuos* are free persons who do not each year renew slavery's ranks, so there is no need for anyone to take upon himself the task of protecting those hundreds of thousands who are slaves only until the age of twenty-one, that is, who are temporary slaves. The hateful spectacle of a great horde of future citizens growing up in the slave huts, subject to the same system of labor, to the same moral training, to the same treatment as the slaves, does not concern our opponents. They do not add the horde of *ingênuos* to the mass of slaves when they inventory their long-term assets, or when they list their current wealth. But for us the condition of the *ingênuos,* like that of the slaves, is an aspect of the same problem.

---

1. *Translator's note:* Victor Schoelcher (1804-93) was a prominent French abolitionist. The source for this quotation could not be located.

Furthermore, is it really true that the abolitionist idea has captured the public mind? We do not inquire into the reasons for claiming, as we do, that most of the people are with us, though without the power to express their opinion. We wish only to know if the cause of the slave has triumphed or whether the final outcome is at least so certain that we can win by default, can cross our arms with the certainty of seeing one and one-half million human beings slowly emerge from bondage to take their place at our side.

How much *real* hope of freedom (we are not willing to rely on mere faith in Providence) can the slave cling to in this moment of history? Let every free man imagine himself in that position and then answer the question for himself.

If he were the slave of a *good* master and himself a *good* slave —a hypothetical condition which no free man could completely achieve and which would require a different background—he would always have some hope of freedom. But good masters are often poor men and sometimes find themselves forced to sell their slave to a bad master. Moreover, they have sons whose inheritances they want to ensure. Conversely, if there are owners who free many slaves, there are also those who never sign a certificate of emancipation. Admitting that the number of manumissions is growing steadily—already one unquestionable result of abolitionism—and that a concerned public opinion, diligent, quick to reward such acts of conscience, has developed in a short time, even so, how many slaves in relation to the total mass are freed, and how many die each year? Manumission as a gift is a hope that every slave can have, but it is the fate of relatively few. In this lottery of liberation, almost all the tickets come up blank; the likelihood is too small to provide a solid basis for future plans. Most of our slaves die in bondage; the freedman has always been the exception.

Setting aside the hope that the master will grant him freedom, a hope which does not constitute a right, what legal way is there by which a slave can escape from bondage? The law of September 28, 1871, without easing the way for him, opened two roads to freedom: that of forced redemption through his savings [*pecúlio*] and that of the annual allotment.[2] The first, unfortu-

---

2. *Translator's note:* Article 4 of the Rio Branco Law legalized a practice evidently customary in Brazil, that of allowing slaves to keep their own savings and to use the money to purchase their freedom. The article reads in part: "The slave is permitted to form a *pecúlio* [savings fund] from what may come to him

nately, serves urban slaves but not those in the countryside, owing to the faulty and erratic administration of this important function of the Rio Branco Law which results from private considerations. Even so, this way to freedom would be open to a large part of the captive population if slavery had not deadened our spirit of initiative, if it had not impaired confidence in labor contracts. That a slave, by contracting his labor to another master as provided for in the Rio Branco Law, cannot acquire enough capital to free himself is a clear demonstration of the character of slavery as a social and economic system.[3] In regard

---

through gifts, legacies, and inheritances, and from what, by consent of his owner, he may obtain by his labor and economy. . . . The slave who, through his savings, may obtain means to pay his value has a right to freedom." The "annual allotment" Nabuco refers to was "the Emancipation Fund" created by Article 3 of the Free Birth Law to free selected slaves each year in each of the provinces of Brazil.

3. That fact proves that slavery is usury of the worst kind, the usury of Shylock demanding each ounce of flesh pledged in his promissory note. In effect, since a slave can deposit his value in cash whenever he has it and demand his freedom, each slave merely represents a debt owed to his master which he cannot pay and for which he serves as collateral. In this sense he is a debt slave, and here we find the most extraordinary usury which, to be exposed as it ought to be, would require the genius of a Shakespeare.

When the Rio Branco Law was passed in 1871, the one-year-old slave could be redeemed by his mother at an insignificant price. However, because she lacked the money, her *cria* was not freed, and today he is a *moleque* [black boy] of thirteen and is worth much more. (The sad vocabulary of slavery used in our age, the shame of our language, will in the future much undermine the liberal pretensions of Brazilian society.) Soon he will be a *preto* [black man] worth twice as much. This means that the debt of the slave to his master more than quadrupled because his mother lacked the means to pay when he was a child.

Let us take a young, strong, and capable slave. (In slavery the greater the physical, intellectual, and moral value of a man, the harder it is to ransom him, because his price is higher. It is in the interest of the slave, therefore, that he be stupid, crippled, lazy, and unfit.) This slave was twenty-one in 1871 and worth 1,500 *milréis* [approximately $825 in U. S. currency]. He did not represent any invested capital, since he was the son of a slave woman who was also the *cria* of the household. Let us suppose, however, that he really represented that amount of capital and that he had been bought in that year. He was thus equivalent to a bill of exchange redeemable by the debtor on sight upon the deposit of that amount if he was to achieve judicial freedom. In 1871, however, this man had no *peculio*, nor could he find anyone to lend him the money.

During the next twelve years his financial state did not change. His hire, if he was rented, or his unpaid labor, if he served in his owner's house, did not leave him any surplus to begin a *peculio*. In those twelve years the rent from this man was never less than 30 *milréis* [about $16.50] per month (serving at home he saved his master an equal expense), which gives a total of 4,320 *milréis* [about $2,375] excluding interest. Deducting from that amount the original price of the slave, there remains 2,820 *milréis* [about $1,550] which he granted to his master because he could not pay him the debt of 1,500 *milréis* [$825] in 1871, in addition to amortizing the whole investment without any profit to himself.

to the emancipation fund of the state, which, as the Baron
Cotegipe observed in the Senate, is vulnerable to manipulations
of interested masters, we will later show by what insignificant
percentages the allotment decreases the slave rolls each year.[4]
Aside from these hopes, both elusive, which abolitionism must
convert into elements of reality, what is left to the slaves? Absolutely nothing.

If abolitionism, ever on guard, sympathetic, concerned for the
fate of those unfortunate people, should ever disappear, they
would find themselves betrayed to the fate which the law has
outlined for them, betrayed to the power of the master, whatever
his character. And death will continue to be, as it is today, the
most likely and only certain way of one day eluding slavery.

This condition—the condition of slavery—its duration, its
nature, is today what it has always been. In the hands of a good
master, the slave can have a life of contentment, like that of a
favorite and well-tended animal. In the hands of a bad master
or a bad mistress (the cruelty of women is many times more
refined and persistent than that of men) there is no way to
describe the lives of these miserable people. If there were a public inquiry in which slaves could freely testify, all Brazilians
except the cynical and the slave merchants, who are themselves
indifferent to the afflictions of others, would be struck with
astonishment by the core of barbarism which exists in our country beneath a thin layer of civilization wherever that layer is
superimposed upon the possession of men by men.

In slavery, not only *quod non prohibitum licitum est,* but also
practically *nada é prohibido*—nothing is forbidden. If every

---

If in 1871 someone had lent him that amount of money to buy his freedom at
an annual interest rate of 12 percent, by 1880 he could have paid his entire debt,
with a wide margin for clothing and illness, and today he would be without
obligation. Since he did not find this lender, however, he continues to pay interest of more than 20 percent on capital which never diminishes.

Calculating the amount of money invested in slaves and the interest from this
money represented by salaries paid or owed, we get some idea of the degree of
usury involved in slavery. It must not be forgotten either that a great part of the
slave population is gratuitous property, that is, a gift of the slave mothers to their
masters. The law of September 28 reduced slavery to pawned indebtedness. The
high interest collected on the security which consists of the debtor himself makes
that speculation the most profitable of all investments. The state itself, which is
not involved in this usury on human flesh extorted at the crack of a whip, tried
for a long time to get 7 percent interest from the master class on its territorial
properties, which were guaranteed by a mortgage on those same slaves.

4. *Translator's note:* The Baron Cotegipe (João Mauricio Wanderley) was a
prominent Conservative senator from Bahia and a staunch defender of slavery.

slave were to tell his life story from childhood on—his family
relationships, the development of his mind and spirit, the scenes
he witnessed, the punishment he suffered, the treatment he experienced, the rewards he received for so many years of labor
which went to increase the fortune and well-being of others—the
effect of Harriet Beecher Stowe's *Uncle Tom's Cabin* or the
Narrative of the Life of Frederick Douglass would seem insignificant alongside some of the stories we would hear.

It will be argued that slavery, like every other institution, results in *abuses,* and one does not debate abuses. But these abuses
are part of the justification and necessity of the institution, and
the fact that they are essential to its existence fully condemns the
entire system. The master who regards his slaves as members of
his family is an exception, as is the master who detests and tor-
tures his slaves. Most proprietors try to derive all the profit they
can from their slaves, and they exploit the system with no particular concern for the moral nature of servile property. But
whether the *bad master* is the exception or the rule, it is enough
that he exists—if he were only a hypothesis, it would be enough
—to make of a segment of the Brazilian legal system a total
denial of all moral reason. For the law allows anyone—Brazilian
or foreigner, *ingênuo* or freedman, the innocent or criminal,
the merciful or brutal, even the *slave*—to exercise over others
better perhaps than himself a power which it has never defined
or limited.

Each day we read advertisements in the press for runaway
slaves, which arouse the greed of slave hunters [*capitães do mato*]
with details which do not offend the human modesty of the society which reads them. In our cities there are open commission
houses, flesh markets, and brothels, but the police close their
eyes to these disgusting scenes. The courageous opposition of
one police commissioner in the city of Rio de Janeiro to the
traffic in female slaves for prostitution is still fresh in the public
mind. Africans shipped from Angola and Mozambique after
passage of the law of November 7, 1831, are still in bondage.
Judicial slave markets continue to take the place of the formerly
public auctions.[5] In a word, human flesh still has its price. In
view of these facts, how could anyone dare to claim that slaves
do not require defenders, as if the bondage in which they exist

---

5. *Translator's note:* A law of August 25, 1869, prohibited public and commercial slave auctions but allowed private sales and "judicial auctions" for discharging debts or dividing property among heirs.

were conditional and not permanent, and as if slavery were something out of date, or its worst features at least now matters of history?

Who knows for certain how many more thousands of slaves will die in bondage? Who knows when the sale of men, women, and children will at last be banned, when the state will no longer have to impose more taxes upon this form of property? No one knows for certain.

What everyone recognizes, however, is that the master still looks upon his right over the slave as permanent. As he once defended this right under the shadow of constitutional safeguard —Article 179 [6]—he now relies upon protection of the law of September 28, 1871. The slave is still *property,* like any other, which the master can dispose of, as with a horse or a piece of furniture. The slave living under various civilizing influences in the cities in some ways escapes that condition. But the Brazilian slave living in the countryside, isolated from the world, far from protection of the state and unknown to *any* of its agents—having at best only his baptismal name on record in the books of the local tax collector—subject to imprisonment for months in a private dungeon where no authority ever goes, or to daily beatings for the smallest offense or for no offense at all, at the mercy of the temperament and character of the master who grants him as charity the clothing and food he needs, subject to being pawned, mortgaged, or sold, literally speaking has only death to call his own.

Neither hope nor sorrow nor tears are his, and so there is nothing that can be compared with this unfortunate person, who is not an abstraction or an invention of the fantasy of his defenders. He exists by the thousands and hundreds of thousands, and the tales of these hundreds of thousands could be told in most terrible detail. No one competes in suffering with this orphan of Fate, this waif of humankind who before his birth trembles under the whip which lashes his mother's back, who has only the remains of milk which a mother employed in suckling other children can spare for her own child, who grows up in the midst of the abjectness of his own class—corrupted, demoralized, brutalized by life in the slave hut—who learns not to lift his eyes to his master and not to demand even the smallest

---

6. *Translator's note:* Article 179 of the Constitution of 1824 guaranteed the right to property, which was not to be expropriated except for the public benefit and with full previous indemnification.

return from his own labor, who is denied affection and personal choice, is unable to express feelings without fear, and is condemned never to possess his own body. Finally he dies without any expression of gratitude from those who worked him so hard, leaving behind his wife, his children, and his friends, if these he had, in the same endless agony.

Compared with the plight of so many thousands of slave families, the unmerited distress of other men becomes secondary in the record of human misery. The slave alone knows the sorrow of belonging to another person, alongside of which the anguish of so many impoverished persons, who have no one and nothing in the world they can call *their own,* is mild. "Only the slave is miserable" is a phrase which could be written with accuracy in the record of human consolation. Beside the tragedy of hope and despair which is the daily ebb and flow of his life, all other lives which float upon a current of freedom, whatever their troubles and grievances, are relatively privileged. Of all men only the slave—he who through his lack of free will is the opposite extreme on the human scale of Shelley's Prometheus—shares with the latter the fate "to suffer woes which Hope thinks infinite; to forgive wrongs darker than death or night."

Certainly, in some ways it can be said, nevertheless: "Your cause, that is, the cause of the slaves which you have made your own, is morally won." Yes, it is won, but before public opinion—dispersed, apathetic, out of reach—and not before Parliament and government, the concrete organs of opinion. It is won before religion, but not before the Church, nor within the community of the faithful, nor among the established priesthood; it is won before science, but not before the scientific bodies, the professors, the men who represent science. The cause has been won before justice and law, but not before the law which is its expression, not before the magistrates, the administrators of the law; before youth, irresponsible, protected by a political "Macedonian privilege" which does not recognize the sources of the views which it adopts, but not for the youths enslaved; before the political parties, but not before the ministries, the deputies, the senators, the provincial presidents, the candidates for leadership of those parties, nor before the voters who form the lower caste of our aristocracy; before Europe, but not before the Europeans established in our country, who in great part either possess slaves or do not believe in a Brazil without slaves and who fear for their own interests; in the minds of the populace, but not before the people. Before the Emperor as a private citizen it is victorious, but not before the Chief of State; before Brazilians in general, but not before Brazilians individually. In short, we have converted moral jurisdictions, political abstractions, forces which remain in the realm of the possible, generous and impotent sympathies, but we have not triumphed before the one court of law which can pronounce the freedom of the black race, the constituted Brazilian nation.

The abolitionist victory is an accomplished fact in the hearts of the great majority of the people. But as long as that victory is not translated into freedom, as long as it is only promised in words but not yet worked into law, as long as it is only *proved* by mercenary sophists but not experienced by the slave himself, such an impractical victory, which fails to achieve the restitution expected by the victims of slavery, will be nothing more than the stirring of human conscience within a paralyzed organism which manages to stand up and stretch but is not yet able to walk.

CHAPTER VI

Hopes for Freedom before Independence

> Generous citizens of Brazil who love your country, recognize that without the total abolition of the infamous African slave trade, and without the subsequent emancipation of the present slaves, Brazil will never affirm her national independence and assure and defend her liberal constitution.
> —José Bonifacio de Andrada e Silva [1]

BY ENCOURAGING slaves to have faith in the progress of social morality, abolitionists do not inspire them with the belief that they will be free within a set period. Failure to fulfill such a promise could feed that desperation among them which is so greatly feared. But when the government, or he whom the slaves conceive to be the government, assures the world and the nation that emancipation *is only a question of form and of opportunity,* that prospect of freedom thus displayed before their eyes has for them a different meaning, a greater certainty, and in this case the disillusionment can have fearful results.[2]

For slaves the encouragement of the abolitionists is like a wish or like the golden dream of freedom treasured by the poor slave mother, the indelible childhood memory of all those brought up in bondage. The hope which abolitionists give is like the words murmured in the slave's ear by his most faithful companion to raise his spirits. The promise of public powers, on the other hand, is an entirely different thing, for among the tenets of the slave's philosophy is belief in the honor of the "White Man," and in the solemn nature of those who can do whatever they wish, and in the certainty that the king will not go back on his word. This kind of promise, therefore, emanating from the highest possible place, is for a slave like the pledge of freedom his

---

1. *Translator's note:* From *Representação a Assembléia Geral Constituinte e Legislativa do Império do Brasil sobre a escravatura* (Paris, 1825).

2. *Translator's note:* In August, 1867, in response to a plea on behalf of the Brazilian slaves from the French Emancipation Committee, the Brazilian government informed the world in the name of the Emperor that abolition was "only a question of form and of opportunity." This announcement and promises of a similar nature made by Pedro II in subsequent speeches to Parliament helped to stimulate antislavery in Brazil and facilitated passage of the Rio Branco Law.

master makes, after which, however long he is made to wait, he
looks upon himself as a free man.

What the victims of slavery do not know is that the promises
of such persons are made not to be carried out, but only to
satisfy the political need to accomplish two other things at the
same time: to keep the slave in bondage and avoid alienating
his master, and to hide the country's shame by representing the
slave as about to achieve his freedom. The word of the king may
have had some value in an absolute monarchy—though, as will
be seen, this was not always the case—but in a constitutional
monarchy the leader's promise is the ancient mask with which
the actors alternate their roles on the proscenium. The "White
Man's honor" rests upon the superstition of a race which lags
behind in its educational development, which worships the white
man's color for the power it represents and grants it virtues
which by itself it does not possess.

What does it matter if so many slaves remember those pledges,
promissory notes drawn upon another generation, at the moment
of death, before their God? Who can hear them then? Those
they leave behind rely forever upon this hope, and the world
continues to believe that slavery is ending in Brazil, without
recognizing that this is happening because the slaves are dying.
It is impossible to number all the assertions of public officials
which contend that the emancipation of the slaves in Brazil is
near, that it is resolved in principle and for its final achievement
depends only upon the best opportunity. Some of these declarations are, in fact, still alive in the memory of all of us and adequately document the complaint we are making.

The first solemn promise that slavery, which became and remains a perpetual condition, would be a temporary one is to be
found in Portuguese legislation of the last century.

To the honor of Portugal, the most renowned of her juris-
consults, Melo Freire, did not admit that Roman law in its most
backward and barbaric part, *dominica potestas,* could be revived
by a vicious commerce as an integral part of the nation's law
after an interval of time as great as that which separates ancient
slavery from the servitude of the black race. His phrase, "Servi
nigri in Brasilia, et quaesitis aliis dominationibus *tolerantur: sed
quo jure et titulo me penitus ignorare fateor,*" [3] is the condemnation of the slave trader and the legal destruction of the whole

---

3. "Black slaves are tolerated in Brazil and in other dominions, but by what
right and with what title I confess I am entirely ignorant."

edifice erected upon the piracy of the old *asientos*.[4] It is the embarrassment contained in this confession of Melo Freire which gives a touch of dignity to the decree of June 6, 1755, which contains the first of the solemn promises made to the black race.

That decree, which legislated the freedom of the Indians of Brazil, made this important exception: "From this general order I exclude only the offspring of the black slave women, who will remain under the control of their present masters *for so long as I do not issue a further order concerning this matter.*" The order thus expressly promised was never given. But another royal decree concerning Portugal's black slaves could not have failed to have repercussions in the Portuguese overseas territories. That document is a strong and praiseworthy brief which nevertheless defames its author, the king, who while thus denouncing slavery tolerated it in his American and African dominions.[5]

---

4. *Translator's note: Asientos* were licenses or contracts granted to European firms to transport slaves to New World colonies.

5. These are the terms of the decree dated January 16, 1773: "I, the king, make known to those to whom this decree comes with force of law that after having ended by means of the edict of September 19, 1761, the great inconvenience which resulted for these kingdoms from maintaining the slavery of black men (the mentioned edict declared the freedom of slaves imported into Portugal after a certain date), I was informed that in the whole kingdom of the Algarve and in some provinces of Portugal there are still persons so lacking in feeling of humanity and religion that they keep slave women in their homes, *some whiter than they though called blacks and negresses, so that through the evil propagation of them they may perpetuate slavery* through a hateful commerce of sin and *usurpation of the freedom of the unhappy persons born of those successive and profitable matings* under the pretext that the wombs of slave mothers cannot produce free children in accordance with civil law.

"And, since that same civil law *which they have so abused* does not allow the descendants of slaves, who are guilty of nothing more than their unfortunate condition of servitude, to be kept in the infamy of slavery longer than the term provided by law for those descended from persons who commit the most terrible crimes against the sovereign power, and *considering the great indecencies that the said servitude brings to my vassals, the confusion and hatred which it creates among them, and the harm which results for the State from having so many vassals wronged, hindered, and rendered useless, so many miserable persons whose unhappy condition makes them ineligible for public office, for commerce, agriculture, and trade, and for contracts of every kind,* I will be served by ending all the above absurdities, ordering:

"As to the past, that all slaves, male and female, whether born of the above-mentioned concubinages or of legitimate marriages, whose mothers and grandmothers are or were slaves, will remain in their present servitude during their lives only: *that, however, those whose slavery originates from their great grandmothers are free and without obligation* if their mothers and grandmothers were slaves; and that all the above persons freed by this my paternal and pious order *become eligible for all offices, honors, and dignities, without the distinctive disgrace of being called* libertos [freedmen], *which superstition of the Romans established in*

This distinction between the fate of the slaves in the colonies and in the kingdom and neighboring islands is like that established between the condition and importance of the two parts of the Portuguese empire. For Brazil slavery was still a very good thing, whereas for Portugal it was dishonorable. The part of the great empire thus identified with this national shame was very limited, not extending in fact beyond Portugal's shores and not including all of that country either. In spite of this, however, the powerful pronouncement against the immorality and abuses of slavery could only have been received by the masters and slaves of Brazil as a forecast of its extension to the colonies.

---

our customs and which Christianity and civil society today make intolerable in my kingdom, as it has been in all other kingdoms of Europe."

No Brazilian can read this notable document published more than a century ago, particularly the parts printed in italics, without recognizing with pain and humiliation:

(1) That if the decree had been extended to Brazil, slavery would have ended at the beginning of the century, before independence.

(2) That though it is a law of the last century, anterior to the French Revolution, it is more generous, comprehensive, and liberal than the law of September 28, 1871: (a) because it *totally frees* the newborn at once, while our law does so only after the age of twenty-one; (b) because it declares the great grandchildren of slave women free and without obligation, and the law of September 28 took into account only the future generation but not the present slaves; (c) because it relieves those it declared free from the dishonorable label of *liberto*, "a superstition of the Romans . . . which Christianity and civil society" made "intolerable" already in that period, whereas our law of 1871 did not remember to erase that blemish and in one of its paragraphs subjected the *libertos* to five years of government inspection and to the obligation of displaying work contracts or of facing the punishment of working in government establishments. In the Council of State, Viscount Rio Branco himself said, before reading that decree whose words he described as *memorable*, that Portuguese law "extended this favor (that of declaring them freeborn) to those babies who were liberated at baptism and to some freedmen of certain classes," and he added, "which cannot be done here without violating the Constitution of the Empire." This being the case proves only that the absolutist king in 1773 and the constitutional Emperor in 1824 held different views concerning the obligations imposed by Christianity (the Constitution was made in the name of the Most Holy Trinity) and civil society.

(3) That today, although Brazilian slavery is the exclusive result, aside from the traffic, of the same causes pointed out in the decree: of the *usurpation of the freedom of the unhappy persons born of those successive and profitable matings,* of the evil breeding of the slave women, of pretexts derived from civil law *which they have so abused;* and despite the far greater number of subjects who are *wronged, hindered, and rendered useless . . . for trade, and for contracts of every kind,* these hard facts are not admitted from the heights of the throne. The *infamy* of slavery continues to fall, not upon the man who inflicts it upon others, having as he does the choice of not inflicting it, but upon the person who endures it, though he has no choice in the matter. This antiquated edict which should now be obsolete appears to represent an epoch of public, religious, social, and political morality much more advanced than that of the present period, represented by the general registration of the slaves.

Later came the agitation for independence. During that wide-spread upheaval the slaves caught a more favorable glimpse of freedom, and all instinctively supported the break with Portugal. Their color itself made them adhere with all their might to Brazil, a country where there was a future for the black race which they could not have in Portugal. Colonial society, by its nature, was open-ended, whereas the mother country was aristo-cratic, exclusive, and entirely closed to the black race. As a result of these circumstances, descendants of slaves plotted for the formation of a country they also could call their own. This powerful element of separation was an unacknowledged factor in the achievement of independence. The relations between slaves, freedmen, and men of color, and between these and known representatives of the independence movement, formed a chain of hope and sympathy which linked the political thought of the latter to the social aspirations of the former. Allied in spirit with the Brazilians, slaves awaited independence and hailed it as the first step toward their freedom, like an unspoken promise of liberty which could not be long delayed.

The document which the Provisional Government addressed to the people of Pernambuco after the Revolution of 1817 proves that independence was associated with emancipation in the thoughts of slaves and their masters, as well as in the minds of the opponents of independence.[6] That proclamation, outstanding for more reasons than one, is not as well known as it should be in the interests of Brazilian patriotism, so I reproduce it. Today it is a political monument raised in 1817 to a province which is cast in the main role in Brazilian history by its initiative, its heroism, its love of liberty, and its gallant spirit, but on whose character slavery stamped the same mark as on that of every other province.

> Pernambucan patriots! Suspicion has crept into the minds of the rural proprietors. They believe that the humane tendency of the present liberal government has as its aim the indiscriminate liberation of the slaves and men of color. *The Government forgives them a suspicion which does it honor.* Sustained by generous sentiments, it can never believe that men, because they are more or less browned by the sun, degenerate from the original type of

---

6. *Translator's note:* Here Nabuco refers to a liberal republican revolt in the northern province directed against Portuguese domination. It was quickly and ruthlessly suppressed, and many of its leaders were executed, exiled, or imprisoned.

equality; but it is equally convinced that the basis of every orderly society is the inviolability of every kind of property. Motivated by these two opposing points of view, it desires a form of liberation which does not allow the cancer of slavery to continue among us; but it wants this liberation to proceed slowly, with order and legality. The Government deceives no one. Its heart bleeds to see such an inspiring age so distant in time, but it does not wish to invoke it prematurely. Patriots! Even those properties of yours which are the most contrary to the ideal of justice are sacred; the Government will establish ways to reduce the evil but will not end it by force. Believe in the word of the Government. It is inviolable. It is sacred.

These words are the most noble yet uttered by a Brazilian government in the whole course of our history. Not even the compromise they seem to make regarding the right of the master over the slave mars the gallantry of the proclamation. This proclamation reveals that slave "property" for its authors is without legitimacy and that it shames and humiliates them. The revolutionaries of Pernambuco understood and deeply felt the inconsistency of a national republican movement which initiated its rule with an acknowledgement of the property right of men over men, and it cannot be doubted that this contradiction was for them a blot upon the independence they were proclaiming. That revolution which, in the words of its supporters, "seemed more like a festival of peace than the tumult of war," that dawn of Brazilian patriotism which began on the 6th of March, 1817, was our only national movement in which the country's representatives blushed with shame—or, better yet, wept with sorrow —to see slavery dividing the nation into two castes, one of which, though it shared the joy and enthusiasm of the moment, would not claim a crumb of victory's spoils.

And yet, what does that document really mean? What is most significant about it is that the necessity of gaining the trust of the rural proprietors did not prevent that government from revealing its support for a slow, orderly, and legal emancipation, from announcing that its heart bled, that slave property was contrary to the ideal of justice, and that it would establish ways to reduce the evils of slavery. Its meaning is that the martyrs of independence recognized that they stood between slavery and the scaffold, fearing that, if hope of ending the colonial system were identified with eradication of slavery, an alliance of "rural proprietors" with Portuguese armed forces would drown in blood that first dream of an independent Brazil.

This occurred in the North. The close association in the South between independence and emancipation is proved by ideas expressed by José Bonifacio de Andrada e Silva and by other members of the Constituent Assembly. In one of the articles of the Constitutional Project [of 1823] it was decided that the Assembly had the duty to create establishments for "the slow emancipation of the blacks and their religious and industrial education." The Constitution of the Empire, on the other hand, does not contain such an article. The authors of the Constitution of 1824 understood that it would have been unpropitious to stain the record of the political emancipation of the nation with allusions to the existence of slavery. The word *libertos* in the article in which freedmen are declared Brazilian citizens and in Article 94, fortunately since revoked, which declared them ineligible to be deputies, could have referred to a previous political order which the Constitution was eliminating.

The rest of our fundamental law makes no mention of slavery, for, in fact, its organizers did not want to spoil their work or to reveal its iniquitous character. With the inclusion of Article 179, which guarantees the inviolability of private property, even one small reference to slavery anywhere in the Constitution would have turned it into a monstrosity. However, José Bonifacio, the leader of the Andradas (his brother Antônio Carlos had been very close to the gallows in the movement in Pernambuco), the man in whom the people of color—the freedmen, the slaves themselves, and all the humble people of the country who dreamed of independence—had placed their confidence, had witten a bill concerning the slaves which was to be voted on in the Assembly.

For modern abolitionism that bill is inadequate, but many of its provisions would bring humane improvement to our laws even today. If it had been adopted in that period, however, and thus the "Patriarch of Independence" had been successful in instilling within our politicians his great and generous views on liberty and justice, slavery would certainly have disappeared from Brazil more than half a century ago.

Articles like the following, for example—which would be rejected with indignation by our present Parliament—express

sentiments which, if they had been set in motion and directed
seriously and continuously by the public powers, would have
done more than any law to humanize Brazilian society.

Article 5. Any slave, *or any other person on behalf of any slave,*
who may offer an owner *the amount for which he has been sold,*
or at which he has been legally valued, shall be immediately made
free.

Article 6. But if the slave, or any person acting on his behalf,
cannot pay the entire price at once, as soon as he can present one
sixth of it the master will be compelled to accept it, and will give
him a free day each week, and additional days at the same rate
when he receives the other sixths, until he has received the full
amount.

Article 10. All free men of color who do not have a profession
or some certain way of making a living will receive from the State
a small grant of land which they may farm, as well as the necessary
financial help to establish themselves, which they will repay over
a period of time.

Article 16. Before the age of twelve, slaves should not be employed in unhealthful and excessive work, and the Council—the
High Council for the Preservation of the Slaves proposed in this
same bill—will watch over the execution of this article for the
good of the State and the masters themselves.

Article 17. In the same manner the High Council in each
province will set standards and hours of labor, as well as regulations regarding the slaves' food and clothing.

Article 31. To ensure the strict execution of the law and to
promote the good treatment, good behavior, and rapid emancipation of the slaves in every possible way, there will be in each
provincial capital a High Council for the Preservation of the
Slaves.

There were various other articles in the same vein concerned
with corporal punishment, the work of slave women during
pregnancy and immediately after giving birth, slave marriages
and moral instruction, public advantages to masters who would
give freedom to families, and the possession of slaves by priests.
There is nothing in the law of September 28 which demonstrates such a depth of concern for the slaves' human nature. In
1871 the legislators merely complied with their duty, without
love, almost without sympathy. But in 1823 José Bonifacio,
recognizing that he was powerless to decree immediate freedom,

showed the most penetrating concern, even a kind of tenderness, for the victims of social injustice; this concern could not fail to go directly to the bondsmen's hearts.

Furthermore, a magnificent—and, read in light of the history of the last sixty years, heartbreaking—call addressed to Brazilians from exile in France reveals José Bonifacio's recognition that a Brazil which maintained slavery was a nation unworthy of free men. "Without the emancipation of the present slaves," he wrote, "Brazil will never affirm her national independence and assure and defend her liberal constitution. Without individual freedom there can be no civilization, no stable fortunes, no morality and justice; and without these gifts from heaven no one can possess honor, a force and a power among nations."[7]

This warm defense, this spontaneous and impassioned advocacy of the rights of the slaves by the most renowned of Brazilians was the result of high-minded patriotism, of a wish to complete his great work. But certainly he also knew that independence with endless slavery was a cruel blow to the personal hopes of slaves in the years before and after that event, since they had been witnesses to the enthusiasm of the age and had breathed the air which had swelled the hearts of everyone. Independence was not a formal, written, enforceable pledge of Brazilians to the enslaved. But it could not have been less than a promise which sprang from a national consensus of purpose, from revolutionary cooperation, and from an unspoken alliance which gathered about the same flag all those persons who dreamed of an independent Brazil; and thus it was understood by the Andradas and by the martyrs of Pernambuco.

---

7. How much the well-known ideas of José Bonifacio concerning slavery helped bring to an end in his own country the political career of the statesman who planned and achieved independence is a question worth studying. Perhaps the person who attempts this investigation will learn that slavery played a large role in this ostracism, and that it was probably slavery too which brought the Pernambucan nationalists to the gallows.

In any case, one finds in the following words, written by Antônio Carlos, one more political effect of the system which, erected upon the foundations of slavery, is by nature a regimen of servility and ingratitude. "Such was the character of José Bonifacio that he lived and died poor; he did not receive from the nation any distinction whatsoever. In the Senate, which the law created for men of merit and virtue, where vice, intemperance, intrigues, and treason have been seated,"—not to speak of the slave traffic—"there was never a place for the founder of the Empire." "Perhaps for this reason," adds Antônio Carlos, "his name will survive better, as did those of Brutus and Cassius, because their busts did not appear in the funeral pageants of the families to which they belonged." *Esboco biogr. e necrol. do Conselheiro José Bonifacio de Andrada e Silva*, p. 16.

CHAPTER VII

Before the Law of 1871

> For five years the hope of freedom emanating from the throne rained down upon the miserable bondsmen like manna upon the Israelites in the desert.
>
> —CRISTIANO OTÔNI [1]

FOR A CERTAIN PART of the slave population the promises of freedom made during the long period from independence until passage of the Rio Branco Law date back only a few years, whereas for others they go back to the end of the First Empire.

The rights of the latter group, the Africans imported after 1831 and their descendants, will be discussed later. For the moment it is enough to point out that those rights are not founded upon more or less debatable promises, but upon an international treaty and a positive and explicit law.[2] The simple fact that at least half the captive population of Brazil was enslaved after that law was passed, with complete disregard for the penalties which it threatened, would seem to relieve us of the need to put forward arguments concerning public promises made to the slaves.

When the law itself is not adequate to guarantee for at least half of the enslaved the freedom it decreed for them (as will later be shown in detail), when an article as clear as this: "All slaves who enter into the territory or ports of Brazil, coming from abroad, are free," was never enforced, and when the command issued by Diogo Antônio Feijó to carry out that law was never honored by either the ministers of the Regency or those of the Second Empire, how much confidence can we place in the nationalist movements which have appeared among us? [3] What faith can we have in acts which seem unrelated to the lot

---

1. *Translator's note:* For information concerning Otôni, see chapter 2, note 4. The source for this quotation could not be located.

2. *Translator's note:* Here and in the following paragraph Nabuco refers to the British-Brazilian treaty of 1826 and the Brazilian law of November 7, 1831. See the translator's introduction.

3. *Translator's note:* Father Feijó, Justice Minister in 1831 and 1832 and later Regent of the Empire, decreed stringent regulations for enforcement of the law on April 12, 1832. However, as Nabuco points out, the law was rarely enforced.

of the slaves, official declarations which seem intended only to produce impressions? In other words, what good are calls to conscience, to loyalty, to the nation's sense of justice when half the slaves are held illegally in bondage? Why ask the state for payment of a debt of honor which it never recognized or entirely forgot, when the state itself brazenly repudiated, on grounds of foreign coercion, that public writ solemnly fashioned by the General Assembly and signed by the Triple Regency?

Useful or not, protests of the slaves should correspond to obligations which have been drawn up on their behalf. To an enormous extent, these government obligations are contained in one law, and that law was written to fulfill another commitment contained in an international treaty. We will later demonstrate, therefore, how and in what terms British diplomacy vindicated the rights of the slaves before the Brazilian government, remembering that there is infinitely more disgrace for us in open denial of justice by Brazilian authorities than in seizure of slave ships in our ports on orders of a foreign government.[4]

With that important declaration behind us, we will limit this discussion to those slaves who neither by themselves nor through their mothers possess a right to freedom which is guaranteed by a specific law. Needless to say, all of these slaves were born in Brazil, with the exception of a few rare Africans still in bondage who were imported during the First Empire.

The facts upon which these slaves may have based some hope, and which certainly compromise the honor of the nation, date from a little before the law of September 28, 1871. Principal among these national compromises in regard to the slaves are the following: liberation of slaves to fight in the Paraguayan War; the 1867 Speech from the Throne and correspondence between European abolitionists and the imperial government;[5] the personal action of Count d'Eu in Paraguay as Commander in Chief of the Army;[6] identification of the promised emanci-

---

4. *Translator's note:* Nabuco is referring to British seizures of slave ships in Brazilian ports which took place in 1850 and hastened an end to the illegal slave trade. Brazilians, particularly those who wished to see a continuation of the slave trade, were naturally greatly offended by these British actions. Evidently this was still a sensitive issue as late as 1883.

5. *Translator's note:* See chapter 6, note 2.

6. *Translator's note:* The Count d'Eu, husband to Princess Isabel, heiress to the Brazilian throne, served as commander of the Brazilian armed forces in Paraguay and in that capacity urged the provisional Paraguayan government, newly installed in 1869, to abolish Paraguayan slavery. This the subservient Paraguayan government quickly agreed to do.

pation with the ending of the war; the creation of the emancipation bill in the Council of State; the agitation of the Liberal
party following establishment of the Conservative Itaboraí ministry; the fall of the latter and rise of the cabinet of São Vicente;
the opposition to the Rio Branco bill; the dire predictions of
the Dissidence; the struggle organized against the government
and the Emperor by planters of the South; the law of September
28, 1871, itself interpreted by those who defended it; and the
vistas into the future which were revealed to us during the
debate.[7]

Without dwelling long on any one of these historic points, we
can discuss them in such a way as to show, beyond any question
of good faith, that each one of them is related to the destiny of
the slaves.

The effects of the decree of November 6, 1866, which granted
gratuitous freedom to the slave of the state who could serve in
the army and which extended the same benefit to wives of those
who were married, could not have been limited to the small
group directly affected. Moreover, with the trying conditions of
the country at that time, when recruitment—hateful to the people because of the sly and burdensome way it was carried out,
because of its political complications, and because in some cases
prospective recruits could substitute others for themselves—
could hardly supply the needed wave of "Volunteers," it was
obvious that the government was considering arming many slaves
after redeeming them from bondage.[8] The titles of nobility
granted to masters who furnished slaves for the army prove that
the government desired to find soldiers among the slaves.

7. *Translator's note:* For accounts of most of these events which preceded
passage of the Rio Branco Law of September 28, 1871, see Conrad, *Brazilian
Slavery,* pp. 70-115.

8. Concerning the question of whether the government should free slaves
owned by private persons to serve as soldiers in Paraguay, the following was the
opinion which Senator Nabuco [Joaquim Nabuco's father] gave in the Council of
State in November, 1866: "This policy would be disgusting if the status of the
slaves were to be unchanged after serving as soldiers, if they were to remain as
slaves like the 8,000 which Rome bought and armed after the battle of Cannae.
But this will not be the case. The slaves thus bought will be liberated and so will
be citizens before they are soldiers. They will be citizen-soldiers. It is the Constitution of the Empire which makes the freedman a citizen, and if there is no dishonor involved in his voting for public officials, how can there be dishonor in
being a soldier, in defending the country which freed him and to which he belongs? Thus at the same time and by the same act a great service is performed
for emancipation, which is the cause of humanity, and another great service for
the war, which is the national cause. . . . If we employed slaves in the cause of
independence, why not employ them in this war too?"

The bondsmen's collaboration with the army prompted the legal and social uplifting of that class. No people, unless it has lost its own sense of dignity, can deliberately debase those charged with defending it, those who make a profession of maintaining its integrity, its independence, and its national honor. Therefore, it was not the army which the government humiliated by searching for soldiers among the lowest ranks of the slaves; it was rather the entire slave population which it lifted up. Between the master whose title was bestowed upon him for freeing a slave to serve in the army and the slave who became a soldier, the greater honor went to the latter. For the bulk of Brazilian slaves these facts meant that the government, to uphold its own dignity, would someday also attempt to grant citizenship to the brothers of those men who had gone to die for their country on the very day when they had become citizens. The effect of such official acts, to which the untutored mind of the bondsman attributes more justice and honest and sustained purpose than they in fact possess, must be tremendous. From that day on, at any rate, the slaves possessed the government's gift of an alliance with a whole social class: the armed forces.[9]

The Speech from the Throne of May 22, 1867, was for emancipation like a bolt of lightning in a cloudless sky.[10] That sibylline oracle in which the clever euphemism, "servile element," deadened the effect of the reference of the Chief of State to slavery and to the slaves (the institution may exist in our country, but its name may not be spoken from the heights of the Throne before Parliament assembled) was like the eruption of a volcano. That document is intimately linked to two others which play an important role in our history: the message of the French Emancipation Council to the Emperor, and the reply of the Minister of Justice in the name of the Emperor and the Brazilian

---

9. In the Council of State on April 2, 1867, Counselor Paranhos (Rio Branco) said, "The methods which the government finally adopted, urged on by the requirements of war, liberating slaves of the state and of the Crown and rewarding citizens who offered freedmen for the army, not only necessarily inspired the persons most eager for that reform, *but also spread hope among the slaves. All of us can testify that these efforts are having their effects.*" José Antônio Pimenta Bueno, *Trabalho sobre a extincção da escravatura no Brasil* (Rio de Janeiro, 1868) , p. 50.

10. "The *servile element* in Brazil," said the Emperor before the General Assembly, "cannot but merit your attention at an opportune time, considering it in such a way that with present property respected and with no great disturbance in our principal industry—agriculture—the high interests linked to emancipation will be attended to."

government. The second of these humanitarian pieces was signed by Counselor Martim Francisco, and the first by the following French abolitionists: the Duke of Broglie, Guizot, Laboulaye, A. Cochin, Andaluz, Borsier, the Prince of Broglie, Gaumont, Léon Lavedan, Henri Martin, the Count of Montalembert, Henri Moreau, Edouard de Pressensé, Wallon, Eugène Yung.

In that message these men, most of whom were known throughout the world, declared: "Your Majesty is powerful in your Empire; a decision of Your Majesty can result *in the freedom of two million men*." Thus it was not the emancipation of future generations which they were requesting in the name of *humanity and justice;* it was the liberation of the existing slaves themselves, these and no others. In the reply of the Justice Minister [Martim Francisco Ribeiro de Andrada] there are no reservations whatever regarding what was understood by the abolition of slavery. The Emperor gives his thanks for the high regard in which he is held by such notable men and does not suggest that there is the least difference of opinion. The reply of the government must be interpreted in accordance with what was being requested, what was promised because of what was asked. It is only in this sense that the meaning of the final words of the Minister of Justice will be accurately revealed. "The emancipation of the slaves, the necessary consequence of the abolition of the traffic," said the government's reply, "*is only a question of form and of opportunity*. When the difficult circumstances of the nation allow, the Brazilian government will consider as an object of the first importance the realization of that which the spirit of Christianity has so long demanded of the civilized world." [11]

Here is a clear and decisive promise, solemnly made before Europe in 1867, in favor of two million persons who—those of whom are still alive—are still waiting for the state to discover the *form* and to find the *opportunity* of achieving *that which the spirit of Christianity has so long demanded of the civilized world* and which has now been accomplished everywhere except in Brazil.

The initiative taken against slavery in Paraguay by the Count d'Eu, husband of the Imperial Princess, as Commander in Chief of our army, was another commitment made before the world. How could that world believe that the Brazilian general, in de-

11. The two documents are published in their entirety in *O Abolicionista,* November 1, 1880.

manding the abolition of slavery in the conquered nation, did not commit the conqueror to the moral obligation of achieving the same thing in his own country? That army, whose bravery and determination enabled its commander to impose his humanitarian will upon the enemy as an order which was at once obeyed, was made up in part of men who had lived in slavery. Perhaps the Count d'Eu forgot this fact when he demanded an end to slavery in the Paraguayan Republic, and perhaps he forgot that there was an incomparably greater number of slaves in the Brazilian Empire. But the world could not forget either fact when it learned of that gallant request and the way it was carried out.

"If you grant [the slaves] the freedom they request," the Prince wrote to the provisional government of Paraguay in Asunción, "you will have solemnly broken with an institution which was unfortunately bequeathed to many of the peoples of free America by centuries of despotism and deplorable ignorance." The reply to this call was a decree of October 2, 1869, the first article of which declared: "From this day forward slavery is totally abolished in the territory of the Republic." The commitment to do everything in the nation's power to imitate Paraguay's example was as clearly manifested by that final episode of the campaign as if it had been engraved into the Treaty of Peace itself. That debt of honor can only be rebuked if we accept the principle that it is legitimate and just for a nation, using the pretext of humanity and Christianity, to destroy, in an occupied and defenseless enemy territory, an institution from which, within its own borders, it fully intends to derive all possible profit until the death of its last victims. Such a notion, however, would reduce war to piracy and the commander of an army to the ringleader of a band of robbers, and it is entirely unacceptable to those who regard "moral law," in the words of John Bright, "as binding upon nations as it is upon individuals."

In regard to the hope which resulted from agitation before and after the parliamentary campaign which created the law of 1871 and from the promises later made, it will suffice for the moment to point out that the opposition to that bill in the legislature must have given the slaves the impression that the end of their bondage was near. The excessive fury of many slaveholders, the disreputable language used against the monarchy on the plantations, where walls also have ears; the role of the Emperor, whose name to the slaves is synonymous with social power and even with Providence, being as he is the defender of their cause; and, finally, the complete failure of the antigovernment campaign—each of these several features of that restless period seemed designed to implant courage into the souls of the slaves, to fill them with a sense of liberty.

From the day when the Speech from the Throne before the Zacarias cabinet unexpectedly and without warning raised the formidable question of the *"servile element"* until the day when the Rio Branco Law was passed in the Senate amid popular acclaim, with the chamber floor covered with flowers, the nation was in a state of uncertainty, disagreeable to the planters but, for the opposite reason, a time of hope for the slaves. The rise of the Viscount Itaboraí to power in 1868, after the promises contained in that speech and in the celebrated letter to the European abolitionists, meant either one of two things.[12] Either the Emperor, perhaps because of the war, was more concerned with the state of the treasury than with slavery reform; or in political matters, in the experience of Dom Pedro II, the straight line was not the shortest distance between two points. As is also known, that ministry fell mainly because of the attitude assumed toward that question by its opponents, and by its friends who wished to see it fall. The call to Viscount São Vicente to replace Viscount Itaboraí was a sign that the emancipationist reform, always to be associated with that statesman's name, as well as with the names of others, was in fact to be undertaken.[13] Unfortunately the President of the Council of Ministers organized a divided cabinet which, therefore, was forced to surrender its place to a combination more conducive to the purpose the nation and the Crown had in mind. This was the Rio Branco ministry.

During this entire period of backsliding and hesitation, the Liberal party, which had included "the emancipation of the slaves" in its program in 1869, aroused the country by every means, in the Senate, in the press, in public meetings. "To postpone the decision indefinitely is unthinkable," Senator Nabuco, president of the Centro Liberal, told the Senate Conservatives the same year. "The Liberal party, aware that you intend to do

12. *Translator's note:* Itaboraí was a Conservative leader and an opponent of the free-birth proposal.

13. *Translator's note:* São Vicente (José Antônio Pimenta Bueno), probably encouraged by the Emperor, had written a free-birth proposal as early as January, 1866. His *Trabalho*, cited in note 9 above, is a valuable source of information concerning the debate over slavery during this period.

nothing, will not agree to this, will continue to air the question."
And in 1870 that statesman insisted even more forcefully:

> Gentlemen, this matter is very grave. It is the most important
> question facing Brazilian society, and it is foolish to leave it to
> chance. Do you want to know the results of inaction? I must speak
> with complete sincerity, with all the power of my convictions. A
> small step will be enough today, but tomorrow a giant stride will
> not suffice. In political matters, opportunity is the main considera-
> tion. Reforms, however small, have real value when society is
> ready for them. Later they do not satisfy anyone, however sweeping
> they may be. If you do not want gradual methods, you will have
> to accept even greater changes in swift succession. If you do not
> desire the consequences of a measure calmly decided by yourselves,
> you will have to accept the dubious results of improvidence. If
> you do not desire the economic inconvenience endured in the
> British and French Antilles, you will run the risk of confronting
> the horrors of Santo Domingo.

How could such agitation in favor of the slaves by one of the
great national parties, itself recently in power, help but inspire
the bondsmen with confidence that their freedom, though perhaps near at hand, perhaps distant, was in any case a certainty?
The battle cry which echoed through the country was not "the
emancipation of the newborn." There cannot be, except in a
figurative sense, *emancipation* of persons who are still nonexistent, but there can be "emancipation of the slaves." The
rights alleged, the arguments produced, were all applicable to
the present generations. An earthquake of this kind could not
restrict its tremendous shock to the area marked for it, could not
shake the land where nothing had been constructed without
cracking the earth nearby. The impulse was not to the interests
of the party but to human conscience, and when there is a desire
to convert a revolution into a reform, it must at least be made
certain that that reform possesses a channel broad enough to
contain the torrent.

Everything said during that period of uncertainty, when the
opposition tried to wrest from the Conservative party the reform
bill which it refused to reveal, constitutes so many more promises
solemnly made to the slaves.[14] In the agitation no one took the

___

14. A very odd thing happened in 1870. The special committee headed by Mr.
Teixeira Junior, with the support of the Chamber, asked the government that
copies of the bills sent to the Council of State in 1867 and 1868 and of the

trouble to explain to them that the measure was not intended to
be in their favor, but in favor of their children only. On the
contrary, there was talk of both present and future generations,
and on the banner raised from the North to the South no legislative articles were inscribed, only a one-word emblem of
struggle: "Emancipation."

Now let us see the promises which can be reasonably inferred
from that same law of September 28, 1871, which was and could
not help but be a tremendous deception for the slaves, who had
heard it said that the Emperor wanted *emancipation* and that
emancipation was to be granted. Regarded in the beginning as
plunderous by the landed aristocracy, that legislative act, which
did not restrict their acquired rights in any way, became in time
their main line of defense. But it is not what is said today that is
important to us; it is what was said before the law was passed.
To measure its importance, it is essential to consider what was
then believed, not by those who passed the bill, but by those
who fought against it. In this case the foresight was all on the
side of the latter—an odd result of moral blindness. It was the
opponents of the law who accurately measured its real consequences, who pointed out its paradoxes and absurdities, and
who predicted that this could not and would not be the final
solution to such a great problem.

opinions of members of the council be urgently submitted to it. To this request
the Minister of Justice (J. O. Nebias) and the Minister of Empire (Paulino de
Sousa) replied that there were no papers whatever in their respective secretariats.

In its report the committee stated: "In a *confidential* manner and with the
repeated recommendation of *the greatest restraint,* a copy of the four acts of the
sessions of the Council of State and of the final bill there examined was shown
to the committee by one of the worthy members of the Cabinet. Under these
conditions, therefore, the committee cannot reveal any of the opinions printed in
these documents." However, according to Article 7 of the law of October 15, 1827,
"the Counselors of State are responsible for the advice they give, etc." The italics
are those of the report.

CHAPTER VIII

The Promises of "The Law of Emancipation"

> The great injustice of the law is that it did not attend to the present generations.
>
> —JOSÉ ANTÔNIO SARAIVA [1]

IN THIS CHAPTER I will study the Rio Branco Law from only one point of view. I will consider the expectations which could reasonably be aroused, by the law itself and by the way it was passed, in anyone who attributes to our legislative power a firm purpose, serious intentions, a sense of national honor, and a spirit of fair play. If we do not look upon that body as determined, thoughtful, patriotic, and just, the law can contain no promises at all, and we might even expect its inadequate enforcement, like that of the law of November 7, 1831, passed when the nation was still at the mercy of the slave traders.

The law of September 28, 1871,[2] let it be said in passing, was a giant step forward for the nation. As imperfect, incomplete, ill-conceived, unjust, and even absurd as it looks to us today, that law was nothing less than a moral blockade of slavery. Its only decisive and irreversible part was this principle: "No one again will be born a *slave*." All the rest was either temporary, such as the surrender of those same *ingênuos* to bondage until

---

1. *Translator's note:* Saraiva was a prominent Liberal politician who was head of the cabinet in 1880, when Nabuco began his antislavery campaign in the General Assembly. In 1885 he was head of the cabinet which directed the Sexagenarian Law (Saraiva-Cotegipe Law) through the Chamber of Deputies. This law provided for the liberation of slaves sixty and older with the condition that they serve their masters three more years as a form of indemnification.

2. Concerning this law I am not open to suspicion. First, I have a strong personal interest in the historic reputation of Viscount Rio Branco, and second, no one contributed more toward preparing that legislative act or toward arousing public opinion in its support than my father, who from 1866 until 1871 adopted it as his primary political goal. "In the Council of State, in correspondence with the planters, and on the rostrum by means of the most eloquent speeches, it was he who caused the idea to ripen and to take on the dimensions of a national cause," Mr. F. Octaviano said of Senator Nabuco in the Senate in 1871. During that whole period, from 1866 to 1871, when the known determination of the Emperor served as a nucleus for the formation of a constitutional force able to overcome the power of slavery, that statesman, along with Souza Franco, Octaviano, and Tavares Bastos, prepared the Liberal party, while São Vicente and Sales Torres-Homem prepared the Conservative party for the reform, to which the Viscount Rio Branco was granted the deserved honor of linking his name, to the applause of all the rest.

the age of twenty-one; or incomplete, such as the system of compulsory redemption; or insignificant, such as the classes of slaves freed; or absurd, such as the right of the slave woman's master to compensation for the eight-year-old child whom he does not abandon to die, to take the form of a bond worth 600 *milréis* [$330]; or unjust, as in the separation of the child from his mother in the case of the latter's transfer to another owner. So much for what is contained in the law. As to what was forgotten, the index of omissions would be endless. In spite of everything, however, the simple basic principle to which it assents is enough to make this law the first act of humanitarian legislation in our history.

Reduced to its simplest terms, the law means the end of slavery within half a century. But this extinction of slavery could not be decreed for the future without causing a widespread desire that it be decreed for the present. It is not only the slaves who are dissatisfied with their children's freedom alone and who want to be free themselves. All of us, in fact, wish to see Brazil relieved and cleansed of slavery, and we are not satisfied with the certainty that future generations will enjoy that privilege. When the law of September 28 said to the slaves, "From this day on your children will be born *free*, and when they reach the age of civil emancipation they will be citizens"—let us forget for a moment the compulsory *services*—it said implicitly to all Brazilians, "Your children or your grandchildren will belong to a nation reborn."

For the slave, that double promise may seem final, but not for the free. The effect of that vision of a decent and respected country for those who will come after us can be none other than to arouse in us the desire to live in such a country. When a government enhances the honor and dignity of its future citizens, those now possessing less honor will naturally protest the delay. It is not likely that the slaves are jealous of their children's good fortune, but what sentiment other than jealousy will assure us, the citizens of a land of slaves, that the next generation, because of an absence of slavery, will enjoy a more virtuous homeland?

It is because of that sense of pride, of national honor, inseparable from real patriotism that we dare to hope that the law of September 28 will not be the final decision determining the personal fate of each slave and each Brazilian. The complaints raised in opposition to the bill were not so persuasive as to cause its rejection, since its flaws, shortcomings, and absurdities are infinitely preferable to the logic of slavery. But the opinions expressed by the bill's opponents showed how, even in their minds, the reform once promulgated would require expansion, development, and ethical adjustments.

The law of September 28 should be looked upon not as a transaction between the state and the owners of slaves, but as an act of national sovereignty. The proprietors had as much right to impose their will upon the country as any other minority. The law is not a treaty which is thought to be unalterable without the agreement of both parties. On the contrary, when it was made, it was with the understanding of both sides—certainly on the part of the slaveholders—that it was only a first step. Those who rejected it claimed that it would be equivalent to immediate abolition.[3] Among those who voted for it, many described it as inadequate and expressed the hope of seeing it completed by other measures, notably the setting of a date for total abolition. However, even if the legislature had unanimously passed a law so broad and meaningful as to constitute a complete end to the question, that legislature possessed neither a special mandate to bind future chambers to its decisions nor the right to make laws which later assemblies could not broaden or revoke. Later we will see what terrible predictions were made at that time, what extraordinary measures were thought essential.

Another remarkable claim is that this law legalized every abuse which it did not prohibit, pardoned all crimes it did not punish, revoked all laws which it did not mention. It is even asserted that the clause which expressly abolished the former revocations of freedom [4] went so far as to revoke in turn the charter of liberation which the law of November 7, 1831, granted to every African imported after that date. Such interpretations in slavery matters—matters in which in the event of doubt, and here there is no doubt whatever, it is the principle of freedom which prevails—are not surprising when even today we read

---

3. "What I predict will certainly occur," said Almeida Pereira in the Chamber of Deputies in August, 1871. "If the government's bill passes, emancipation will be achieved in this country within two years. (Applause.) Mr. Andrade Figueira: And they are aware of this. Mr. C. Machado: It will be the beginning of complete emancipation. Mr. Andrade Figueira: The President of the Council declared in his report in the Council of State that this would be the result."

4. *Translator's note:* Article 3 of the Rio Branco Law revoked an old law which allowed a master to re-enslave a person whom he had liberated if that person had been "ungrateful."

advertisements placed by public authorities for the judicial sale of *ingênuos*.[5]

Nevertheless, that interpretation, which exists today only because most of our magistrates are accomplices of slavery, as they were so long of the traffic, deviates too much from public opinion to endanger the character of the law of September 28. Leaving aside the proslavery interpretation of the law, let us see in what ways the need to reform it was obvious from the beginning in the eyes of those who fought against it. Then, employing the arguments of those who supported it, let us consider in what ways it needed to be expanded and endowed with broader powers. Let us begin with the latter.

In general, it can be said that the law is incomplete because it ignores measures proposed much earlier in Parliament; for example, the Wanderley Bill of 1854, which would have prohibited interprovincial traffic in slaves.[6] The law which freed the newborn might well have localized slavery within the provinces. Similarly, major points most strongly advocated in the Council of State—for example, the fixing of a maximum price for manumission, the revocation of the savage punishment of the lash and the law of June 10, 1835, the ban on separation of families which was incompletely formulated in the law of September 15, 1869—were left out of the government's proposal; and thus, after passage of the so-called emancipation law, the Brazilian Black Code, civil and penal, remains on the whole as barbarous as it was before.

The main direction taken by those who wished to broaden the law was toward fixing a terminal date. In this matter Souza

---

5. In regard to one of these advertisements, I had the honor to direct a protest to the Viscount Paranaguá, President of the Council, in which I wrote: "The law of November 7, 1831, is revoked *de facto;* and now the moment has arrived for the government to demonstrate that this cannot be the fate of the law of September 28, 1871. The *traffic in ingênuos* which is beginning to appear must be stopped. It is not by hushing up such scandals that this can be achieved. That official advertisement of Valença [an agricultural community in the province of Rio de Janeiro] opens a very sad page in the history of Brazil which Your Excellency must eliminate at once. By undertaking the sale of the *ingênuos'* services with or without government announcements, the law of September 28, 1871, will soon be looked upon by the world as the most monstrous lie to which a nation can resort to conceal a crime. The question is this: *Can the* ingênuos *be sold or not?* The government has the duty to salvage the dignity of that whole immense class created by the law of September 28."

6. *Translator's note:* This proposal introduced into the Chamber of Deputies by João Mauricio Wanderley (later Baron Cotegipe) in August, 1854, was intended to prohibit the interprovincial slave trade as a means of preventing the loss of much of the North's slave population to the wealthier South. This bill was rejected by the Chamber. See Conrad, *Brazilian Slavery*, pp. 65-67.

Franco played the most important role, and the date which I
suggested in the Chamber of Deputies in 1880 [7] was nothing
less than the plan outlined by that statesman in the following
proposal, which he presented to the Council of State in 1867:

> That the declaration of the day on which slavery in the Empire
> will cease to exist should be set for the tenth year of the execution
> of the above-named law, the relevant article being the following:
> Article 23. In the tenth year of the execution of that law the
> government, having collected all available information, will pre-
> sent it to the General Legislative Assembly, along with statistics
> on the slaves freed in virtue of its execution, and the number of
> slaves still existing in the Empire, so that, with its recommenda-
> tion, a date may be fixed on which slavery will entirely cease to
> exist.[8]

The provision (he added in 1868) which is most notably lacking
(in the bill under discussion in the Council of State) is that which
concerns the establishment of a date on which slavery will end in
the entire Empire. The silence of the bill on this very important
point seems intended to avoid calls for a very early date, which
would shock the slaveholders, and to avoid as well the delicate
question of indemnification. *However, it will not satisfy those who
are demanding a clear commitment to the elimination of slavery.*

On the other hand, the terminal date was opposed within the
liberal group itself as being too distant in time. Pimenta Bueno,
later the Marquis of São Vicente, had proposed December 31,
1899, as the date for total abolition with indemnification. This
was the time span discussed in the Council of State,[9] where some

7. *Translator's note:* According to Nabuco's proposal of 1880, slavery would
have ended at the end of that decade.

8. The outstanding Liberal leader thus believed that in the legislative session
of 1879 it would be possible "to decree the complete abolition of slavery" at the
end of the first or second half of the present decade.

9. In a bill introduced on May 17, 1865, Viscount Jequitinhonha [a senator
from Bahia and long an opponent of slavery] proposed, among other measures, a
terminal period of fifteen years. This period, if it had been adopted, would have
ended slavery in 1880. Two years later, however, in the Council of State, while
delivering his thoughts on the Pimenta Bueno terminal date (the end of the
century), that same statesman condemned it, revealing himself as determined to
adopt the program of freedom for those born after promulgation of the law.
Jequitinhonha, whom the Viscount Jaguari called "the first statesman who pledged
himself to the abolition of slavery" (the praise would have been more just if he
had said "in the Second Empire"), was a convinced, frank, and open abolitionist.
Nevertheless, that statesman, when discussing the absurd question which most
concerned the Council of State, whether the free children of slave women would
be *ingênuos* or *libertos,* in which the principle "the offspring follows the womb"

judged it much too long for the slaves to bear and others saw it as much too remote in time to be legislated in 1867. The length of the terminal period was indeed absurd. The opinion of Counselor Nabuco was, "I am not in agreement with that article of the (São Vicente) bill which sets slavery's terminal date on the last day of 1899." He added, "If we cannot decide on a shorter period, it is better to say nothing. If each of us will estimate when slavery could end, considering the probable effects of the natural factors of birth and death and the provisions contained in the bill, *the declaration of a quarter of a century is not flattering to Brazil.*"

During the discussion of the bill in the Senate, however, a shorter period—twenty years—was recommended by Senator Silveira da Mota.[10] This compromise would have allowed slavery to last *without any limitation whatsoever* until 1891, a date now approaching. However, even this date seemed too distant to Senator Nabuco, who said in the Senate: *"I support the idea of a terminal date, not, however, as a substitute for the main purpose of the bill, but as a complement to it."*

The terminal period which the proposed law established for slavery was fifty or sixty years. Along with freedom at birth, the law was to have other results, so it was hoped that once it was passed "the strife among the parties would cause gradual emancipation to give way to *the broadest and fastest possible process of liberation."* [11] For this reason the terminal date was only a way of protecting the interests of the existing slave generations, to fill up in some way the great void of injustice contained in the law, revealed in the phrase of Mr. Saraiva which serves as an epigraph to this chapter.

The law did *not attend to the present generations;* but it was made in their name, was wrought by the compassion and concern which their fate aroused inside and outside the country, which spread the news to the world that Brazil had freed her slaves.

(*partus sequitur ventrem*) played such a crucial role, allowed himself to become entangled in a cobweb of Romanism by allying himself with those who wanted to put the label of *liberto* on persons who had never been slaves. However, these and other errors in no way reduce the abolitionist glory of Montezuma [Jequitinhonha's adopted revolutionary name], whose stand before slavery was always that of an opponent, convinced that it was literally, in his phrase, "the cancer" of Brazil.

10. *Translator's note:* José Inácio Silveira da Mota represented the province of Goiás in the Senate from 1855 to 1889.

11. This statement is from a speech delivered by Nabuco de Araújo during discussion of the antislavery bill.

For this reason, during the entire discussion the predominant mood was one of sorrow, since so much was being done for those who had not yet been born and so little for those who had passed their lives in bondage.

Now let us turn to the arguments of the bill's opponents. The injustice of liberating the newborn while leaving the existing slaves to their fate could not and did not go unnoticed by friends of the law, and it was thrown into their faces by their opponents. The concern of the latter for the elderly slaves bent under the weight of years could not be expressed more pathetically than it was, for example, by the farmers of Piraí in the words which I italicize: "Founded upon the most obvious relative injustice among the slaves," said the planters of that rural county, " (the proposal) concedes the privilege of freedom to those who, through their blindness perhaps, were born after that date, meanwhile keeping enslaved *the individuals who, because of their long, profitable, and abundant services, have a greater claim to freedom."*

This was the loud and formidable cry of the enemies of the bill: "You liberate the future generations," they said "and do nothing for those who for thirty, forty, or fifty years and more have been immersed in the degradation of slavery." To this the supporters of the reform replied: "We do not forget the present generations. For them there is gradual liberation." Or in the phrase of Nabuco, "The slaves must put their trust in gradual liberation." The commitment of the country to the living could not have been more solemn. It said to them: "For the moment we are decreeing the freedom of your children still unborn, but your freedom will not be long delayed. The law established means. It created an emancipation fund which will liberate all of you. It arranged for you to go to the emancipation societies for the money you need for your freedom."

On the other hand, the law was denounced as slavery's ruin. We have seen what was said in the Chamber of Deputies. Everywhere, in fact, it was declared that abolition would come soon after the law. The fears of the Marquis of Olinda that the state would be "sent into convulsion" were not verified.[12] But such

12. "If we do not follow the plan which I have just outlined (that of doing absolutely nothing) , I can imagine no measure which can save the nation from being reduced to a state of turmoil. One word which raises the idea of emancipation, however adorned (he meant *disguised*) it may be, opens the door to endless tragedy." Pimenta Bueno, *Trabalho sobre a extincção da escravatura no Brasil*, pp. 38, 41.

fears sprang from a grasp of the logic of human affairs which this phrase of Viscount Itaboraí reveals: "It is not necessary for the slaves to be very clever to understand that parents have the same rights as their children, nor can it be imagined that they will watch with indifference the end of their hopes of freedom, which they have cherished in their hearts."

Here clearly is an aspect of the law of September 28 which its opponents correctly recognized as out of step with justice. The bill's enemies cried out: "You must do for the present generations at least as much as is required to avoid making what is done for future generations seem like trickery to the living." If this demand did not carry enough ethical weight to prevent the chambers from passing the bill, now that it is an official law those who raised the point are themselves obliged to humanize it.

To those who fought the reform of 1871 Mr. Cristiano Otôni declared two years ago from the rostrum of the Senate: "What patriotism suggests is that we immerse ourselves in the law of September 28 in order to study its flaws and omissions, to correct and overcome them." The flaws and omissions denounced by the opposition were mainly neglect of the present generation and the servile status of *ingênuos* until the age of twenty-one. The most active enemies of the law recognized at that time that "the Brazilian nation had taken on serious commitments before other nations," and that the pledge to free the slaves through a special fund was a debt of honor. "For five years," said Otôni, "the hope of freedom emanating from the throne rained down upon the miserable bondsmen like manna upon the Israelites in the wilderness." [13]

---

13. José do Alencar, a minister of the cabinet of Itaborai denounced that period of preparation in terms which, rather than dishonoring Dom Pedro II, are a credit to him. "We are not dealing with a law, we are dealing with a conspiracy of power," said Alencar, a famed novelist of Ceará, who in this matter allowed himself to be led by his personal interests rather than his best instincts. "Since 1867 that power has plotted, wearing down the resistance of politicians called to lead, weakening the resistance of political parties. Since 1867 it has been covertly preparing this *coup d'état*, which must either confirm absolutism or unmask it." That the Emperor used his personal power, particularly from 1845 until 1850, in favor of suppressing the slave trade, resulting during that period in the measures of Eusébio de Queirós, and that he used it from 1866 until 1871 in favor of the freedom of the newborn, resulting in that latter year in the Rio Branco Law, are facts which the Emperor, if he should wish to write his memoirs and give an account of what happened in the various cabinets of the two periods, could establish historically with countless documents. His part in what has been done is very great—almost the essential part—since he could have accomplished the same things with other men and other means without fear of revolution.

In regard to the *ingênuos,* for example, with what apparent logic and sense of civic dignity did the foes of the law denounce the creation of that class of future citizens reared in slavery with all its vices? Even Mr. Cristiano Otôni himself, in a speech in the Agricultural and Commercial Club, used such terms in respect to that class: "And what citizens are these? How can they later enter society, having been *de facto* slaves, not knowing how to read and write, not having the slightest notion of the rights and duties of the citizen, abounding in all the vices of the slave hut? (*Applause.*) Vices of mind and vices of heart (*Applause.*)" [14]

Such *applause* from those directly responsible for "the vices of the slave hut" is at best unconscionable. By its nature the argument is abolitionist. And when formulated by those same persons who hoped to retain those *ingênuos* as *de facto* slaves, it is poorly placed compassion and hardly a condemnation of the political potential of the freedman.

Despite this, however, when Mr. Paulino de Sousa,[15] in an argument directed against Viscount Rio Branco, denounced "that favored class of *ingênuos*—whom the Vicount Itaboraí had called *free slaves*—reared in slavery until the age of twenty-one, that is, during those years when their character, tendencies, and personal habits are being formed," that Conservative leader,

---

What I am saying, in fact, is that if, since his rise to the throne, Dom Pedro II, with no greater use of his personal power than he exercised, for example, to carry on the Paraguayan War until the complete destruction of Lopez's government, had given abolition his unflagging attention, even as the main concern of his father's regime was the achievement of independence, slavery by this time would have disappeared from Brazil. It is a fact that but for the Emperor the worst traffickers in slaves would have become counts and marquises of the Empire, and that His majesty always demonstrated a distaste for the traffic and an interest in free labor. But, compared with the aggregate of power which he either exercises or possesses, what has been done for the slaves during his forty-three-year reign is small indeed. It is enough to observe that even today the capital of the Empire is a slave market! Observe, on the other hand, what Czar Alexander II did during only six years in power.

We have no reason to be disturbed by those who say we are contradictory because we appeal to the Emperor while being opposed, at least very largely, to *personal government.* The exercise of the prestige and amassed power which the Emperor personifies in Brazil on behalf of the liberation of the slaves would be, in the fullest sense, the expression of national will. With slavery there is no free government or true democracy. There is only government by caste and rule by monopoly. The slave huts cannot possess democratic representatives, and the subjected and impoverished population does not dare to have them.

14. C. B. Otôni, *A emancipação dos escravos* (Rio de Janeiro, 1871), p. 97.

15. *Translator's note:* Paulino José Soares de Sousa was a senator from the province of Rio de Janeiro and a consistent opponent of abolition from the 1870s until the eve of abolition.

while obviously not wishing to do so, demonstrated one of the
capital defects of that law which, in accordance with civic
dignity, was so in need of changes. There is no reason (and here
our Constitution permits no doubt) why the former slave should
not become a citizen. But there are serious reasons why the
ingênuos, citizens like any others, should not be reared in slavery.
Now that these *ingênuos* exist, however, is it not the responsibility of those who so clearly recognize that mistake in the law to
make certain that "the character, tendencies, and habits" of
hundreds of thousands of Brazilian citizens will develop far from
the unhealthy atmosphere of the slave hut, which those who
know it best admit is a true Den of Dogs for every respectable
trait?

It can thus be concluded that every word uttered against the
law by its opponents from the point of view of civilization re-
verberates back to them as an obligation to alter and expand it.
In that sense Mr. Cristiano Otôni gave a fine example. On the
other hand, the hope, encouragement, and expectations with
which the reform's supporters filled the spirit and imagination
of the slaves constitute so many additional promises whose ful-
fillment the slaves may rightfully demand. The law was not the
shameful repudiation of the commitment made to the world in
1866 by the Brazilian Minister of Foreign Affairs. On the contrary, the law was the recognition of that commitment, its solemn
ratification.

What has been done so far to pay that debt of honor? In these
pages will be seen the real and promised effects of the law as
compared with the effects of death; private initiative and the
slave masters' kindness and good will have accomplished much
more than the state, but ten times less than death. "Death frees
300,000," said the unquestioned authority whom I have cited so
often, Mr. Cristiano Otôni, "private persons free 35,000, and
the state, *which committed itself to emancipation,* 5,000 in the
same period." [16] The slave markets survive, families are still being broken up, the ways to escape slavery outlined in the law are
still blocked. Slavery remains as it always was. Its crimes and
atrocities are constantly recurring, and the slaves find themselves
in the same personal plight, with the same expectations, the same
future prospects that have been theirs since the first Africans
were trooped into the Brazilian backlands. If we do not go

---

16. *Translator's note:* Otôni was referring to the number of slaves freed by the
emancipation fund, which was minimal before 1880.

beyond the law of 1871, that law will remain a national lie, a sham to mislead the world, the Brazilian people, and, sadder still, the slaves themselves.

Yet their cause finds support upon other grounds: the illegality of slavery, which should not, however, be looked upon as more solid grounds of support than these national commitments. In order to prove the extent of slavery's illegality among us, we must know its origins and its history. We must learn of the piracy from which it derived its privileges in a succession of endorsements which were no more valid than the first transactions.

CHAPTER IX

The African Traffic

Andrada! tear out that banner from the skies!
Columbus! close up the ports of your seas!
—Antônio de Castro Alves [1]

SLAVERY among us in this century has no sources other than the commerce in Africans. Various crimes against the indigenous race in the North have been denounced, but such incidents are rare. Among the slaves there certainly are descendants of mixed-bloods enslaved long ago, but such exceptions do not deprive Brazilian slavery of its purely African character. The slaves are either imported Africans themselves or their descendants.

Explorers tell us in horrifying pages what the traffic in slaves on the African continent was and, unfortunately, still is today. What it was like on the slave ships we know through the oral tradition of its victims. Later we will see what happened to them after they finally landed on our beaches, from the time the bonfires were lit to announce their arrival until the caravans of *boçais* [raw slaves] took their places beside the *ladinos* [acculturated Africans] on the plantations. It is sufficient now to point out that, during its long course, history does not reveal another generalized crime which in its perversity, terrors, and boundlessness of personal crimes, which for its duration, morbid aims, and brutality of complex system of techniques, for the profits wrested from it, the number of its victims, and all its results, can be even distantly compared with the African colonization of America.

To attempt to describe the traffic in slaves in East Africa (wrote Dr. Livingstone) I had to remain well inside the truth so as not to accuse myself of exaggeration; but the topic did not allow me to succeed. To paint its effects with colors too strong is quite simply impossible. The sights I witnessed, though they were incidents common to the traffic, are so repulsive that I am constantly

---

1. *Translator's note:* Antônio de Castro Alves (1847-71) was a noted writer whom Nabuco once appropriately called "the poet of the slaves." The lines in this quotation are from one of his many poems about slavery, "Tragedia no mar (O navio negreiro)"—"Tragedy at Sea (The Slave Ship)"—which was written in 1868.

trying to cast them from my thoughts. As to the most disagreeable
memories, I succeed at last in subduing them in my mind, but
scenes of the traffic return to my memory uninvited and cause me
to tremble in the silence of night, horrified by the vividness with
which they are reproduced.[2]

These words of Livingstone eliminate the need of other descriptions of the persecution which has victimized Africa for
centuries because of the color of its people.

Castro Alves in his "Tragedia no mar" ["Tragedy at Sea"]
drew an accurate picture of the Dantesque torment of the
quarterdecks and the deep holds of the slave ships.[3] Whoever has
heard the horrors of the traffic described will always have before
his eyes a picture reminiscent of the painting by Géricault, *The
Wreck of the Medusa*. Southey's ballad of the sailor who had
taken part in that accursed voyage, whom sorrow granted no
repose, whose conscience, implacable and avenging, persecuted
him from within, expresses the mental agony of so many persons
who, having a spark of conscience, were engaged in that contraband of blood.

Once landed, the living skeletons were conveyed to the regime
of the plantations, to the environment of coffee. The work of
the traffic had ended and that of slavery had begun.

In this volume I will not discuss the history of the slave trade
and therefore will refer only incidentally to the humiliations
that trade's insatiable and sanguinary greed imposed upon Brazil.
From 1831 until 1850 the Brazilian government found itself, in
effect, a pawn of Great Britain in a diplomatic struggle which for
our nation was of the saddest kind, since we were unable to
enforce our treaties and laws. Instead of coming patriotically to
an understanding with Britain for complete destruction of the
piracy which infested our ports and coasts, as nearly all the
powers of Europe and America had done in that period, the gov-

2. *Translator's note:* This is a retranslation from Nabuco's Portuguese translation. The original source could not be located.

3. Those ships, known as floating coffins, which they were in more than one
sense, cost comparatively little. A vessel of one hundred tons worth seven *contos*
served for the shipment of 350 slaves. Testimony of Sir Charles Hotham, commander of the British squadron in western Africa, April, 1849, *First Report from
the Select Committee on the Slave Trade* (London, 1849), sec. 604. The total cost
of transportation of that many slaves (ship, crew's salary, provisions, the commander, etc.) did not exceed 10 *contos* [in 1849 about $6,000], or in round
numbers 30 *milréis* [about $17] per head. *Ibid.*, secs. 604-11. A captured brig of 167
tons had 852 slaves aboard, and another of 59 tons carried 400. After seizure many
of these ships were destroyed as unfit for navigation.

ernment allowed itself to be victimized and to surrender its
authority to the benefit of the slave dealers, rather than to accept
with gratitude help of the foreigner in rescuing our flag from the
control of pirates. Britain waited until 1845 for Brazil to reach
an agreement with her; and it was only in that year, when for
the lack of a treaty the English were about to lose the fruits of
twenty-eight years of work, that Lord Aberdeen produced his
bill. The Aberdeen Bill, it can be said, was an embarrassment
which slavery forced upon the Brazilian government.[4] The
struggle between Britain and the traffic was a bitter one, and for
the honor of humanity it could not—and should not—have
ended with Britain's retreat. It was this fact that our statesmen
did not understand. The darkness which enveloped them because
of slavery did not allow them to recognize that in 1845 our
century's sun was already too high in the heavens to shine down
upon such piracy in our hemisphere.

Only in one sense was the Aberdeen Bill less than honorable
to England. As stated at various times in the British Parliament,
Britain did to a weak nation what she would not have done to a
powerful one. One of the last slave cargoes to Brazil, that of the
so-called Africans of Bracuí interned in 1852 in Bananal in
São Paulo, was transported under the flag of the United States.
When British vessels encountered slave ships which raised the
stars and stripes, they allowed them to continue their voyages.
The attitude of the British Parliament in passing a law giving
the courts of Britain jurisdiction over Brazilian ships and subjects employed in the traffic, even when taken in Brazilian territorial waters, would have been greatly to England's credit if that
law had been part of a system of equal measures against *all* flags
usurped by the agents of that piracy.

But, whatever the weakness of Britain in not confronting the
strong as well as the weak, the Brazilian who reads the diplomatic
history of the most active period of the traffic will see the magnitude of the power which the combined slave-trade interests exercised over our nation.

That power was such that a memorandum on the slavery question sent by Eusébio de Queirós to the cabinet as early as 1849

---

4. *Translator's note:* The Aberdeen Bill of 1845 authorized British admiralty
courts to judge and condemn Brazilian ships captured while engaged in illegal
slave trading. Though much resented in Brazil, the act was justified by Great
Britain on the basis of the British-Brazilian anti-slave-trade treaty of 1826, which
condemned the slave trade as piracy. For an account of the passage of the law, see
Bethell, *Abolition of the Brazilian Slave Trade,* pp. 242-66.

began as follows: "To suppress the African traffic in the country *without provoking a revolution* requires us: (1) to attack new importations vigorously, overlooking and pardoning those carried out before passage of the law; (2) to direct the repression against the traffic at sea or at the moment of landing, while the Africans are in the hands of their importers." The same statesman, in his celebrated speech of 1852, in trying to show how the traffic was ended solely in the interests of the planters, whose estates were passing into the hands of speculators and traffickers as a result of debts contracted for the supplying of slaves, acknowledged the pressure exerted by agriculture in complicity with that trade upon all the governments and parties between 1831 and 1850:

> Let us be frank (he said). In Brazil the traffic was linked to the interests, or, more correctly, to the presumed interests, of our planters. And in a country where agriculture has so much power, it was natural that public opinion, which has so much influence not only in representative governments but even in absolute monarchies, would express itself in favor of the traffic. Why does it surprise us that our politicians bowed before that law of necessity? Why is it surprising that all of us—friends or enemies of the traffic —bowed before that necessity? Gentlemen, if this was a crime, it was a very widespread crime in Brazil. But I maintain that when in a nation all the political parties hold power, when all of its politicians have been called to exercise that power and all of them agree on one policy, that policy must have been based upon very powerful considerations. It cannot possibly be a crime, and it would be bold to call it a mistake.[5]

If the word "slavery" were substituted for the word "traffic," that eloquent passage so warmly applauded by the Chamber might eventually serve as an apology for today's politicians who may wish to justify our time. The fact is, however, that there always was a difference between the declared enemies of the traffic and its defenders. With that reservation made in favor of a few public men who were *without complicity* in the trade, and another in regard to the decency of the opinion that violation of a moral law cannot be called a *crime* or a *mistake* if an entire nation commits it, the rationalizations of the great Minister of

5. *Translator's note:* Eusébio de Queirós Coutinho Mattoso Camara, *Questão do trafico, Discurso proferido na Camera dos Deputados* (Rio de Janeiro, 1852), p. 15.

Justice of 1850 do not exaggerate the degradation to which our political system had fallen until quite recent times.

A few facts will illustrate the point. By the Convention of 1826 the African slave trade was to be regarded as equivalent to piracy at the end of three years, and the Brazilian law which declared it such bears the date of September 4, 1850. The immediate freedom of Africans legally captured was guaranteed by the same convention when it ratified the treaty of 1817 between Portugal and Great Britain, and the decree which *emancipated* the *free* Africans was dated September 24, 1864.[6] Finally, the law of November 7, 1831, is not enforced even today, and those whom it declared to be free are still in bondage. In this question of the traffic, we drink the dregs from the very bottom of the cup.

It is for this reason that we are ashamed to read the accusations made against us by men like Sir Robert Peel, Lord Palmerston, and Lord Brougham, and to see British ministers demanding the freedom of Africans whom our own law declared free with no result whatsoever.[7] Under the pretext of wounded national pride, our government, which found itself in the constrained position described by Eusébio de Queirós, practically concealed the trafficking expeditions organized in Rio and Bahia under the banner of its sovereignty. If what was done in 1850 had been done in 1844, there would certainly not have been an Aberdeen Bill.

The question should not have arisen between Brazil and England, but between Brazil and England on one side and the traffic on the other. If history ever passed up an opportunity to record a worthy and honest partnership, it was the one which we failed to establish with that nation. The principle that the slave ship is without any right to the flag's protection would be far more honorable for us than all the arguments derived from international law intended to perpetuate the enslavement of aliens brought by force into our territory.

---

6. *Translator's note:* Nabuco refers here to the so-called *emancipados*, Africans removed from captured slave ships by British or Brazilian officials, freed in Rio de Janeiro, and then held as free "apprentices," ostensibly for a period of fourteen years. For an account of their conditions in Brazil, see Robert Conrad, "Neither Slave Nor Free: The *Emancipados* of Brazil, 1818-1868," *Hispanic American Historical Review* 53, no. 1 (February, 1973).

7. *Translator's note:* Prime Minister Robert Peel, Lord Palmerston, and Lord Brougham were three of the most prominent among many British statesmen and politicians who criticized Brazil for her failure to stop the slave trade during the first half of the nineteenth century.

The power of the traffic was irresistible, however, and until 1851 no less than a million Africans were cast into our slave huts. The figure of 50,000 per year is not exaggerated.

Later we must consider the amount of money Brazil used up in this way. Those one million Africans cost her no less than 400,000 *contos,* and of these 400,000 *contos* which flowed from our agricultural economy for twenty years, 135,000 *contos* represent the total expenses of the slave traders and 260,000 their profits.[8]

For years that huge national loss was not recognized by our politicians, who supposed that the traffic enriched Brazil. Obviously, much of that capital reverted to agriculture when the plantations fell into the hands of the slave dealers who had taken mortgages on them in exchange for slave shipments and thus became permanent masters over their own contraband. It was Eusébio de Queirós who said it in the following passage from his speech of July 16, 1852, to which I have already referred:

> To this (the imbalance between free men and slaves caused by the progressive increase of the traffic which in the years 1846, 1847, and 1848 had grown threefold) were joined the interests of the planters. Believing in the beginning that by buying the greatest possible number of slaves they were increasing their wealth, without noticing the very serious threat to the country, our planters sought only to acquire new workers, *buying them on credit with payments over three or four years, paying a painful rate of interest.* (There follows here a statement about the mortality of Africans cited in a later chapter.) Thus the slaves died, but the debts remained, and with them the lands mortgaged to speculators who bought the Africans from the traffickers to resell them to the planters. (*Applause.*) *Thus our landed property was passing from the hands of the planters to those of the speculators and traffickers.* (*Applause.*) This experience awakened our planters and made them understand that they had found their ruin where they had

8. "Taking 6£ to be the cost of the slaves, and proceeding upon the assumption of one out of three being captured, the cost of carrying over the remaining two would be, at 9£ a man, 18£; to which must be added 9£ as the loss on the one taken, making the cost of two slaves in Brazil 27£, or 13£ 10s. per head. If the price of a slave on landing in Brazil were 60£, there would be a profit, notwithstanding the capture of one-third, and including the cost of the two ships, which took over the two-thirds of 46£ 10s. a head? I think that would be so." Testimony of Sir Charles Hotham, *First Report from the Select Committee,* sec. 614. My own estimate is the same, taking 40£ as the average price of the African in Brazil.

sought their wealth, and from that moment the traffic was entirely condemned.

A great part of the same capital was employed in the improvement of Rio de Janeiro and Bahia, but the rest was exported to Portugal, which thus derived from the traffic, as it had derived from slavery in Brazil, no less wealth than Spain had acquired from the same sources in Cuba.

Nobody, however, thinks to deplore the resources consumed in that ignoble trade, because its moral damage casts a shadow over the aborted profits and all the material damage to the nation. The Brazilian who today reads the documents of the traffic, preserved forever in the archive of one of the gloomiest enterprises ever launched by unprincipled speculation, to the tarnishment of the civilizing accomplishments of commerce, sees only the enormity of the crime and the statistics which provide the measure of it. The economic side is secondary. The fact that this was the main cause, according to Eusébio's own demonstration, of both a threefold growth in the trade from 1846 to 1848 and its destruction two years later, merely demonstrates the blindness with which the whole nation supported that revolting piracy. The few men who were deeply offended by this state of affairs, the Andradas, for example, were never able to change it. The bold traffickers in new Negroes, strengthened by their ill-acquired fortunes, were omnipotent, and they denounced as foreigners, allies of England, and partners in the humiliation inflicted upon the country those who dared to raise their voices against the commerce.

True patriotism—that which reconciles the country with humanity—no longer claims that Brazilians had the right to go with their flag, in the shadow of international law created to protect and not to destroy mankind, to steal human beings in Africa and ship them to our shores.

Sir James Hudson [9] once characterized the argument "of national dignity" which our government always used in the following terms: "A dignity which it is trying to maintain at the cost of national honor, of the destruction of the country's interests, and of the gradual but certain degradation of its people." Those words were not deserved when they were written in 1850, but

---

9. *Translator's note:* The British minister in Rio de Janeiro in 1850, whose diplomacy helped to end the slave trade.

they can be applied with the greatest justice to the long period from 1831 until that year.[10]

That is the feeling of the present generation. All of us now swear that if ever again in our history some other force, irresistible like the traffic, by intimidating the government, prostituting justice, corrupting the authorities, silencing Parliament, makes itself master of our flag and subjugates our laws with the aim of inflicting a long and heinous martyrdom upon the people of another continent or another country, that piracy will endure no longer than the time required to crush it, along with every accomplice, with the aid of any nation which will help us.

To be respected, national sovereignty must confine itself to its own borders. The stealing of aliens for slavery is not an act of national sovereignty. Each shot fired from the British cruisers to prevent the imprisonment of human beings on our plantations and to free them from permanent slavery was a service to the *national honor*. That green and yellow cloth hoisted at the stern of slave ships was a profanation of our flag. The law forbade this insult to it, and the slave traders were without authority to raise it on the floating coffins which spread the realm of the baracoons from the coasts of Angola and Mozambique to the shores of Bahia and Rio de Janeiro.

These ideas may be expressed today with the noble pride of that kind of patriotism which does not confuse national boundaries with the circle of depredations traced on the map of the globe by any band of adventurers. The question is, however, whether the present generation, which sincerely detests the traffic and is as far removed from it as from the Holy Office or absolutist government, should not now put an effective end to the trade by annulling that part of its dealings which lack the least spark of legality. If this generation is in fact committed to this, then it must abolish slavery, since slavery today is nothing less than that same traffic rendered permanent and legitimized, that traffic which even then our law had declared criminal, but which nevertheless was pursued on a scale never before witnessed.

---

10. *Translator's note:* Nabuco gives more credit to the Brazilian government for suppression of the slave trade than it deserves. In the speech which Nabuco cites above, Eusébio de Queirós argued that Brazil had acted alone and spontaneously to end the slave trade, not because of British pressure, but in spite of it. For a scholarly treatment of the abolition of the Brazilian traffic which contradicts this older Brazilian view, see Bethell, *Abolition of the Brazilian Slave Trade.*

CHAPTER X

The Illegality of Slavery

Nations like men should greatly cherish their reputations.

—EUSÉBIO DE QUEIRÓS

WE HAVE SEEN what the traffic was. This hellish trilogy, whose first scene was Africa, the second the high seas, the third Brazil, is the sole origin of our slavery. The human conscience cannot question certain principles: a system based upon such foundations is monstrous in the eyes of humanity; our law could not reduce Africans—that is, aliens—to slaves; in a system of justice which is not the brutal legalization of piracy, the claim to possession of the children of those Africans, a claim based upon their birth, is equally worthless. Before strict legality, or before the legality set apart from the competence and morality of the law, the greater part of the slaves among us are free persons criminally enslaved.

In fact, the overwhelming majority of those persons, particularly in the South, are either Africans imported after 1831 or their descendants. In 1831, as we have seen, the law of November 7 stated in its first article: "All slaves who enter the territory or ports of Brazil, coming from abroad, are free." As is known, that law was never enforced, because the Brazilian government could not contend with the slave traders. But this does not mean that the law is any less the charter of freedom for all those imported after that date.

It is a notorious fact that before 1831, owing to the ease of acquiring Africans, the mortality among our slaves, both those of the Coast and the Creoles, was enormous. "It is well known," Eusébio de Queirós told the Chamber of Deputies in 1852, "that the greater part of those unfortunate persons (the imported slaves) are destroyed quickly in the first few years by the sad state to which they are reduced by ill-treatment on the voyages, and by the change of climate, food, and all the customs which make up life." [1] However, of those Africans imported before 1831 (almost all captured in their youth), very few can exist today with fifty years of slavery in America added to the age at

1. Speech of July 16, 1852. To those causes, according to official evidence, must be added a longing for their native land.

which they arrived from Africa. Even without the terrible mortality among the newcomers, to which Eusébio testified, it can be affirmed that almost all the Africans still alive were criminally introduced into our country.

However, let us look at highly believable testimony concerning the mortality of the *crias* more or less up to the period in which the transatlantic traffic was effectively suppressed.

It is an incontestable fact (declares Mr. Cristiano Otôni) that while the price of slaves was low few *crias* survived on the plantations. If you traveled through the counties of Piraí, Vassouras, Valença, Paraíba do Sul, observing the groups in service . . . almost all were Africans. You noticed one exception (and there were not many others), a great plantation whose orphaned owner was receiving an education in a foreign country. This one was notably populated by Creoles [Brazilian-born blacks]. Why? Because, according to a contract, some of those who survived belonged to the overseer. Always personal interest. In all the discussions among the planters this kind of calculation was heard: "You buy a Negro for 300$000 [about $175 in 1850]. In a year he harvests 100 *arrobas* [about 3,200 pounds] of coffee, which at least produce his cost clear. From then on everything is profit. There is no advantage in tolerating the *crias* who will be capable of similar labor only after sixteen years." As a result, pregnant black women and those nursing their babies were not excused from hoeing. In some, hard labor prevented normal development of the fetus. In others, it reduced the flow of milk. In almost all, the children were neglected, and as a result sickness and death were the fate of the poor babies. How many grew up? There are no statistics to tell us, but if only 9 or 10 percent survived among those abandoned in the capital, as the Viscount Abaeté once proved in the Senate, of those born into slavery certainly not more than 5 percent survived.[2]

"We must speak with the greatest frankness, because the subject is grave," a former Foreign Minister, a deputy entirely loyal to agricultural interests, told the Chamber. "It must be recognized that most proprietors, to avoid uncertainties which might arise in the future, tried to register their slaves as having been imported before the law of 1831." That same orator then took it upon himself to demonstrate the illegality of slavery:

2. Otôni, *A emancipação dos escravos*, pp. 66-68.

If we give too much credence to the opinion of the noble deputies, that is, that the fetus, according to the Roman law adopted as our own, follows the status of the womb, not only will the slaves imported after that date be free, but all their descendants as well. Let us place the issue in its true light. If, as I have shown, in only ten years—from 1842 until 1852, as official documents prove—326,317 Africans were imported, and since we do not know how many might have been imported in the earlier period of eleven years following the 1831 law, I ask you: how many of the present slaves could be strictly regarded as slaves, if the view which I oppose prevails? [3]

Less than half, certainly, if the law of November 7, 1831, *prevails*. But the history of that law is a tragic page in our past and in our present. Most of the slave-trading pirates sailing under the Brazilian flag—certainly the most famous, those credited in the English Blue Books [Parliamentary Papers] with the greatest number of victims—were foreigners and Portuguese, to the shame of Portugal, and Brazil as well. The Africans they hunted in the depositories of Africa and disembarked on the coast of Brazil found no one to set them free as the law required. The only pleas on their behalf were made by British ministers and were heard in the British Parliament.

Read the following passage from a speech of 1842 delivered by Lord Brougham. Would it not have been more honorable for us if, instead of its being delivered in the British House of Lords by that great orator (Lord Brougham later requested the repeal of the so-called Aberdeen Bill or Brazil Act), that speech had echoed in our Chambers?

In the first place (he said) they have the recorded declaration of an honourable man in the senate of Brazil, that the law abolishing the slave-trade, was notoriously a dead letter, having fallen entirely into disuse. They have in the next place a petition or memorial from the provincial assembly of Bahia to the senate, urging a repeal of the law, not that they gave themselves any trouble about the prohibition—with that they could easily deal, by wholly disregarding it; but the provision that all slaves imported after 1831, the date of the law, should be free—embarrassed

3. Session of November 22, 1880, speech of Mr. Moreira de Barros [a leading opponent of the abolitionists from São Paulo], *Jornal do Comércio*, November 23, 1880.

the operations of the purchaser, and made it very inconvenient
to hold recently imported negroes.

I find another provincial assembly, that of Minas Geraes, urging
the same suit on like grounds. After dwelling upon the dangers
resulting to the country from the want of new negroes, the
memorial adds: "Above all . . . the worst of all these perils is the
immorality which is the result of our citizens being accustomed to
violate the laws under the very eyes of the administrators thereof."

I verily believe, that the whole history of human effrontery
presents no passage to match this—no second example of equal
audacity. We have here a provincial Legislature coming forward
on behalf of pirates . . . and their accomplices, the planters who
profit by the piracy, purchasing its fruits; on behalf of these great
criminals urging a repeal of the law which they openly avow is
continually broken by them, and which they declare they will
continue to set at nought, as long as it continues unrepealed; but
demanding its repeal upon the ground, that while it remains, they
being resolved to break it, are thus under the necessity of com-
mitting the additional immorality of breaking it under the eye of
the judges sworn to enforce it.[4]

We have here a queer situation: the law of November 7, 1831,
which cannot be enforced except on rare occasions, also cannot
be abolished.

Under our law, certificates of emancipation cannot be revoked,
and any government which dares propose to the Chambers the
legalization of enslavement of Africans imported after 1831
would find the nation not disposed to do what it does not allow
individuals to do. The scandal continues through the indifference of public powers and the impotence of judges, both groups
composed in part of owners of Africans, and not because of any
serious suggestion that the law of 1831 was ever revoked.

Many of our public men, recognizing this as the greatest weakness of our slavery, tried to confirm in some way the ownership
of Africans illegally enslaved, fearing the downfall of our agricultural system if it were verified that they were holding illegal
property. We should not condemn our politicians for the views
they expressed on slavery when we see them obsessed by fear of
social cataclysm; but today we know that such fears are no longer

---

4. *Translator's note:* From *Hansard Parliamentary Debates,* 3d series (1830-
91), p. 939.

reasonable, and that the humanization of the country can only result in its progressive development and greater well-being.

Until recently, on the other hand, it was feared that, if the law of November 7 were enforced by the magistrates, this could bring legal action by slaves imported *before* 1831 who claimed to have arrived after that date. At the present time, however, the Africans legally imported are all at least fifty-two years of age and, with some rare exceptions, having been imported when they were over fifteen, they have now almost reached their seventies. If one of these unfortunate persons, by cheating justice, managed to make use of the law of November 7 to escape from a bondage which has lasted longer than the average human life, Brazilian society would not have much to be sorry for in this isolated and almost impossible misuse of a law a million times violated.

There is no doubt that the generation of 1850 believed, as Eusébio expressed it, that "to allow that legislation (the law of November 7) to exist in the present was equivalent to dismissing its effects in the past" and that "the slaves, having now been mixed among the others," would no longer be allowed to appeal for benefits which the law conceded. However, there is no doubt either that that generation did not have the courage to pass into law the prevailing principle of 1850, of legalizing property rights over Africans imported after 1831, but instead left this task entirely to the passive complicity of the legal authorities and the consensus of the nation. What occurred was entirely natural. The generation educated to tolerate the slave traffic was succeeded by another which regarded that traffic as the greatest of crimes. If it did not dig the names and acts of the traffickers out of the Black Book of the Ministry of Justice [5] for fear of causing unwarranted embarrassment to innocent people, that generation was no less disposed to condemn the acts by which for half a century highwaymen of commerce, for money and money alone, soaked their hands in the blood of millions of unfortunate persons who had not harmed them in any way. In turn, the present generation, wishing to destroy entirely the intimate connection which still exists between the nation and the traffic in Africans, today demands the enforcement of a law which *could not be* and

---

5. *Translator's note:* Nabuco seems to be referring to the annual reports of the Brazilian Ministry of Justice, which frequently described the illegal slave trade in some detail. "Black Book" is apparently a play on words, inspired by the British Parliamentary Papers (Blue Books), which contain an abundance of documentation on the international slave trade.

was not revoked, a law which all Africans still in slavery, being *bona piratarum*, have the right to look upon as their certificate of emancipation sanctioned by the Regency in the name of the Emperor.

Considering the large-scale mortality of slaves, it is not merely probable but undeniable that the present enslaved generations are composed *overwhelmingly* of Africans of the last epoch (when the traffic had legally ended and the slaves had become more valuable) and their descendants. Sales Tôrres-Homem [6] said as much in the Senate in a highly eloquent passage addressed to those who upheld the legality of *slave property:*

> Listening to the petitioners speak so grandly of property rights, one is shocked that they so easily forget that the greater part of the slaves who work their lands are descendants of those whom an inhuman traffic criminally introduced into this country with an affront to laws and treaties! They forget that during the period from 1830 until 1850 more than a million Africans were thus delivered over to our agriculture, and that to obtain that quantity of human cattle it was necessary to double and triple the number of victims, strewing their blood and their bodies over the surface of the seas which separate this country from the land of their birth.[7]

With slavery thus recognized overwhelmingly as the continuation of the illegal traffic which from 1831 until 1852 introduced into Brazil approximately a million Africans, with its manifest illegality proved to the point that "a simple review of the property deeds would be enough to end it" [8] (that is, by reducing the number of slaves to the point that resources of the state could liquidate it), is it not now time to demand release of the traffic's victims from the bondage in which they have lived so long? Let the Brazilian people remember that for fifty years these Africans have worked without pay, in virtue of an act of sale carried out in Africa for less than ninety *milréis.* Let them remember that until today these poor people, hoping for Brazil's honest re-

---

6. *Translator's note:* Francisco de Sales Tôrres-Homem was a noted mulatto veteran of radical politics who in 1871 was a senator representing the northeastern province of Rio Grande do Norte.

7. *Translator's note:* This outstanding speech may be found in *Discussão da reforma do estado servil na Camara dos Deputados e no Senado, 1871,* 2 vols. (Rio de Janeiro, 1871), 2:282-99.

8. *Manifesto da Sociedade Brasileria contra a Escravidão* (Rio de Janeiro, 1880).

pentance, have awaited the expiation of a crime practiced against
them first by the slave hunters in their country, then by exporters
on the coast, by pirates of the Atlantic, by the importers and
shipowners of Rio de Janeiro and Bahia (mostly foreigners), by
traffickers on the coast hired by the latter, by the slave merchants
ashore, and finally by their buyers, whose money encouraged and
enriched all the other groups.

"Nations like men should greatly cherish their reputations."
But, so far as the slave trade is concerned, the truth is that we
cannot save even a scrap of our reputation. The nation's crime
could not have been more disgraceful, and we have not yet
started to make amends. When Brazil is judged, a million witnesses will rise up against us from the backlands of Africa, from
the depths of the ocean, from the baracoons of the beaches, from
the cemeteries of the plantations, and this mute evidence will be
a thousand times more valid than all the protestations of generosity and nobility of the nation's soul.

CHAPTER XI

The Fundamentals of Abolitionism

> Little time now remains before all humanity will
> establish, defend, and guarantee the following
> principle through international law: There is no
> property right of man over man. Slavery contra-
> dicts the rights which human nature confers, and
> the principles recognized by all humanity.
>
> JOHANN BLUNTSCHLI [1]

IT WAS NOT NECESSARY for me to prove the illegality
of a system which is contrary to the fundamental principles of
modern law and in violation of the very notion of what *man* is
before international law. No government should have the right
to place itself outside the community of civilized nations, and
in truth it will not be long before slavery is regarded legally as
it is now regarded morally: as an attack against all humanity.
Each country's laws are subject to certain fundamental principles
which are the bases of civilized societies, the violation of which
in one country amounts to an offense against the others. These
principles form a kind of natural law, the result of man's achievements in his long evolution; they are the sum of the rights with
which the individual is born in each community, however humble he may be. The right to live even before birth, for example,
is protected by the code of every nation. With the distance which
separates the modern world from the ancient, it would be as easy
to legalize infanticide in England or in France as to revive slavery
there. In fact, slavery belongs to a class of fossilized institutions
and exists in our age only in a backward portion of the globe
which unfortunately evades the general consensus. Like canni-
balism, female bondage, the irresponsible authority of fathers,
piracy, religious persecution, political proscription, the maiming
of prisoners, polygamy, and so many other institutions or customs, slavery is a condition which does not naturally belong at
the level to which mankind has arrived.

The theory of personal freedom accepted by all nations is that
which Bluntschli, the eminent Swiss publicist, disciple of
Savigny, defines in the following four paragraphs of his *Droit*

---

1. *Translator's note:* From Johann Bluntschli, *Le droit international codifié*,
trans. M. C. Lardy, 2d ed. (Paris, 1874).

international codifié [*Codified International Law*]: (1) "There is no property right of man over man. Every man is a person, that is, a being capable of acquiring and possessing rights." [2] (2) "International law does not recognize the right of any government or private person to possess slaves." (3) "Foreign slaves become entirely free at the moment they step upon the soil of a free State, and the State which receives them is obliged to respect their freedom." (4) "Slave trading and slave markets are not tolerated anywhere. Civilized states have the right and duty to speed the destruction of those abuses wherever they are found." [3]

Those cardinal principles of modern civilization reduce slavery to a brutal reality which cannot seek recourse in the laws of the individual state, since those laws totally lack the authority to sanction it. In theory, a country's laws could authorize enslavement of its own nationals only, not of aliens. Brazilian law does not have the moral power to sanction the enslavement of Africans, who are not citizens of the Empire. If it can enslave Africans, it can also enslave Englishmen, Frenchmen, Germans. If it does not enslave Europeans but only Africans, that is because

---

2. Sec. 360. This is the note that accompanies the paragraph: "This principle, manifest in nature and known to Roman jurists, was nevertheless scorned by the nations for centuries at great cost to themselves. Although slavery is contrary to nature, efforts were made to justify it in antiquity, basing it upon its admitted existence in all nations. European civilization weakened that shameful abuse of power, which was embellished with the name of property and likened to the right of property over domestic animals. Slavery was ended and mankind's natural right finally triumphed. Serfdom was abolished in Italy, England, France; later in Germany; and in our own time in Russia. Thus a *European law* slowly developed, banning slavery in Europe and lifting personal freedom to the level of mankind's natural right. Since the United States of America also passed judgment against Negro bondage and forced recalcitrant states to grant individual freedom and political rights to people of color, and since in 1871 Brazil established the legal foundations for the liberation of her slaves, that humanitarian right has penetrated into America and is today recognized by the entire Christian world. The Chinese civilization had proclaimed this principle in east Asia long before. In the future, no nation should be permitted, under the pretext of sovereignty, to introduce or maintain slavery in its territory; however, temporary measures taken by a government to end slavery gradually should be respected. The sovereignty of nations cannot be exercised in such a way as to annul the highest and most general right of humanity, because together those nations make up the human organism and should respect the recognized rights of mankind." In this note it is stated with reason that the civilized world ought not to use collective force against a country like Brazil, which has already taken transitory measures and has condemned slavery in principle; but as long as slavery lasts, it is clear that *our sovereignty will continue to be exercised in order to annul the highest and most general right of mankind:* personal freedom.

3. Let it be said in passing that, unfortunately, slave trading and slave markets still exist (1883) in our capital cities, under the eyes of foreigners and without any limitation or control of morality whatsoever, as open and barbarous as the breeding grounds of central Africa which supply the harems of the Orient.

the latter do not enjoy the protection of any government. But in regard to the power which Brazil possesses to suppress the freedom of persons existing within her territory, this cannot go beyond her own citizens.

If the slaves were *Brazilian citizens,* Brazil's laws could perhaps (in theory) be applied to them; however, in fact they could not be, because under the Brazilian Constitution citizens cannot be reduced to the condition of slaves. The slaves, however, *are not* Brazilian citizens, since the Constitution grants that privilege only to *ingênuos* and *libertos.* Not being Brazilian citizens, the slaves either are aliens or have no country, and the laws of Brazil cannot authorize the enslavement of either one or the other, who (under the terms of international law) in so far as personal freedom is concerned are not subject to Brazilian law. The illegality of slavery is thus beyond remedy, whether it be considered within the specific texts and dispositions of the law, or from the point of view of the competence of that same law.

The foundations of abolitionism are not limited, however, to a concern for unfulfilled pledges or repudiated national promises, or to the sentiment of national honor understood as the moral need to comply with treaties and laws related to freedom and to conform with the most positive tenets of civilization. Aside from all this, and beyond the irremediable illegality of slavery in view of modern social thought and existing Brazilian law, abolitionism is also founded upon a series of political, economic, social, and national aims of the widest range and significance. We do not want to end slavery simply because it is illegitimate in the sight of the advancement of moral concepts of cooperation and solidarity; or simply because it is illegal in the presence of the laws of the era of the slave traffic; or simply because it is a violation of the public faith as expressed in treaties like the Convention of 1826, in laws like that of November 7, 1831, in solemn commitments such as the letter of Martim Francisco, the initiative of Count d'Eu in Paraguay, and the promises of statesmen responsible for the advancement of public affairs.[4]

Obviously we desire to end slavery for these reasons, but for the following reasons as well:

1. Because slavery, as it destroys the nation economically, blocks its material progress, corrupts its character, demoralizes its basic components, saps its energy and determination, coarsens

---

4. *Translator's note:* For more on these events, see chapter 7 above and Conrad, *Brazilian Slavery,* pp. 76, 86-87.

its politics, accustoms it to servility, impedes immigration, dishonors manual labor, retards the emergence of industries, causes business failures, diverts capital from its natural course, drives out machines, arouses hatred among classes, produces a misleading appearance of order, well-being, and prosperity, while it hides the chasms of moral anarchy, misery, and destitution which from north to south are carved deeply into our entire future existence.

2. Because slavery is an enormous burden which retards Brazil in its growth in comparison with other South American countries that do not know it; because this system, if continued, must bring as a consequence the dismemberment and ruin of the nation; because an accounting of its losses and diminishing profits reduces to nothing its boastful claims and adds up to an enormous and continuing national injury; because only when slavery has been entirely abolished will the normal life of the nation begin, will there exist a market for labor, will individuals rise up to their true level, will wealth become legitimate, and will regard for others cease to be a mere act of compliance; because not until slavery is ended will the elements of order be founded upon freedom, and freedom cease to be a privilege of class.

3. Because only with total emancipation can members of a community, whose elements are now struggling against one another and among themselves, undertake the work of a common motherland, strong and respected. These contending elements are the slaves, who are outside the social body; the masters, who see themselves attacked as representatives of a condemned system; the enemies of that system, who are unable to reconcile themselves to it; the inactive mass of the population, who are victims of land monopolization and execration of labor; Brazilians in general, who are condemned by slavery to form, as they are now forming, a nation of impoverished men and women.

Each one of these purposes, urgent in itself, would suffice to make us reflect upon the need to end, after so many years, a social system so contrary to the interests of the entire order of a modern people. Brought together, however, and intermingled, these purposes impose this suppression upon us as a vital reform which cannot be postponed without peril. Before studying the harmful influences exercised by slavery upon each of the parts of our national organism, let us see what slavery is in Brazil today at the moment of writing, when there seems little reason to expect any real or immediate improvement.

CHAPTER XII

Slavery Today

> Barbarous in origin; barbarous in its law; bar-
> barous in its pretensions; barbarous in the instru-
> ments it employs; barbarous in consequences;
> barbarous in spirit; barbarous wherever it shows
> itself, Slavery must breed barbarians, while it de-
> velops everywhere, alike in the individual and in
> the society to which he belongs, the essential ele-
> ments of Barbarism.
>
> —CHARLES SUMNER [1]

SINCE the law of September 28, 1871, was passed,
the Brazilian government has been trying to make the world
believe that slavery has ended in Brazil. Our propaganda has
tried to spread to other countries the belief that the slaves were
being freed in considerable numbers and that the children of
the slaves were being born *entirely* free. Slave mortality is an
item which never appears in those fraudulent statistics, behind
which is the philosophy that a lie spread abroad allows the government to do nothing at home and to abandon the slaves to
their fate.

The record of manumissions—highly creditable to Brazil—
dominates the official picture and obscures slave mortality, while
crimes against slaves, the number of Africans still in bondage,
the hunting down of fugitive blacks, the fluctuating price of
human flesh, the rearing of *ingênuos* in slavery, the utter same-
ness of our rural prisons, and everything unbecoming, humiliating, and bad for the government are all carefully suppressed.

In this respect I will cite a unique—perhaps the most remarkable—result of that policy. The biography of Augustin Cochin
written by Count Falloux contains a reference to an article on
the law of September 28 written by that outstanding abolitionist.[2] After referring to ardent statements favoring Brazilian abolition which Cochin had made in his book, *L'abolition de
l'esclavage,* his biographer and friend declared:

---

1. *Translator's note:* From Charles Sumner, *The Barbarism of Slavery* (Washington, D.C., 1860).

2. *Translator's note:* Augustin Cochin was a prominent French abolitionist and
author of *L'abolition de l'esclavage,* 2 vols. (Paris, 1861).

This appeal was heard. Emancipation was decreed in 1870 (*sic*), and M. Cochin can reasonably claim a part in that great work. His book had produced a lively sensation in America. The leaders of the abolitionist movement had put themselves in touch with the author. He himself had sent respectful but urgent solicitations to the Brazilian government. The Emperor, who had not forgotten them, spoke a great deal with M. Cochin when he came to Europe. M. Cochin did not entirely approve of the new law. He found it very slow, very complicated; it did not entirely satisfy his great hopes. But, in spite of its flaws, it promised enough real progress to merit his approval. He devoted to it an article which was published in the *Revue des Deux Mondes*, perhaps the last writing to come from his pen. Today (1875) the emancipation law begins to bear fruit; the development of production increases with the development of free labor; the government, surprised by the tremendous results obtained, tries to accelerate them, devoting six million francs per year to the liberation of the *last* slaves.

These final words, one of which I have italicized, are significant and fully express what the government since then has wanted Europeans to believe. In 1875 the emancipation fund had hardly been distributed *for the first time,* and already the development of production had increased with the development of free labor. The government was surprised by the tremendous results of the law and was devoting six million francs per year (2,400 *contos*) to the liberation of the last slaves.[3] The man who wrote this, Count Falloux, was an authority whose relations with the House of Orléans had probably given him an opportunity to obtain official information concerning a matter of special interest to the biography of the Imperial Princess. The abolitionist sympathies of Cochin were essential for the recognition of the unchanging condition of the slaves, which was masked by such information, and this caused him to write: "The new law was needed, but it is incomplete and inconsequential. This is the truth."

The Brazilian people, however, understand the entire matter. They know that after passage of the law of September 28 the life of the slaves did not change, except for those few who managed to redeem themselves by begging for their freedom. It is essential

3. *Translator's note:* In fact, according to the June 1, 1877, report of the Ministry of Agriculture, by that date only 2,258 slaves had been freed by the emancipation fund in a period of nearly six years, and during that period only 1,295 *contos* (about $712,000) had been applied directly to freeing the slaves. For the poor effects of the emancipation fund, see Conrad, *Brazilian Slavery,* pp. 110-13.

that we outline the condition of the slave today as it appears before the law, before society, before justice, before the master, and before himself, so that it will not someday be said that in 1883, when this book was being written, abolitionists no longer faced the traditional slave system but another kind of slavery, modified for the bondsman by humane, protective, and comparatively just laws. I will sketch this picture of our slavery with strokes perhaps too rapid for a topic so vast.

Whoever arrives in Brazil and opens one of our daily newspapers finds there a photographic image of modern slavery more accurate than any painting. If Brazil were destroyed by a catastrophe, one issue of any of our great newspapers chosen at random would adequately preserve forever the forms and qualities of slavery as it exists in our time. The historian would need no other documents to re-create its entire structure and pursue all its effects.

In any issue of any major Brazilian paper—with the exception, I understand, of those of Bahia, where the press of the capital ceased the publication of slave advertisements—one would find, in effect, the following kinds of information which describe completely the present condition of the slaves: advertisements for purchase, sale, and rental of slaves in which invariably appear the words *mucama, moleque, bonita peça, rapaz, pardinho, rapariga da casa de familia* (free women advertise themselves as *senhoras* in order to differentiate themselves from slaves) ; official announcements of slave sales, a queer kind of document, of which the latest example from Valença is one of the most thorough; [4] advertisements for runaway slaves accompanied in many

4. "Valença. Auction. In a magistrate's sale of this jurisdiction, which will take place on the 26th of October of the current year in the Municipal Chamber of this city, before the ordinary judges, and in conformity with Decree No. 1,695 of September 15, 1869, the following slaves will be auctioned." There follows a list of more than a hundred slaves, from which I copy the following items: "Joaquim, from the Mina coast, ruptured, 51 years old, valued at 300$000 [$165]; Agostinho, black, afflicted with elephantiasis, valued at 300$000; Pio, from Mozambique, a muleteer, 47 years old, valued at 200$000 [$110]; Bonifacio, from Cabinda, 47 years old, sick, valued at 1:000$000 [$550]; Marcelina, Creole, ten years old, daughter of Emiliana, valued at 800$000; Manuel, from Cabinda, 76 years old, blind, valued at 50$000 [$28]; João, from Mozambique, 86 years old, valued at 50$000." There follow evaluations of the services of various *ingênuos* also placed on sale. Offered in this official advertisement are Africans imported *after* 1831, children born *after* 1871, the blind, the sick, elderly people over eighty, and finally *ingênuos* placed as such on sale. It is a recapitulation of slavery in which no generation is forgotten and no abuse avoided, and thus it merits preservation as a document of moral paleontology of great interest to posterity. In Itaguaí a slave was recently put up for judicial auction with the following words: "Militão, fifty years old, insane, valued at 100$000 [$55]." Advertisement of April 23, 1883.

papers by the well-known vignette of a barefoot black with a
bundle on his shoulder, in which the slaves are often distinguished by the scars of punishment they have suffered and for
whom a reward is offered, often as much as a *conto,* to anyone
who can catch him and bring him to his master—an encouragement to the bush-captain's profession; rather frequent notices of
manumissions; stories of crimes committed by slaves against their
masters, but particularly against agents of their masters, and of
crimes committed by the latter against the slaves, barbarous and
fatal punishments which nevertheless comprise only a very small
part of the lordly misuse of power which occurs, since this kind
of abuse rarely comes to the attention of authorities or the press,
owing to a lack of witnesses and informers willing to testify to
this kind of crime.

One finds, finally, repeated declarations that slavery among
us is a very mild and pleasant condition for the slave, better for
him, in fact, than for the master, according to these descriptions
a situation so fortunate that one begins to suspect that, if slaves
were asked, they would be found to prefer slavery to freedom;
which merely proves that newspapers and articles are not written
by slaves or by persons who for one moment have imagined
themselves in their condition.

More than one foreign book of travel containing impressions
of Brazil reproduces these advertisements as the best way to
illustrate local slavery. In reality, no ancient documents are
preserved in hieroglyphics on Egyptian papyrus or in Gothic
letters on parchment of the Middle Ages which reveal a social
order more removed from modern civilization than that which
is exposed by these dismal messages of slavery, which seem to us
to be only a temporary expedient and which nevertheless continue to form the principal feature of our history. The legal
position of the slaves can be summed up in these words: the
Constitution does not apply to him. In order to contain some of
its more enlightened principles, our Constitution could not sanction slavery in any way. "No citizen can be forced to do or not
to do anything except in virtue of the law," [says the Constitution of 1824]. "The home of every citizen is an inviolable asylum.
. . . The law will be applied equally to every person. . . . All
privileges are abolished. . . . From this time forward whipping,
torture, the use of hot branding irons, and all other cruel punishments are abolished. . . . No penalty can be inherited, nor will
the infamy of the criminal be passed on to his kinsmen regardless
of its degree. . . . *The right to property is entirely guaranteed."*

For slavery to have been provided for in this code of freedoms, the following restrictions would have had to be included as well: "Aside from the citizen, for whom these rights are guaranteed, and the foreigner, to whom they will be extended, there exist in this country slaves, a class possessing no rights whatsoever. The slave will be forced to do or not to do whatever his master orders, whether in virtue of the law or in violation of the law, which does not grant him the right to disobey. The slave will not possess any inviolable asylum, whether in his mother's arms, under the shadow of the cross, or in his deathbed; in Brazil there are no places of refuge. The slave will be the object of every privilege revoked for all other persons; the law will not be equal in its application to the slave because he is outside the law, and his material and moral well-being will be as much subject to the control of the law as the treatment of animals; for him the punishments of *whipping* and *torture,* abolished for all others, will continue to exist, to be carried out, moreover, with medieval instruments and with the greatest deliberation when used to force confessions or in day-to-day scrutinization of the most intimate secrets. In this class, the punishment of slavery, the worst of all penalties, will be transmitted, along with the infamy which characterizes it, from mother to children, even if they are sons of the master himself."

Thus we have a *free* nation, daughter of the Revolution and the Rights of Man, compelled to employ its judges, its police, and if need be even its army and navy to force men, women, and children to work night and day without compensation.

Any word which would unmask this unfortunate social constitution would reduce the list of Brazilian freedoms and the regimen of the total equality of its democratized monarchy into a transparent fraud. For this reason the Constitution did not speak of slaves or regulate their condition. This in itself was a promise to those unfortunate people that their status was only temporary, if we are to attribute logic to the shameful spectacle created by those who established our nation.

In 1855 the government commissioned one of our most eminent lawyers, Teixeira de Freitas, with the task of consolidating the nation's laws. His work, *Consolidação das leis civis [Compendium of Civil Laws]*, now in its third edition, appeared without one reference to slaves. By the terms of the Constitution, slavery *did not exist* in Brazil, and the first general codification of our laws continued this artful fiction. The truth is, to admit that we are—or are not—a nation of slaves offends our national sensibilities, so no attempt is made to regulate their condition.

"It should be observed," wrote the author of *Consolidação das leis civis*, "that slavery is nowhere dealt with in our text. We have slavery among us, of course, but since this evil is an unfortunate exception, condemned to extinction at some more or less remote time, let us also make an exception, placing slavery outside the compendium of our civil laws. Let us not stain those laws with shameful provisions which cannot serve posterity. Let the *condition of freedom* stand without its hateful opposite. The laws concerning slavery (which are not many) will then be classified apart and will form our Black Code." [5]

All of this would be most *patriotic* if it in any way improved the lot of the slaves. But when the slaves are not legislated upon because slavery is repugnant, an affront to patriotism, a sight which a sensitive nation's nerves cannot bear without a crisis, and other equally unreasonable excuses (since in Brazil slavery is practiced night and day and all are accustomed, to the point of complete indifference, to its cruelty and inhumanity, to the moral vivisection which it endlessly imposes upon its victims), this fear of *staining our civil laws with shameful provisions* only serves to keep the slaves in their present barbarous condition.[6]

---

5. *Translator's note:* No Black Code as such was ever compiled, although various legal handbooks were published to acquaint slaveholders with their rights and responsibilities.

6. Slavery often places us in difficulties abroad which, though well known in foreign chancelleries, are not familiar to us at home. One such difficulty concerned a proposal to celebrate an extradition treaty with France. In 1857 no such treaty could be agreed upon because Brazil brought up the question of the return of runaway slaves. In 1868 another attempt was made to write a treaty, and a new problem appeared: France insisted upon a guarantee that slaves whose extradition was requested would be treated like other Brazilian citizens. Transmitting a copy of the treaty, Sr. Paranhos [Brazilian Foreign Minister] wrote to M. Roquette: "In the proposal I did not refer to cases concerning slaves, because there was no necessity to do so, since they would come under the general rule. Moreover, I find it completely distasteful *to write that word (slavery) in an international document.*" However, the French government, which also had its honor to defend, did not share that distaste and was duty-bound to guarantee the future of the former slaves whom it might send back to Brazil. As a result, M. Gobineau [author of *Essai sur l'inégalité des races humaines*, then French Minister to Brazil] insisted upon a protocol providing that when the extradition of a slave was requested the French government would have full right to grant or refuse surrender of the accused, to examine each case, and to request explanations which seemed required. Such a protocol, said the Minister of Napoleon III, would not take the form of a secret clause. Instead, with no intention to give it useless notoriety, France would reserve full freedom to publish it, but this, as far as I know, was never done. However, the question arises: how much longer will we maintain an institution that forces us to falsify the Constitution, our books, laws, treaties, and statistics in an attempt to hide the shame that yet remains visible to the entire world and causes our cheeks to turn the color of crimson.

The provisions of our Black Code are very few. Slavery is not indentured servitude which imposes a certain number of specified responsibilities upon the servant. It is the possession, domination, sequestration of a human being—his body, mind, physical forces, movements, all his activity—and it only ends with death. How can we define in legal terms what the master can do with the slave and what the slave cannot do under the supervision of his owner? As a rule the master can do *anything*. If he wants to shut the slave up inside his house forever, he can do so. If he wants to prevent him from establishing a family, he can do so. If the slave has a wife and children and the master desires that he neither see them nor speak to them, if he decides to order the son to whip the mother, if he wishes to usurp the daughter for immoral purposes, he can do so. Imagine all the most extraordinary injuries which one man can inflict upon another without killing him, without separating him by sale from his wife and children under fifteen, and you will have what slavery is *legally* among us. The House of Correction, in comparison with this other condition, is a paradise. Excluding thought of the crime of condemning an innocent person to imprisonment as an example to others—which is worse than the fate of the most unfortunate slave—there is no comparison between a system of fixed obligations, of dependence upon law and its administrators, and a system of proprietary subjection to a person who can be a madman or a barbarian.

Concerning the slave's civil capacity, according to the law of September 28, 1871, he is allowed to form a *pecúlio* [personal liberation fund] which he may derive from gifts, legacies, inheritances, and, *with the consent of his master*, from his labor and personal thrift. But application of this law depends entirely upon the master, who owns the slave and everything the slave possesses, in a country where the protection of bondsmen by the courts is neither spontaneous nor effective. Concerning the family, it is forbidden, under penalty of invalidating the sale, to separate a husband from his wife or a child from his father or mother, except when the child is over fifteen (Law no. 1,695 of September 15, 1869, Article 2).[7] But a wedding depends upon a master's authorization, and if he is not allowed to separate a

---

7. *Translator's note:* Nabuco was evidently unaware that Article 4 of the Rio Branco Law had lowered the age of the child who could be separated from his mother from fifteen to twelve. In both the law of 1869 and the Rio Branco Law the only penalty for an infraction of this provision was annulment of the sale.

family by sale, he can break up that family whenever he desires and for as long as he likes by a simple command.

To recapitulate, I will sketch in broad strokes what slavery is *legally* in Brazil in 1883:

1. The present bondsmen, born before September 28, 1871, and today at least eleven and a half years old, are slaves until they die, *exactly* like those of earlier generations. The number of these, as will be seen, is more than a million.

2. Whoever is subject to slavery is compelled to obey without question every order received, to do whatever he is told, without the right to demand a thing: neither pay nor clothing, improved food nor rest, medicine nor change of duties.

3. The man so enslaved has no duties—to God, to his mother and father, to his wife or children, or even to himself—which the master *must* respect and allow him to perform.

4. The law does not fix maximum hours of labor, a minimum wage, rules of hygiene, food, medical treatment, conditions of morality, protection of women. In a word, it interferes as much in the organization of the plantation as it does in the supervision of draft animals.

5. There is no law whatever which regulates the obligations and prerogatives of the master; whatever the number of slaves he may possess, he exercises an authority over them which is limited only by his own judgment.

6. The master can inflict moderate punishment upon slaves, says the *Criminal Code,* which compares his authority to the power of a father; but in fact he punishes at will, because justice does not penetrate the feudal domain. A slave's complaint against his master would be fatal, as it has been in practice, and in fact the master is all-powerful. The attitudes of today are what they were in 1852. It is as dangerous now, and just as useless, for a slave to complain to the authorities as it was then. To accuse his master, the slave requires the same will power and determination that he needs to run away or to commit suicide, particularly if he hopes for some security in his servitude.[8]

---

8. In 1852 the Council of State had to discuss ways to protect slaves from the masters' barbarity. Several slaves in Rio Grande do Sul had denounced their common master for the death of one of his house servants. The master had been imprisoned and placed on trial, and there was an attempt to guarantee the informants against the family's future vengeance. The Justice Division proposed that the Legislative Power be asked to pass a measure which would officially allow a mistreated slave to initiate legal action to force his master to sell him to another person. The Council of State (Olinda, Abrantes, José Clemente, Holanda

7. The slave lives in total uncertainty regarding his future; if he thinks he is about to be sold, mortgaged, or pawned, he has no right to question his master.

8. Any person released from the House of Correction or even confined within it, however perverse he may be, whether he be a Brazilian or foreigner, can own or buy a family of respectable and honest slaves and expose them to his whims.

9. Masters can employ female slaves as prostitutes, receiving the profits from this business with no danger of losing their property as a result, just as a father can be the owner of his son.

10. The state does not protect the slaves in any way whatsoever. It does not inspire them with confidence in public justice but instead surrenders them *without hope* to the implacable power which weighs heavily upon them, morally imprisons or constrains them, arrests their movement, and in short destroys them.

11. The slaves are governed by exceptional laws. The use of the lash against them is allowed, despite its prohibition by the Constitution. Their crimes are punished by a barbaric law, that of June 10, 1835, the sole penalty of which is execution.[9]

Cavalcanti, Alves Branco, and Lima e Silva) voted against the proposal of the Justice Division (Limpo de Abreu, Paraná, Lopes Gama), "having in mind the danger involved in passing laws on this matter, risking the safety or at least tranquillity of the family, since it is not at all desirable to change our slavery system but better to keep it as it is, and because it is better to avoid discussion in the Legislative Body of any new measures concerning the slaves, when everything that can and should be done has already been done with the effective suppression of the traffic." Paraná ceded to the majority, Araújo Lima as well, and Councillors Maia Lopes Gama and Limpo de Abreu made up the minority. It would be unjust to omit the fact that Holanda Cavalcanti recommended seizure of abused slaves by the government and by the Council of State. The Emperor sided with the majority.

9. In the Council of State a proposal was made for revocation of Article 60 of the Criminal Code, which permits whipping, and of the law of June 10, 1835. Supporting this proposal initiated by the committee he headed, Councillor Nabuco made some statements which are summarized in the minutes of the session of April 30, 1868:

"Councillor Nabuco upholds the need to abolish the exceptional law of June 10, 1835. That it has been ineffective is proved by the statistics on crime: the crimes it was intended to prevent have increased. It is an unjust law because it eliminates the principles regarding criminal imputation and the relationship between a crime and its penalty, since serious and less serious crimes are confused, and aggravating and extenuating circumstances are not taken into consideration, as if slaves were not men and as if they lacked passions and the instinct to survive. That the penalty of death, and only death, is not an exemplary punishment for the slave, who sees death as merely the cessation of slavery's evils. That frequent suicides among slaves and the ease with which they confess crimes and surrender to authorities fully prove they do not fear death."

12. The belief has been spread throughout the nation that
slaves often commit crimes in order to become convicts, in this
way escaping from slavery, since they prefer the chain gang to
the plantation, as Roman slaves preferred to fight wild beasts, in
the hope of achieving freedom if they survived. For this reason
a jury of the interior has absolved criminal slaves to be restored
later to their masters, and lynch law has been carried out in more
than one case. Here we have slavery as it really is! Death by
suicide is looked upon by the bondsman as the *cessation of the
evils of slavery,* imprisonment with hard labor such *an improvement in his condition* that it can be *an incentive to crime!*
Meanwhile we, a humane and civilized nation, condemn more
than a million persons, as so many others were condemned before them, to a condition alongside which imprisonment or the
gallows seems better! [10]

13. Not all the powers of the master, which, as we have seen,
are practically without limit, are exercised directly by him, absent as he often is from his lands and out of contact with his
slaves. Instead, these powers are delegated to individuals without
intellectual or moral education, who know how to command
men only by means of violence and the whip.

It is odd that masters who exercise this unlimited power over
their human property look upon the law's least intervention on

---

"He claims that the penalty of whipping cannot exist in our penal law, since
Article 179, Paragraph 19, of the Constitution abolished this penalty and deemed
it a cruel punishment. It is a punishment which demoralizes but does not
correct. Furthermore, it is a punishment which is out of step with the principle
that the penalty should conform to the crime, since the same number of lashes
replaces imprisonment for life or imprisonment for ten, twenty, or thirty years.
The endurance of the slave is what determines the number of lashes he receives,
and thus the maximum number of lashes is the same in both serious and less
serious cases. That the execution of this punishment results in many abuses, since
in some cases it is evaded and at other times it has resulted in death."

Baron Bom Retiro, opposing the abolition of punishment by whipping, said
on the same occasion: "With whipping abolished there will still be galley punishment [chain gangs] and imprisonment with hard labor, and neither of these will
be effective in the case of the slave. For many of them imprisonment with hard
labor, since it is regulated as it should be, *will be an improvement of their condition, if not an incentive to crime.*"

10. The preference of many slaves for chain-gang life to that which they
suffer in private prisons induced the ministry of Councillor Lafayette Rodrigues
Pereira in 1879 to propose solitary confinement as a substitute for the chain gang.
Calming those senators who seemed uncertain about the results of this kind of
punishment, the President of the Council convinced them with this argument:
"It is recognized today that there is not a human being, even the strongest, who
can tolerate solitary confinement for ten or twelve years, *which is similar to a
new death penalty.*"

behalf of the slaves as intolerable oppression. The resistance of our agricultural community to that part of the law of September 28 which granted the slave the right to accumulate his own *pecúlio* [emancipation fund], and to use that fund to acquire his own freedom once he had saved it, proves that not even this crumb of freedom was willingly dropped from their table. The planters of Bananal, for example, whose names indicate that they represent the agricultural families of São Paulo as well as those on the borders of Rio de Janeiro province, stated in a petition addressed to the Chambers: *"Either property exists with its essential characteristics, or it decidedly does not exist.* Forced liberation, with the various measures relating to it, is armed vengeance which threatens every home, every family, the destruction of agriculture, the death of the nation." Significantly, when an attempt was made in the Council of State to give slaves the right to possess their own savings, the Marquis of Olinda declared, *"We are not creating ethical law."*

The worst side of slavery is not its great abuses and passions, nor its terrible retributions, nor even the death of the slave. It is, rather, the daily pressure which slavery imposes upon the slave: his constant fear for himself and his family; his dependence upon the good will of the master; the spying and treachery which surround him, forcing him to live forever shut up in a prison of Dionysus, whose walls repeat every word, each secret confided to another, and, even worse, each thought which he may unintentionally reveal in the expression on his face.

It is said that among us slavery is mild and the masters are good. The truth is, however, that all slavery is the same, and the goodness of the masters depends upon the resignation of the slaves. Whoever would try to compile statistics on crimes committed either by slaves or against them, whoever would inquire into slavery and hear the complaints of those who suffer it would see that in Brazil, even today, slavery is as hard, barbarous, and cruel as it was in any other country of America. By its very nature slavery is all this, and when it stops being this it is not because the masters have improved. It is because the slaves have resigned themselves totally to the destruction of their personalities.

As long as slavery exists, it will contain within it every form of barbarousness. It can only be administered with comparative mildness when slaves obey blindly and subject themselves to every abuse. Their smallest thought, on the other hand, awakens the sleeping monster in all its ferocity. Slavery can only exist through absolute terror inflicted upon the spirit of mankind.

Let us suppose that the two hundred slaves of a plantation refuse to work. What can a *good* master do to force them to perform? Strictly moderate punishments will perhaps have no effect; the stocks and imprisonment do not accomplish the purpose, which is to make them work. To subdue them through hunger is neither humane nor practical. The good master thus faces the choice of either abandoning his slaves or subjugating them by means of exemplary punishment inflicted upon the principal persons among them.

The limit of the master's cruelty is therefore to be found in the meekness of the slave. When meekness ceases, cruelty begins; and since the situation of the owner of men among his people in revolt would be the most dangerous and, to his family, the most frightening experience possible, each master at each moment in his life lives exposed to the likelihood of becoming barbaric and, to avoid greater calamities, is compelled to be severe. In fact, slavery cannot be otherwise. Charge the most tolerant men with the administration of religious intolerance and you will have new *autos-da-fé* as terrible as those of Spain. It is slavery which is evil and obliges the master to be evil. Nature cannot be changed. The good master of a bad slave would be more than a *fortunate accident*. What we are familiar with is the good master of the slave who has renounced his individuality and become a moral corpse; but the master is *good* because he treats the slave well, materially speaking, not because he tries to raise up a degraded man or to awaken dead human dignity.

Today in Brazil slavery is what it was in 1862 in the United States, what it was in Cuba and the West Indies, what it cannot avoid being, just as war cannot help being bloody. Slavery is barbarous, exactly as Charles Sumner described it.

CHAPTER XIII

The Influence of Slavery upon Brazilian Nationality

(With slavery) Brazil will never perfect her existing races.

  —José Bonifacio de Andrada e Silva [1]

As is generally recognized, Brazil is one of the largest countries on the globe, with an area of more than eight
million square kilometers. Yet a great part of her territory has
never been explored, and her known areas are sparsely populated. The national population is calculated at between ten and
twelve million. There is, however, no serious basis upon which
to compute it, unless we accept the refined census lists of 1876,
which would shock any novice in the science of statistics.
Whether that population be ten or twelve million, however, the
greater part of it is descended from slaves, and thus slavery acts
upon it like a heritage from the cradle.

When the first Africans were taken to Brazil, the first settlers
did not realize that they were establishing for the future a people
overwhelmingly composed of descendants of slaves, nor would
this have deterred them if they had, since they were not Brazilian
patriots. Even today many people believe the importation of one
or two hundred thousand Chinese would have no serious ethnic
and social consequences even after five or six generations. The
principal effect of slavery upon our population has thus been to
Africanize it, to saturate it with Negro blood, just as the main
result of any great effort to introduce immigrants from China
would be to Mongolize it, to saturate it with yellow blood.

Forced into slavery, the black race, by merely surviving and
propagating, became an ever more significant part of the population. The celebrated phrase so jarring in Father Campos's report of 1871: "Vagabond Venus incites to the greatest excesses
that ardent blood of Libya," translated into prose describes the
primitive beginnings of a major part of our people. This was the
first act of vengeance on the part of the victims. Each slave womb
gave the master three or four *crias* whom he transformed into
cash. These in turn multiplied, and thus the vices of African

---

1. *Translator's note:* From *Representação à Assembléia Geral Constituinte e
Legislativa do Imperio do Brasil sobre a escravatura* (Paris, 1825).

blood came into widespread circulation throughout the nation.

If the black race had multiplied without mixing or if the white race had multiplied faster, as in the United States, the problem of the races would be other than it is, entirely different —perhaps more serious and perhaps to be solved only by the expulsion of the weaker and less developed race as incompatible with the other. But this did not happen in Brazil. The two races mixed. There occurred the most varied combinations of the elements of each, and to them was joined a third race, that of the aborigines. Of the three main currents of blood mixed in our veins—the Portuguese, the African, and the Indian—slavery corrupted mainly the first two. Thus we have the first effect upon our population: the crossing of characteristics of the black race as they occur under the conditions of slavery, with those of the white, the mixing of the servile degradation of the one with the brutal arrogance of the other.

At the start of our colonization Portugal unloaded in our territory her criminals, her errant women, the dregs of her entire society; and from time to time immigrants of another kind arrived as well, among them fortunately a large number of Jews.[2] Brazil at that time was like the Congo of yesterday. In the sixteenth and seventeenth centuries the will to emigrate was not developed enough in Portugal, as it has been since the end of the eighteenth century, to motivate people to look to Portuguese America for the wealth and well-being which they did not find at home. The few Portuguese who risked crossing the Atlantic in sailing ships to set themselves up in the Brazilian wilderness were a minority of adventurous, totally fearless people indifferent to the worst discomforts of the struggle for existence, a minority which even today in Portugal is not large and could not conceivably have been so two or three centuries ago. Although Portuguese imperial control was extended throughout the world —to South America, to west, south, and east Africa, to India, and even to China—Portugal did not have the power and substance needed to control that huge empire more than nominally. For this reason the territory of Brazil was divided among *donatários* [grantees] who lacked the means, the capital, all the needed resources for colonizing their captaincies, which were in

---

2. In his abolitionist novel, *Os herdeiros de Caramuru,* Dr. Jaguaribe Filho, one of the most convinced defenders of our cause, transcribes a letter written on August 9, 1549, by the famous Jesuit, Father Manuel de Nóbrega, in which he reveals how slavery built our nation's primitive beginnings.

fact given over to the Jesuits. The European population was too small to occupy those unlimited expanses of territory, but was nevertheless attracted by its wealth; so, with Africa in the hands of the Portuguese, the peopling of America with blacks began. A bridge, so to speak, was extended between Africa and Brazil, over which millions of Africans passed, and the habitat of the black race was extended from the shores of the Congo and the Zambesi to the banks of the São Francisco and the Paraíba do Sul.

No one can read the history of Brazil in the sixteenth and seventeenth centuries and part of the eighteenth (with the exception of that of Pernambuco) without concluding that in all respects it might have been better if Brazil had been discovered three centuries later. If it had been found free and unoccupied a hundred years ago, that huge region, more favored by nature than any other, would probably have made more progress by now than her history records. The population would be smaller but more homogeneous. The occupation of the land would perhaps not be as greatly extended, but that settlement would not have taken the form of a ruinous and sterilizing exploitation. The country would not have reached its present level of development, but neither would it reveal the symptoms of a premature decadence.

One of the eminent personalities of Portugal has asserted that "the enslavement of the Negroes was the hard price which had to be paid for the colonization of America, because without it Brazil would not have become the country we know." [3] This is a fact: without slavery Brazil would not have become the country we know. But those who paid that price, and are paying it still, are not the Portuguese but ourselves, and in every way that price is too hard and too high when compared with our languid, meager, and unnatural development. The Africanization of Brazil by slavery is a mark planted by the mother country upon her own image, into her language, and upon her only enduring national achievement.

The famous author of the above sentence is the same who leaves us this description of the slave cargoes: "When the ship arrived at its destination—a remote and deserted beach—the cargo was put ashore, and into the bright light of the tropical sun emerged a column of skeletons covered with pustules, their

3. J. P. Oliveira Martins, *O Brazil e as colonias portuguezas*, 2d ed. (Lisbon, 1881), p. 50.

bellies swollen, their knee joints ulcerated, their skin torn, consumed by insects, with the stupid and sickly air of idiots. Many could not even stand, but stumbled and fell and were transported like sacks on the shoulders of men." [4] It is not with such elements as these that a nation is morally quickened.

If in the sixteenth century Portugal had been capable of understanding that slavery is a mistake and had possessed sufficient power to punish it as a crime, "Brazil would not have become the country we know." Perhaps it would still be a Portuguese colony (which seems unlikely), but it would be progressing like Canada or Australia, healthy, strong, and virile. It is conceivable that without slavery Brazil would have lacked the forces needed to repel the foreigner, as it repelled the Dutch, and that without slavery Brazil would have passed under the control of another nation and would not be Portuguese.

No one can say what history might have been. Between a Brazil snatched from the Portuguese in the seventeenth century because they refused to allow the traffic, a Dutch or French Brazil exploited with slaves, or a Brazil exploited with slaves by the Portuguese themselves, no one can say which would have been better for the history of our region. But between two Brazils, a Portuguese Brazil exploited with free Africans and the same Brazil developed with slaves, the first would be a more powerful nation at this time than the second. And between what actually occurred (the exploitation of South America by a handful of Portuguese surrounded by an enslaved people imported from Africa) and the severe prohibition of slavery in Portuguese America, between the spreading of slavery throughout its territory, its almost inextricable occupation by slavery down to its very roots, and the gradual colonization of its territory by Europeans, however slow the process might have been, there can be no doubt that the latter would have been infinitely more advantageous to the destiny of that huge region.

It is said that the white race would not be capable of acclimatizing itself in Brazil without the immunity bestowed upon it by miscegenation with Indians and Africans. In the first place, the bad element of the population was not the black race, but that race reduced to bondage; in the second place, there is nothing to prove that the white race, particularly southern peoples, mixed as they are with Moors and blacks, cannot exist and

---

4. Ibid., p. 57.

develop in the tropics. In any event, if the white race cannot adapt to the tropics in conditions of total fruitfulness, that race will not indefinitely prevail in Brazil. The powerful development of mixed races must eventually surpass it, and European immigration will be inadequate to maintain the permanent supremacy of a species of man to whom the sun and the climate are hostile. This being the case, Brazil even now by necessity would be merely a brief experiment in human adaptation; but nothing is less certain than this alleged physical incapacity of the white race to exist and prosper in one whole region of the world.

Assuming that without slavery the number of Africans in Brazil had been the same as it was, or even greater if this seems preferable, the crossbreeding of the races would inevitably have taken place, but with one difference. The family would have existed from the start. The mixing of the races would not have occurred as a result of concubinage, through the promiscuity of the slave huts or the master's abuse of his power. The child would not have been born under the lash, would not have been carried into the fields on the back of a mother driven to the daily task of hoeing her master's lands. That mother's milk would not have been used like the milk of a she-goat, to feed other children, while for her own child there remained only the leftover drops to be squeezed from a tired, dry breast. Women would not have done the labor of men, would not have been made to work in the fields under the burning midday sun, and during pregnancy could have attended to their condition. It is not the crossing of races that we are concerned with, but procreation in slavery, in which the best result for the mother was that the child succumb. Let us imagine what this barbarous practice must have meant to millions of women over three centuries, expressed in the following words by the planters of Piraí in 1871: "The most productive part of slave property is the generative womb." Let us consider the development of the white family as a moral entity over three generations, and we will better understand how large was the return to that family of one single female slave purchased by its founder.

The history of African slavery in America is an abyss of degradation and misery whose depths cannot be fathomed, and unfortunately this is the record of Brazil's development. Looking back at the past from the point at which we have arrived, we Brazilians, descendants of the race which wrote that sad human chapter, or of the race whose blood was used to write it, or of a

fusion of the two, should not waste our energy blaming ourselves for that long history which we cannot wash away, for that
heredity which we cannot elude. What we should do is muster
all our power for the purpose of eliminating slavery from our
being, so that this national misfortune will be reduced in us
and will be passed on to future generations weakened, rudi-
mentary, wasted away.

Many of the effects of slavery can be attributed to the black
race, to its backward mental development, to its still barbarous
instincts, to its crude superstitions. The fusion of Catholicism, as
it was offered to our people by the fanaticism of the missionaries,
with African fetishism—an active and extensive influence among
the lower elements of our population, intellectually speaking,
which through the wet nurse, through the contacts of domestic
slavery reached even the most notable of our men; the effects of
African diseases upon the physical constitution of part of our
people; the corruption of language, social manners, and education; and so many other effects of crossbreeding with a race at a
particularly backward period of its development all might have
happened without slavery. But even if we take into account what
was most characteristic about that race, it can be argued that if
that race had been brought to Brazil at a time when religious
fanaticism did not exist, when there was no greed beyond the
reach of the law, when there was no shortage of acclimatized
populations and, most important, no slavery, domestic and personal, the crossbreeding of whites and blacks would have been
accompanied not by the bastardization of the more advanced
race by the more backward, but by the gradual elevation of the
latter.

In conclusion, there can be no doubt that slavery brought
from Africa to Brazil more than two million Africans; that,
because of the master's interest in the production of the slave
womb, it favored as much as it could the fertility of black
women; that descendants of that population make up at least
two-thirds of our present population; that for three centuries
slavery, working its effects upon millions of individuals, who
included during much of that time most of the people, impeded
the normal appearance of the family in the basic strata of the
nation, reduced human procreation to a venal interest of the
masters, kept that whole mass of humanity in a purely animal
condition, did not feed it, did not properly clothe it, robbed it
of its savings, never paid it wages, allowed it to be consumed

by diseases and to die in abandonment, prevented it from developing habits of foresight, voluntary labor, personal dignity and responsibility, and made of it a plaything for every low passion, for every sensual desire, for all the cruel vindictiveness of another race.

It is almost impossible to follow the movement of such a vast process, which countless times has involved descendants of the slaves themselves, into all the moral and intellectual byways it has taken and still takes. Nor is there a social agent which has the same deep and wide-ranging psychological effect as slavery when it becomes an integral part of the family. This influence can be characterized by observing that slavery enveloped our entire populated space from Amazonas to Rio Grande do Sul in an environment destructive to all the manly, generous, humanitarian, and progressive qualities of our species. It created a crude, money-grubbing, selfish, and backward national vision, and for centuries it cast in this pattern the three heterogeneous races which today constitute the Brazilian nationality. In other words, it made the air itself *servile,* to use the medieval legal phrase, like the air of the villages of Germany where no free man could live without losing his freedom. *Die Luft leibeigen war* is a phrase which, when applied to all of Brazil, best sums up the national legacy of slavery. It created an atmosphere that envelops and stifles all of us, and this in the richest and most admirable of the world's dominions.

CHAPTER XIV

The Effects of Slavery upon the Territory and Population of the Interior

> There is not a slaveholder in this House or out of it but knows perfectly well that, whenever slavery is confined within certain special limits, its future existence is doomed. . . . Slavery cannot be confined within certain specified limits without producing the destruction of both master and slave. [1]
>
> —HIRAM WARNER OF GEORGIA [1]

IN 1880 the Provincial Assembly of Rio de Janeiro sent to the General Assembly a petition in which the following passage appears: "The picture which presents itself to the view of the traveler who passes through the interior of the province is one of desolation. Particularly precarious is the situation in the lowland counties, where the original fertility of the soil has been exhausted and neglect has transformed the fertile valleys into deep stagnant pools which sicken all who go near them. The unfortunate inhabitants of the countryside, without leadership, without public assistance or any examples to follow, are outside the social community. They neither consume nor produce, and they hardly draw sufficient nourishment from the soil if they cannot hunt and fish in the game preserves of the great landholders. Thus they are regarded as a veritable plague, and it should not be overlooked that this situation will become even more serious when to these millions of pariahs are added the one and a half million slaves who today form the core of the great estates."

These words, which were not to have been expected from a proslavery assembly, describe the effects of the slave system. Wherever it goes, it burns the forests, and mines and exhausts the land; and when it moves on, it leaves behind a devastated countryside in which a miserable population of wandering vagrants is just able to survive.

What is found in Rio de Janeiro exists in every other province where slavery established itself. André Rebouças, in describing the present conditions of the Recôncavo of Bahia, that ancient

---

1. *Translator's note:* From Hiram Warner, *Slavery in the Territories* (Washington, D.C., 1856).

paradise of the slave traffic, drew a picture of the sorry condition of the land, even the most fertile, wherever the plague of slavery has passed.[2] Whoever goes by ship to Nazaré and stops in Jaguaribe and Maragogipinho, or travels by rail to Alagoinhas and beyond, recognizes that slavery, even when revived and invigorated by the steamship and locomotive, is in itself cause of a more or less slow but certain death. On the banks of the river or along the railroad tracks nothing is to be found but signs of decadence and the first stages of atrophy. A rude pottery industry is attempted in some places in the most primitive manner; in Jaguaribe ancient buildings which date from the era of flourishing slavery, such as the church, contrast sharply with today's paralysis.

The fact is that the vast regions exploited by colonial slavery have an unmatched look of sadness and desertion. In them there is no alliance of man with the earth, no feature of permanent habitation, no sign of natural growth. The past is visible, but there is no sign of a future. The present is the gradual wasting away which comes before death. The population does not permanently possess the soil. The great landowner conquered it from nature with his slaves, exploited it, enriched himself by consuming it, later went bankrupt because of the extravagant use nearly always made of badly acquired fortunes, and at last returned it to nature, wrecked and exhausted.

Thus it is that in the northern provinces slavery was liquidated or is being eliminated through the ruin of all the old establishments. The wealth acquired from sugar was abundantly employed in the purchase of slaves, in the hedonistic luxury of the seigneurial life. With the elimination of entailment, the properties passed out of the hands of the old landed families into the possession of others as a result of mortgages or in payment of debts; and descendants of the ancient heirs and territorial lords in Bahia, in Maranhão, in Rio de Janeiro and Pernambuco are today reduced to the most precarious condition imaginable, forced to retreat to the great asylum of slavery's squandered fortunes, the refuge of the public bureaucracy. If by some chance the government were to dismiss all its pensioners

---

2. *Garantia de juros,* p. 202.

Translator's note: André Rebouças was a mulatto engineer, teacher, economist, and prominent abolitionist. The Recôncavo is the region surrounding the Bahia de Todos os Santos (Bay of All Saints), which for centuries has been a major center of the sugar industry.

and employees, we would get a glimpse of the true condition to which slavery reduced representatives of the families which profited by it in the eighteenth and nineteenth centuries, of how slavery nearly always consumed itself by the destruction of the wealth which it produced. And what we have seen is nothing compared with what we are going to see.

For a long time to come, the whole Brazilian North will remember that the end result of slavery is the impoverishment and misery of the country. Nor is it surprising that cultivation of the soil by a class without any interest whatever in the labor extorted from it should produce these results. As we know, land tenure under slavery consists of division of the entire cultivated territory into a certain number of large properties.[3] These feudal estates are then isolated from all contact with the outside world. Even the peddlers who enter them arouse the master's suspicion, and the slaves who are born and die within the narrow confines of the sugar or coffee estates are all but convicts. The division of a vast province into true penal colonies incapable of progress, small Ashantis in which one will alone rules, administered at times by persons who have risen out of slavery or, more often, by overseers who are themselves merciless slaves, cannot bring any permanent benefit to the parceled territory, not even to the free population which by grace of the landlord inhabits it in a state of permanent dependence.

For this reason too, progress of the interior has been insignificant during three hundred years of national life. The cities, which are not stimulated even artificially by the provincial governments, are, so to speak, dead. Almost all are decadent. All supplies which go to interior areas are concentrated in the capitals. It is with the agent in Recife, Bahia, or Rio de Janeiro that the sugar or coffee planter carries on his business; therefore, in other parts of the province commerce does not exist. What is true of Bahia and Pernambuco is true of every other province. Provincial life is concentrated in the capitals, and the life led there, the small steps taken toward growth and progress prove

3. The report of a committee nominated in 1874 to study the conditions of the agriculture of Bahia, bearing at the top of the list the signature of the Baron of Cotegipe, read: "The old and vicious system of land grants and of the rights of occupation produced the phenomenon of land possession confined to a relatively insignificant population which neither cultivated it nor consented that it be cultivated. The committee recommends the land tax as the way to avoid this evil, or abuse rather, which created an impoverished class in the midst of so much unused wealth." That *impoverished class* is the great majority of the nation.

that centralization, far from spreading vitality into the provinces, causes life to decline. This lack of local centers is so serious that the map of every province could be drawn with only the capitals indicated without neglecting any flourishing town. Many of the capital cities themselves are made up of an insignificant cluster of houses whose material components and everything they contain would not adequately serve to build a North American city of the tenth rank. Life in other places is precarious; everything that contributes to health and well-being is missing. There is no running water; there are no gas lights. The district does not collect taxes from even one moderately rich resident, does not possess the rudiments, or even a blueprint, of the practical equipment of a *city*. These are the marvelous results of three hundred years of slavery.

With this premature decrepitude of towns which were never able to grow, many of which must die without surpassing what they are today, compare the creativity of an American city of the Far West or the rapid growth of the settlements of Australia. In the United States a village grows up in a few years, passes through successive stages, and rises upon a plan in which the sites of all the buildings needed to establish the community's moral life have been previously marked out; and when it becomes a city it is a complete entity whose several parts have grown up harmoniously.

These cities are centers of small regions which also developed in a way radically different from that of our agricultural zones. Our isolated coffee and sugar plantations, organized on a foundation of slavery, with inhabitants of the land cast as hangers-on, political clientele, or hired assassins, where owners do not allow contracts between their people and strangers and are often themselves divided by ruinous boundary disputes, since justice lacks power to deal with potentates—such estates cannot generate the appearance of self-governing country towns which stimulate surrounding regions with the use of their wealth and resources. Consider Cabo or Valença, or any other city of the interior of any province, and it will be clear that it lacks a life of its own, does not play any decisive role in the social economy. A few towns, such as Campinas or Campos, which appear to thrive, are in a stage of meteoric splendor that the others also experienced, the temporary nature of which a calm observer can easily recognize.

What is true in the North is true in the South, and would be even more obvious if coffee were unseated by *Hemyleia Vasta-trix,* the coffee blight. As long as sugar's golden age endured, the North offered a spectacle which fooled many people. The houses, the so-called *palacetes* of the landed aristocracy in Bahia and Recife, the liveries of the footmen, the litters, the sedan chairs, and the noble carriages distinguished the flourishing monopoly of sugarcane—at a time when the sugar beet had not yet appeared on the horizon. Similarly, the agricultural wealth of the South, which is in fact greatly exaggerated and hard to estimate, but which is nevertheless substantial and, in some cases, enormous in relation to the general condition of the country, is the result of the temporary affluence of coffee. Competition must appear, as it did with sugar. It is true that the latter can be extracted from various plants, whereas coffee is the product of the coffee tree alone. However, several countries are now planting coffee and will produce it more cheaply, particularly in relation to transportation costs, although Ceylon has already revealed the dangers inherent in coffee monoculture.

When the reign of coffee is past (the low prices are already a forecast of what will come), the South will find itself reduced to the condition of the North. Putting São Paulo and the extreme south aside, let us look at the provinces of Rio de Janeiro and Minas Gerais. Where there is no coffee they are both feeble. Ouro Prêto today is no more important to the national life than was Villa Rica in the days when the house of Tiradentes was leveled by a judicial decision; Mariana, São João d'El-Rei, Barbacena, Sabará, Diamantina—all are either decadent or scarcely able to ward off decline.[4] It is to the coffee counties that we must look for the opulent part of Minas Gerais.

The situation of São Paulo is peculiar. Although it is now the bulwark of slavery, in that province and in those of the extreme south that institution did not cause as much damage as it did in other regions. It is true that São Paulo has used much of its capital to purchase slaves from the North, but its agriculture does not depend as much upon slavery for its solvency as does that of Rio de Janeiro or Minas Gerais.

São Paulo's enterprise and resourcefulness have been much exaggerated in recent years since, after noting the good results of the Santos-Jundiaí Railroad, it built new railroad systems with-

---

4. *Translator's note:* The towns referred to here are ancient mining towns of the province of Minas Gerais. Tiradentes was a revolutionary leader of the late eighteenth century whose execution transformed him into a famous martyr.

out the aid of the national government. However, the *Paulistas* are not, as they have sometimes been called, the Yankees of Brazil —which has no Yankees—nor is São Paulo the most advanced province or the most American, or the province with the most liberal spirit. It might reasonably be called the Louisiana of Brazil, but not the Massachusetts. Nevertheless, it is also undeniable that São Paulo will reveal greater resiliency than its neighbors, having entered into its period of prosperity as the power of slavery declines.

In Paraná, Santa Catarina, and Rio Grande do Sul, European immigration is infusing new blood into the veins of the people, who are reacting against slavery as the freshness of the soil and the gentleness of the climate are opening greater opportunities to free labor than were ever open to slavery. Similarly, in the Amazon Valley slavery's power over the land was always nominal; the small population developed in a different way, far from the slave huts. Steamship navigation on Brazil's vast Mediterranean began only thirty years ago. The great basin of the Amazon is yet to be explored. Its tributaries, the Madeira, the Tocantins, the Purus, the Tapajós, the Xingu, the Juruá, the Javari, the Tefé, the Japurá, and the Rio Negro, are watercourses of more than a thousand, two thousand, or even three thousand kilometers, which remain largely in the hands of the original Indian population, lost to industry, to labor, to civilization. The backwardness of this vast region can be conceived of through the description of it left by Couto de Magalhães, the explorer of the Araguaia, in his book *O selvagem* [*The Savage*]. It is a territory, he tells us, covered either by rain forests through which the inhabitants travel in canoes as in the Paraguayan swamps, or by open and unpopulated plains containing an occasional thin grove of trees.

The three million square kilometers of the two provinces, Pará and Amazonas, which share the Amazon basin, enough space for nearly six countries the size of France, including unoccupied lands almost as large as all Europe without Russia, do not contain 500,000 people. The condition of that region is such that in 1878 the Brazilian government made a twenty-year concession of the valley of the upper Xingu, a tributary of the Amazon whose course is estimated at about two thousand kilometers, with all its products and everything to be found within it, to a few businessmen from Pará. Parliament did not ratify this grant, but the fact that it was made proves that, practically speaking, the basin of the Amazon is *res nullius*. Despite their vastness, the rubber forests have been greatly destroyed, and this natural wealth of the immense valley is menaced with extinction, since the nature of the extractive industry is exploitative and therefore tends to deplete through its use of both land and slave labor. And in the Amazon Valley even the peddler is an agent of destruction, just as the slaveholder has been in the North and South.

> Everywhere that civilized man penetrates along the inhabited banks of the rivers (President Brusque said in his report of 1862 to the Provincial Assembly of Pará) , he finds the surviving remains of that population (the Indian) who now wander about without any hope for the future. And the poor village, usually built by Indians themselves in a choice place where the land offers them the best possible harvest of the little manioc they plant, disappears completely soon after its hopeful establishment. The peddler, a fierce cancer that invades the natural arteries of legal trade in the major settlements, tricking the unwary consumers, is not satisfied with the fabulous profits which he thus obtains, but recklessly travels enormous distances and so turns up as well at the Indian's hut. The people of the village are then quickly converted into a band of servants who are rashly assigned, by cruel rather than humane methods, to the various kinds of work necessary for the collection of natural products. Since the village is soon abandoned the garden plots are lost, the hut disappears, and the miserable Indian in return for so much sacrifice and labor often receives nothing more than *a pair of trousers and a shirt*.[5]

These peddlers, who according to the Bishop of Pará [6] "make the headmen drunk in order to dishonor their families more easily," who "engage in every form of depravity," are nothing but the product of slavery, acting upon the greedy and reckless spirit of men without moral education.

The semblance of prosperity that rubber extraction gives to the Amazon Valley is like that created by the cultivation of sugar and coffee with methods and attitudes that go with slavery. Everywhere it is the same. The progress and development of the capital city contrast sharply with the decadence of the rural areas. Where slavery exists there are no local centers, no regional life,

---

5. Canon Francisco Bernardino de Souza, *Comissão do Madeira, Pará e Amazonas* (Rio de Janeiro, 1874) , p. 130.

6. Ibid., p. 132.

no municipal spirit. The parishes do not draw benefits from the proximity of the rich and powerful. The aristocracy in possession of the land does not involve itself with that land, does not try to turn it into a permanent and profitable home containing comforts normal to a happy population. The families are all nomads who gravitate toward the same place, the capital of the Empire. The sugar or coffee plantation serves to supply the money which will be spent in the city and which will pay for the annual season of boredom and hibernation. The soil is enriched neither by the savings of the poor nor the generosity of the rich. The small landholding does not exist except through indulgence.[7] The middle classes, the driving force of nations, are nowhere to be found. There are only opulent slave masters and the very poor. The nation is in fact made up of the very poor, since the descendants of slaveholders rapidly fall into that same condition themselves.

It is a sad picture, this struggle of men against the land with the use of slave labor. Nowhere does the soil acquire life. The buildings erected on it are a form of temporary and extravagant luxury destined for rapid decline and eventual abandonment. The people live in huts penetrated by wind and rain, without floors or windowpanes, without furniture or conveniences, with the hammock of the Indian or mat of the Negro for a bed, a water vessel and a pot for utensils, and the guitar dangling beside the image of the saint. This is the situation in the countryside. In the small cities and towns of the interior the dwelling places of the poor, those without jobs or small businesses, are little better than the wretched thatched huts of the peasant or squatter. In the capitals, with their elegant streets and aristocratic suburbs, poor districts like the Afogados in Recife extend out from the entrances to the city with their rows of shacks which in the nineteenth century are like the haunts of beasts. On the busiest streets of Bahia and on Rio's beaches, alongside the stately old residence which belonged to some bygone heir or

---

7. "As a rule the planter looks upon the peasant or dependent, to whom he grants or sells a small plot of land, as a cause of antagonism, an enemy who attempts to usurp his property, who brings lawsuits against him, who urges his slaves to flee or to rob him of his plantation products to sell them cheaply at the tavern of the same well-established ex-dependent, who thus enriches himself at another man's expense. As a result of this, the worker, having lost all hope of becoming a landowner, is not willing to work in the fields of the plantation or to process its products." *Parecer das commissões da Fazenda e especial da Câmara dos Deputados sobre a criação do credito territorial* (1875), p. 21.

some ennobled slave trader one sees the miserable and squalid den of the African, which is like the grotesque shadow of that bygone wealth, or of the giant pit which swallowed it up.

Whoever beholds the railroads we have built, the immense coffee crop we export, the material progress we have made may well believe that the results of slavery have not been totally disastrous to the nation. However, it must not be forgotten that the present appearance of prosperity is the result of one product only—at a time when the population of the country is more than ten million—and that forced liquidation of that product would be nothing less than a financial disaster. In the South slavery has reached its apogee at a time of considerable development, at a time when that region still has virgin lands, like those of São Paulo, to develop and a precious export crop to produce. At this moment this enterprise—and it is nothing less—is providing some benefits to its associates: profits divided among all the intermediate commercial classes (commission houses, sackers, exporters) whose crumbs support an enormous clientele of every profession, from those who perform well at the polling places to the doctor, lawyer, priest, and justice of the peace; and finally, part of which, and no small part at that, is absorbed by the national treasury to maintain the immense adjunct of our budget, the public bureaucracy. With a portion of the revenue from slavery, the government grants 7 percent guaranteed interest to the English companies that build our railroads; and thus foreign capital, attracted by high interest and the safe credit of an apparently solvent nation, invests its capital in enterprises like the São Paulo Railroad guaranteed by both Brazil and coffee.

However, this illusion of prosperity, of national progress, created by the production of sugar and cotton in the North, rubber in the Amazon Valley, gold in Minas Gerais, does not deceive the person who studies the contrasts fashioned by slavery under its dark shadows. The reality he finds is a people more enslaved to the vast territory it occupies than master over it, in whose eyes work has been systematically debased and to whom it has been taught that nobility is best achieved by making others work. The reality he finds is that of a people unacquainted with the school, of a people indifferent to all those sentiments, instincts, passions, and needs which fashion from the inhabitants of a common country not only a society but also a nation.

When Mr. Silveira Martins said in the Senate: "Brazil is coffee and coffee is the Negro" (not willing, of course, to use the word "slave"), he characterized Brazil as a plantation, a commercial enterprise under the control of a small group of profiteers.[8] In a few choice words he described today's slaveholding Brazil. That a country with more than ten million people, much larger than European Russia, almost the size of Europe without Russia, more than a third the size of the British Empire which spans five continents, can be described in such a way is enough to make us recognize what slavery has done to that country.

This terrible scourge not only whipped the backs of black men, it also lacerated the flesh of an entire people. Because of powerful social laws springing from human morality, that edifice of plunder could not bring forth anything good. It was, in fact, an affliction which scarred the land and the society with every symptom of premature decline. Wealth passed from the hands of those who founded it into the hands of their creditors; few are the grandsons of planters who are still in control of the properties that their fathers inherited. The adage "Rich father, noble son, poor grandson" expresses the long familiar results of slavery's customary ways, which squandered all the wealth, often in foreign countries, and, as we have seen, in great part eliminated from the nation's reserves the capital accumulated under that system.

Slavery devastated part of our territory but did not march on to embrace all of it, since it possesses not the initiative to migrate but only the urge to enlarge itself. For this reason Brazil is still the biggest piece of *terra incognita* on the map of the world.

> In a slaveholding State (said Mr. T. R. Cobb of Georgia) the greatest evidence of wealth in the planter is the number of his slaves. The most desirable property for a remunerative income, is slaves. The best property to leave to his children, and from which they will part with greatest reluctance, is slaves. Hence, the planter invests his surplus income in slaves. The natural result is, that lands are a secondary consideration. No surplus is left for their improvement. The homestead is valued only so long as the adjacent lands are profitable for cultivation. The planter himself, having no local attachments, his children inherit none. On the contrary, he encourages in them a disposition to seek new lands. . . . The result is that they, as a class, are never settled. Such a

---

8. *Translator's note:* Gaspar da Silveira Martins was a Liberal senator from the southern province of Rio Grande do Sul.

population is almost nomadic. It is useless to seek to excite
patriotic emotions in behalf of the land of birth, when self-interest
speaks so loudly. On the other hand, where no slavery exists, and
the planter's surplus cannot be invested in laborers, it is appropriated to the improvement or extension of his farm, the beautifying
of the homestead where his fathers are buried.[9]

It was this that occurred in Brazil, and nowhere was the cultivation of the land more destructive. The recent drought of
Ceará revealed in the most disastrous way imaginable one of
the curses which always accompanies, if it does not precede,
slavery: the destruction of the forests by burning.[10] "Fire and
the hoe," writes Senator Pompeu, "are the cruel instruments
with which a population ignorant of the elementary rules of
rural economy and heir to the customs of the aborigines has for
two hundred years ceaselessly leveled the virgin forests of our
mountains and valleys, with no other purpose than to reap the
harvest of a forest clearing for a single year." [11] Everywhere we
look we observe the results of this system, which has reduced a
beautiful and exuberant tropical country to the condition of
those regions where the creative force of the land has been exhausted.

To sum up (in a field of observation which would require
another book), the effects of slavery upon our land and the
people it supports were in every sense disastrous. In regard to
the country's exploration, the results are evident in the geo-
graphic map of Brazil, on which the shaded areas indicating
slavery's domination are insignificant when compared with the
unexplored or unpopulated areas. In regard to the occupation of
the land, we have seen what it was and is. Agriculture is characterized by improvidence, routine methods, indifference to the
machine, a total disregard for the future, the desire to extract
the greatest immediate profit possible with as little personal
effort as possible, regardless of potential harm to future generations.

The feudal division of the land instituted by slavery, along

---

9. *An Historical Sketch of Slavery from the Earliest Periods* (Philadelphia,
1858), p. 215.
10. *Translator's note:* Ceará, a state of the northeast, probably has suffered
more than any other from the disastrous droughts which have periodically
afflicted the entire region.
11. Tomás Pompeu, *Memoria sobre o clima e seccas do Ceará* (Rio de Janeiro,
1877), p. 42.

with slavery's monopoly over labor, impedes the formation of communities of hard-working people and the extension of commerce and trade into the interior. In every sense slavery was and is an obstacle to the material development of the local communities. It exploited the land without concern for local needs, without recognizing its obligations to the people beyond its borders. It burned, it planted, it abandoned. It consumed the profits in the purchase of slaves, in the luxuries of city living. It did not build schools or churches. It did not construct bridges, did not improve rivers or canalize streams, did not establish asylums. It did not build roads or construct houses, not even for its slaves. It did not encourage industry, did not increase the monetary value of the land, did not make improvements, did not nurse the wealth of the soil, did not employ machines, did not contribute in any way whatsoever to the progress of the surrounding region.

What it did was sterilize the soil through destructive planting, brutalize the slaves, impede the development of towns, and encircle its seigneurial estates with defiled regions, regions devastated by the institutions it supported, a spectacle that the free man instinctively recognizes. Upon the whole population of our interior, on the fringes of our capital cities or in the open spaces of the backlands, its effects were: dependence, misery, ignorance, subjection to the will of the landlords, for whom forced recruitment was a common procedure.

Slavery denied to the poor man even for a limited time a slice of land that he could call his own and that he could cultivate as though it were his own. It denied him a house which gave him an inviolable refuge from which he could not be evicted at will and denied him a family, safe and respected. Finally, for more than three centuries the people have been accustomed to consider work in the fields as fit only for slaves. Almost entirely descended from bondsmen, that population has preferred to widen the gap which separated it from slavery, not doing willingly what the slaves were made to do by force.

I have often been told stories about how money was offered to one of our back-country people if he would do some light task, and how he had refused to do it. Such reports are not surprising, since such people are not offered reliable wages. If they were offered regular positions which improved their circumstances, they would probably respond to such opportunities. But if they do not accept them, it being frequently pointed out that persons of this kind represent a class of Brazilians numbering in the millions, a class of Brazilians who refuse to work for wages, what greater proof could there be of the terrible effects of slavery? For centuries slavery did not allow the development of a labor market and was only served by slaves. The free worker had no place in society, being a vagrant, a beggar, who thus never acquired a permanent occupation; nor did he find about him the incentive which awakens in the poor man a vision of well-being gained through labor by individuals of his own class, who started at his own level.

And how do they live, these millions of human beings—for there are millions who find themselves in this intermediate state which is neither slavery nor citizenship, whose only contribution to the community which grants them no protection is the shedding of their blood in war? How do they nourish themselves, these millions who are the only source of recruits for the army, since the agricultural fief robbed the military of the masters and their sons and denied it the slaves, the plantation dependents, the squatters, and the whites as well?

We have seen their homes. They consist of four walls divided inside into two or three stinking cubicles, low and drafty, open to the wind and rain, little more than a sheep's pen, less than a stable. In such hovels live whole families of Brazilian citizens! The food corresponds to the indolent habits of the household. Manioc flour makes up the main item of nourishment, to which is added, as an article of luxury, Norwegian codfish or jerked beef from the Rio de la Plata. "They live directly from hunting and fishing," writes Mr. Milet, referring to the millions of free pariahs of slavery whom he estimated at a fifth of the Brazilian population, "from the immediate fruits of their farm labor, from the raising of cattle, and from the products of a primitive industry." They live, he writes, "outside the general movement of international trade." [12]

This was the population that migrated inland, living like gypsies, attaching themselves to the coffee or sugar plantations where they received asylum, clustering in small groups in the unoccupied parts of the agricultural estates, setting up their four mud walls where they were permitted to do so in exchange for conditions of vassalage which converted the new residents into serfs bound to the soil.

---

12. *Miscelânea econômica*, p. 36.

Wherever we look, the results are the same. *Latifundia per-
didere Italiam* is a phrase which rings like a tangible truth to
the Brazilian. Those who have traveled in the United States or
Switzerland should take a moment to compare the spectacle of
Brazil, to compare the different ways in which people occupied
the land. It is said that Brazil is a new country. Yes, in some parts
it is a new country, almost a virgin country, but elsewhere it is
an old country. More than three hundred years ago the soil was
first violated, the forests humbled, the sugar fields set to seed.
Take Pernambuco, for example, where in the sixteenth century
João Pais Barreto established the colony of Cabo, which during
the Dutch occupation in the seventeenth century possessed a
good number of sugar mills, which fought inch by inch against
the Dutch West India Company in order to follow the path of
Portugal. Compare that heroic province, more than three hundred years old, with the colonies of Australia and New Zealand,
or with the states which most recently joined the United States,
countries which, so to speak, belong to yesterday. If slavery had
not existed, our growth would certainly not have been as rapid
as that of the countries occupied by the British. Portugal would
not have been able to arouse us, to develop us with her capital,
as England developed her colonies. The value of human beings
would always have been cheapened and, therefore, the value of
the nation and of the state as well. On the other hand, without
slavery we would not possess today a people created outside the
sphere of civilization, a people deriving many of its characteristics from the hardships imposed upon it, from the brutal regimen to which it was subjected, a people descended from the
most backward and primitive race. The heredity of the other
race, more advanced certainly, but cruel, inhuman, avid for
illicit profits, burdened with atrocious crimes, responsible for
millions of victims during three centuries of slavery, would also
then have been much improved.

Slavery everywhere has moved over the land and over the
people who accepted it like a wind of destruction. Whether
found in the dungeons of ancient Italy or in the villages of
Russia, on the plantations of the southern states or on the sugar
and coffee estates of Brazil, it always brings ruin, disease, and
death. For a certain time, with the bright metallic luster of its
tiny core, it succeeds in hiding the darkness which surrounds it
on all sides. When its flame has died down, however, it becomes
apparent that the part which burned brightly was an insignificant

spot compared with the dense, deserted, lifeless mass of the whole
system. It may be said, therefore, that just as material does not
disappear but is only transformed, the suffering, curses, and sup-
plication of the slave before God, condemned as he is to perpetual bondage, a child deformed by the lust for wealth, are
not extinguished with him but are spread like a heavy fluid,
fatal to mankind and to nature, over slavery's *valley of tears,*
which he inhabits.

> It is a dreadful picture (says the German historian of Rome), this
> picture of Italy under the rule of the oligarchy. There was noth-
> ing to bridge over or soften the fatal contrast between the world of
> the beggars and the world of the rich. . . . Riches and misery in
> close league drove the Italians out of Italy and filled the peninsula
> partly with swarms of slaves, partly with awful silence. It is a
> terrible picture, but not one peculiar to Italy: wherever the gov-
> ernment of capitalists in a slave-state has fully developed itself, it
> has desolated God's fair world in the same way. As rivers glisten
> in different colors, but a common sewer everywhere looks like
> itself, so the Italy of the Ciceronian epoch resembles substantially
> the Hellas of Polybius and still more decidedly the Carthage of
> Hannibal's time. . . . All the arrant sins that capital has been
> guilty of against nation and civilization in the modern world,
> remain as far inferior to the abominations of the ancient capitalist-
> states as the free man, be he ever so poor, remains superior to the
> slave; and not until the dragonseed of North America ripens, will
> the world have again similar fruits to reap.[13]

In Brazil those seeds, cast in every direction, flourished long
ago. And if the world did not reap those fruits and is not even
aware that we are reaping them, it is because Brazil plays no role
in the world and is hidden from civilization "by the last rem-
nants of the dark mist which still envelops our America." [14]

---

13. Theodor Mommsen, *History of Rome,* vol. 5, chapter 11.
14. Antônio Cândido, Chamber of Deputies of Portugal, session of January
8, 1881.

CHAPTER XV

The Social and Political Results of Slavery

> It is not simply as a productive factor that slavery is valued by its supporters. It is far rather for its social and political results—as the means of upholding a form of society in which slaveholders are the sole depositaries of social prestige and political power, as the "cornerstone" of an edifice of which they are the masters—that the system is prized. Abolish slavery and you introduce a new order of things.
>
> —JOHN ELLIOTT CAIRNES [1]

HAVING SEEN the effects of the slave system upon our territory and population, we can understand its social and political results as mere consequences. A free state built upon a foundation of slavery would be a new thing in the world. The governments of the ancient world did not rest upon the same basis of individual freedom as those of modern states, and they constitute a very different social order. Only after the French Revolution did there come into being—in the United States— the remarkable spectacle of democracy combined with slavery. The fact is, however, that the states of the South never did establish free governments. Indeed, taking the Union as a whole, American liberty dates from Lincoln's Emancipation Proclamation, which declared the freedom of millions of slaves in the southern states. Far from being free territories, the states south of the Potomac were sustained by the violation of every human right. American leaders such as Henry Clay and John Calhoun, who accepted slavery or were identified with it, did not understand the intensity of the antagonism which was later to reveal itself in such a frightful manner. What happened in North America—the rebellion in which the North rescued the South from the suicidal act of separating itself from the Union to form a slave power, and the way that rebellion was crushed—proves that slavery in the United States had not infected the entire social order, as it did in Brazil. Instead, it left the better part of that order intact and still strong enough, despite its great com-

---

1. *Translator's note:* From John Elliott Cairnes, *The Slave Power* (New York, 1862).

plicity with slavery, to prevail over the section which formerly had been the master of its will.

Among us there is no dividing line whatever. Not one part of Brazil is different from any other part. Contact was synonymous with contagion. The entire bloodstream, from the great arteries to the smallest veins, provides a channel for the same contamination. The whole body—with its blood, its vital organs, its breath, its strength and movement, its muscles and nerves, its will and intelligence, not only its character but also its temperament, its vigor more than anything else—is affected by the same disease.

In the case of Brazil we are not dealing merely with an institution which placed an immense number of persons outside society, as was done in Greece and ancient Italy, and assigned to them the social function of toiling for the citizens. Not only are we dealing with a society based upon slavery—as was the civilization of the ancient world—and permeated by it in every social class; we have as well a society largely composed of the cast-off waste material of that huge system.

In the southern states of the American union, with their color line, the slaves and their descendants were not part of society; slavery had blended the population on a very small scale. Though it destroyed the land, barred the development of industry, set the stage for economic failure, repelled immigation, in short, caused all the effects of the sort we have seen in Brazil, American society was not composed of elements created by that process. Attempting to change all this, the Fourteenth Amendment to the Constitution ordered the incorporation of Negroes into the social community, demonstrating that the divisions which artificially prevent races or classes from reaching their natural level are less than permanent.

As long as slavery lasted, however, neither the slaves nor their free descendants took part in any way in the intellectual and active life of that parasitical society which they had the task of sustaining with their blood. When emancipation came, and after it political equality, Virginia and Georgia suddenly saw the functions of government turned over to those same slaves who until then were, socially speaking, inanimate objects, and who for this reason could only function during this first political experiment as tools of outside opportunists such as the carpetbaggers. Thus this period can be thought of as a continuation of the Civil War. The separation of the two races, which was the system adopted by North American slavery—maintained by a scorn for blackness which later sought justification in harsh educational principles, in the curse of Cain, and in the descent-from-the-ape theory—continues to characterize the relationship between the two great sectors of the American population.

In Brazil the exact opposite occurred. Though based upon racial differences, slavery never developed obstacles based on color, and in this regard Brazil was infinitely more reasonable. From the arrival of the *donatários* until today, the contacts between the races produced, as we have seen, a mixed population. The slave, upon receiving his certificate of emancipation, also receives his badge of citizenship. Thus no permanent social castes exist among us, not even a fixed separation of classes. The slave as such *hardly exists* for the society, since the master could neglect to register him and, even having done so, could substitute another person for him. Even the registration itself has been meaningless, since there is no government inspection of the plantations and the masters are under no obligation to give an account of their slaves to the authorities. The human being who, insofar as social protection is concerned, is thus indistinguishable from any other privately owned thing finds himself on the day following his emancipation a citizen like any other, with every political privilege and the same degree of political qualification. Even while still in the shadow of captivity, the slave is permitted to buy slaves (and who can tell?), perhaps some son of his former master. This is an indication of the confusion of classes and of individuals, of the unlimited degree of social mixing which goes on between the slave and the free. Thus most Brazilians are made into political hybrids, if it may be so expressed, in whom two opposite tendencies engage each other in struggle: those of the master by birth and those of the slave domesticated.

Slavery among us remained open-ended, indiscriminately extending its privileges to all: to whites and blacks, *ingênuos* and freedmen, aliens and natives, the rich and the poor, the slaves themselves. Thus it acquired a reinforced capacity to absorb and, simultaneously, a flexibility immeasurably greater than it would have possessed had it been the monopoly of one race, as it was in North America. That system of absolute equality certainly opened a better future for the black race in Brazil than in the United States. Macaulay said in the House of Commons in 1845, the year of the Aberdeen Bill: "I do not deem it unlikely that the black population of Brazil will be free and contented within eighty or a hundred years; I do not envision, however, a reasonable likelihood of a similar change in the United States." [2] This forecast of the black man's relative contentment in the two countries seems today as realistic as the supposition was incorrect that the United States would preserve slavery longer than Brazil. In this case, what deceived the great British orator was color prejudice, which to him seemed to be a political and social impulse reinforcing slavery, when in fact the strength of slavery in Brazil lay in its capacity to banish prejudice and to open the doors of the institution to every class. For this same reason, however, the ethnic chaos among us has been the greatest imaginable, and the confusion reigning in those regions where national unity is being forged with all those heterogeneous elements reminds one of the splendid disorder of incandescent worlds.

To use a chemical analogy, Athens, Rome, and Virginia were simple mixtures in which the various elements kept their particular properties. Brazil, on the other hand, is a compound, for which slavery represents the agent of affinity, the force of attraction which brought the parts together. The problem we need to solve is to find a way to convert that compound of master and slave into that of the citizen. The problem in the United States was quite different, since in that country these two classes did not mix. Among us slavery affected not only those below the Roman category of the *libertas* [freedman]; it had its effects with and above the sphere of the *civitas* [citizen] as well. With the exception of the slaves, who always exist in the lower regions of the social scale, it leveled every other class, but it did so through a process of degradation. It is for this reason that it is so difficult, when analyzing slavery's results, to discover anything—whether in the disposition of the people, in the condition of the country, or even in the high places farthest from the stench of the slave huts—upon which the slave system did not act in one way or another and which should not be included in the national slavery synthesis. All show symptoms of retarded or impeded development or, worse yet, of unnatural precociousness. If we study the several political groupings, those who would preserve the nation's heritage intact and those who would direct it toward change, it is clear that the major ones are declining and that the

---

2. *Translator's note:* The source of this Macaulay quotation could not be located. It appears here in a retranslation from Nabuco's translation into Portuguese.

conservation of the nation's institutions and the promotion of its progress are today problems beyond solution, for which slavery, and slavery alone, is the unknown quantity. There is space merely to point this out, not to prove it.

An important class whose development is impeded by slavery is that of the landless farmers and the rural and backland inhabitants in general. We have already seen to what level this abundant part of our population has been reduced. For them, lacking independence, reliant as they are upon the chance whims of others, the words of the Lord's Prayer, "Give us this day our daily bread," have a real and concrete meaning. We do not refer here to workers who, released from one factory, find work in another, or to families who can emigrate, or to manual workers who offer their services in the labor market. We are dealing here with a population without resources, without assistance, a population taught to think of labor as an activity suitable only for slaves. We are referring to a population without markets for its products, far from the realm of wages—if such an El Dorado even exists in our country—and therefore without any alternative but to live and raise its children in the conditions of dependence and misery in which they are allowed to vegetate.

The following is a description of a segment of that rural class —the most fortunate segment—which one of our sugar planters read with genuine humanitarian feeling at the Agricultural Congress in Recife in 1878:

> The planter who does not process his own sugar leads a precarious existence. He is not compensated for his work, his dignity is not respected, his interests are at the mercy of the sugar mill owner on whose lands he lives. There is not even a written contract which commits the interested parties; everything depends entirely upon the will of the mill owner. In exchange for a place to live, often of the very worst kind, and for some land granted to him for planting manioc, necessarily a small piece and always the least productive—in exchange for this the sharecropper divides all the sugar obtained from his cane into equal parts, and the mill owner gets all the molasses and rum from that sugar, all the cane husks, which are a good fuel for the sugar mill, all the buds of the cane, a succulent food for the cattle. It is the lion's share, and terribly unjust, since all the expenses of planting, cultivating, cutting, and stacking of the cane stocks and their transportation to the mill are the sole responsibility of the sharecropper.

When it is not for the sentiments of fair and generous people, the poor sugarcane planter of this class cannot even be certain of the security of his home. From one moment to the next he can be wantonly evicted, and he faces the threat of finding strangers even at the kitchen door of his dismal hovel, there to hurry him on his way, bringing the most terrible misfortunes upon his family.[3]

And this is a privileged class, that of the sharecroppers, beneath whom there are others who own nothing, who inhabit the land and have nothing to sell to the proprietors, who lead a vagabond existence remote from all social responsibility and beyond the government's protection.

There are still other classes—workers, industrialists, and, in general, merchants—whose progress is retarded by slavery. Slavery does not suffer the existence of a true working class, nor is it compatible with a wage system and the personal dignity of the artisan. The latter, so as not to fall under the social stigma imposed by slavery upon its workers, tries to exaggerate the social distance which separates him from the slave. He thus imbues himself with a sense of superiority which is nothing more than baseness of character on the part of the person who escaped from slavery or is identified with it through his parents. Moreover, there are no strong, respected, and informed working classes in countries where the employers of labor are accustomed to commanding slaves. Similarly, the workers among us do not enjoy the smallest political influence.[4]

Slavery and industry (like slavery and immigration) are always mutually exclusive terms. The spirit of slavery creeping into every corner of the nation eliminates every human faculty which tends to stimulate industry. It destroys initiative, inventiveness, and personal ambition; and it eradicates each of the factors required for industrial development, the growth of capital, abundant workers, technological training, and confidence in

---

3. A. Victor de Sá Barreto, *Congresso Agrícola do Recife*, pp. 323-24.

4. The following distribution of voters of the Município Neutro (the county containing the city of Rio de Janeiro) in 1881 clearly indicates how well the workers are represented. Among the 5,928 voters who represented the capital of the nation, there were 2,211 public employees (civil or military), 1,076 merchants or commercial employees, 516 proprietors, 398 medical doctors, 211 lawyers, 207 engineers, 179 teachers, 145 pharmacists, 236 artists, and the rest were divided among various professions, including priests (76), bookkeepers (58), customhouse clerks (56), solicitors (27), and so forth. Such statistics require no additional comment.

the future. In Brazil agriculture is the only industry which has flourished under Brazilian control; commerce has prospered in the hands of foreigners alone. And, despite these facts, think of the condition of agriculture, which we will later describe. In our country, then, the industrial age is singularly retarded, and it is only now in fact that we are beginning to enter that age.

The large national trading companies, both exporting and importing firms, do not possess capital comparable to that of foreign companies. Retail trade, in its whole active sector, the consolidated part with an existence of its own, is practically a foreign monopoly. At times in our history this fact has provoked popular demonstrations favoring the nationalization of retail trade. Such a demand, however, is typical of the spirit of exclusivism and distaste for competition, however legitimate, which slavery taught our people. And in more than one place such demands have been accompanied by uprisings carried on in the same spirit and motivated by religious fanaticism. Those who have supported the policy of closing Brazil's ports and annulling all the progress achieved since 1808 have not understood that to deny foreigners the right to engage in retail trade would not cause that trade to revert to Brazilians but would simply create instead a permanent shortage of goods, since it is slavery and not our nationality which prevents retail trade from becoming predominantly national.

In regard to commerce, slavery functions in the following way: owing to lack of confidence and routine procedures, it impedes trade in all interior areas outside the provincial capitals. With the exceptions of Santos and Campinas in São Paulo province, Petrópolis and Campos in Rio de Janeiro, Pelôtas in Rio Grande do Sul, and a scattering of other towns, there are no commercial houses outside the capital cities where anything can be found beyond a small stock of items essential to life, and even these are crude or adulterated. Thus, just as nothing exists to reveal the intellectual development of the backlanders—neither bookstores nor newspapers—trade is also absent, except in the old-fashioned, still unspecialized, primitive form of the public market. For this reason, whatever is not ordered directly from the capital reaches the consumer through the peddler alone, that pioneer of commerce whose story is that of our backlands, who personifies the extent to which slavery is compatible with local trade.

Commerce, nevertheless, is the wellspring of slavery as well as its banker. During the past generation it supplied the slave system everywhere with Africans, either newly imported or acculturated. Many of the agricultural estates fell into the hands of the slave dealers; the fortunes made by the traffic (with which counterfeiting was sometimes closely identified), if not sent abroad or converted into palatial estates, were used up in the payment of usurious rates of interest. For the present generation the link between commerce and slavery is no longer dishonorable to the former, but their mutual dependence remains the same as always. The principal customers of the merchants are slaveholders, just as slaveholders are the leaders of the mercantile class. Coffee is always king on the beaches of Rio and Santos, and, with industry and free labor absent, commerce can find no useful role except to serve as the agent of slavery, buying everything slavery offers and selling slavery everything it needs. It is for this reason too that commerce fails to thrive in Brazil, that it does not open up new prospects to the nation. It is an inactive force, without purpose, and fully aware that it constitutes nothing but an appendage to slavery or, more precisely, the mechanism through which human flesh is converted into gold and circulated at home and abroad as bills of exchange. Commerce knows that if slavery fears it, as it fears all conductors of progress —the merchant's shop, the railroad station, the primary school (and the latter most of all) —slavery also needs it and seeks to live with it on the best possible terms. But as long as slavery endures, commerce will be the handmaiden of a single class, will lack the independent status of a national agent. Commerce will never flourish within a system which does not allow it to enter into direct relations with the consumer, which does not even elevate the backland people to the level of consumers.

Among the classes which slavery artificially generates, the largest is that of the public employees. The close relationship between slavery and the epidemic of bureaucratism is no more open to doubt than the relationship between it and the superstition of the All-Providing State. Under that system the government is counted on for everything. Being the only active organization, the state covets and absorbs all disposable capital by means of taxation and loans, distributing it among its clients by means of public employment, absorbing the savings of the poor through inflation and rendering precarious the fortunes of the well-to-do. Any twenty or thirty Brazilians to be met wherever our most cultivated society gathers can provide the example. All of them either once were, or now are, or will one day be public employees, and if not they themselves, then their sons.

As we have observed, bureaucratism is the refuge of the descendants of the rich and noble families who squandered the fortunes acquired through slavery, fortunes which, like those won through gambling, may be said as a rule neither to grow nor to bring contentment. Aside from this, bureaucratism is a political sanctuary, since it shelters every needy intellectual, all those who are ambitious and talented but without resources, a group which includes the great majority of our men of merit. Make a list of our poor statesmen, the best and the second best, who solved their personal predicament either by making rich marriages—by generally becoming, that is, the humble clients of slavery—or who solved their financial problem by accumulating public jobs. On those two lists you will have the names of nearly all our political leaders. What this means is that opportunity is shut off on all sides, that many avenues which could provide a livelihood to men of talent with no gift for business—careers in literature, science, journalism, or teaching—are at best narrow alleyways. And others in which practical men of industrious tendencies could prosper are so many additional closed doors, owing to a lack of credit and commerce and the primitive structure of our economic life.

Under these circumstances, several roads offer themselves to the Brazilian starting out in life, all of which lead to public employment. The so-called independent professions such as law, medicine, engineering, which in fact depend heavily upon the benevolence of the slave system, have important points of contact with bureaucratism. This is the case, for example, when lawyers are given political commissions, when doctors teach in the academies, or when engineers are employed on public works. Aside from these professionals, who gather up, so to speak, the crumbs of the national budget, there are others—businessmen, capitalists, unclassifiable types—who want contracts, subventions from the state, guaranteed interest, public works contracts, and even cash advances from the government.

The class which thus lives with its eyes turned toward the munificence of the state is very large and a direct result of slavery. Having monopolized the land, debased labor, perverted feelings of personal self-esteem into contempt for anyone who labors under another's command or does not force others to work, slavery does not consent to any other career for Brazilians. Since necessity is irresistible, this hunger for public employment brings a constant expansion of the budget which the nation, unable to finance through its income, pays with the very capital needed for its subsistence and which, nevertheless, is balanced finally only by incurring new public debts.

Beyond being artificial and premature, the current development of that class of persons remunerated by the treasury is past our power to support. As we have seen, by closing off every other road to improvement through industry, commerce, science, and letters, slavery created alongside that active army of public employees a reserve of pretenders whose number is beyond our ability to count. However, with the exception of those who are idly consuming their inheritances and those who are exploiting slavery with the spirit of the owners of men, they can be estimated with some exactness by reference to the census statistics on those who are able to read and write.[5] At a time when servility and adulation are the stairway by which one rises, and independence and character are the stairway by which one descends; at a time when envy is a prevailing passion, when there is no criterion for promotion or evidence of capacity beyond protection and patronage, when no one not calling attention to himself is called upon for anything, and no one resents injustice except its victims; at such a time public employees are the government's serfs, living with their families on the government's lands, subject to eviction without prior notice, a condition equivalent to destitution, in a dependent status which for the strong alone does not result in a crippling of character. The student of slavery quickly sees its results in all the symptoms characteristic of the grave overdevelopment of bureaucratism as it exhibits itself in Brazil. Do we have, however, the consolation that while discouraging the various professions, while reducing Brazil to a nation of paupers, slavery nonetheless managed to make of the slaveholders, of the agriculturists, a superior class? Are they at least rich and, more important yet, educated, patriotic, and worthy of representing the nation intellectually and morally?

---

5. *Translator's note:* According to the census of 1872, 1,564,391 Brazilians in a total population of 9,930,478 were literate, including less than one in every thousand slaves (1,403 literate slaves among a total slave population of 1,510,806).

In regard to wealth, we have already seen that slavery ruined a generation of farmers, that that generation was in fact replaced by those who supplied them with slaves. From 1853 until 1857, when debts accumulated through the traffic should have been in a process of liquidation, the mortgage debt of the city and province of Rio de Janeiro rose to 67,000 *contos* [nearly $39 million]. The present generation has not been more fortunate. A large part of their profits was converted into human flesh at high cost, and if today an epidemic should depopulate the coffee plantations, the capital which the whole agricultural sector of the Empire could raise for new planting would be so small as to shock those who believe that agriculture is in a flourishing condition. Furthermore, for fifteen years there has been constant talk of *assistance to agriculture.* In a brief work by Mr. Quintino Bocaiúva, *A crise da lavoura* [*The Crisis of Agriculture*], which was published in 1868, that noted journalist wrote: "Agriculture cannot be restored without two simultaneous kinds of assistance which can no longer be delayed: the establishment of agricultural credit and the acquisition of productive workers." The first type of support was to take the form of "a huge bond issue" to be based upon the real estate holdings of the Empire, which would thus be converted into currency. The second type of assistance was to take the form of Chinese immigration.

For fifteen years agriculture has been described repeatedly as languishing in a state of *crisis,* in need of *assistance,* writhing in agony, close to bankruptcy. Every day we hear the government denounced because it does not make loans or increase taxes to enable planters to buy even more slaves. A law of November 6, 1875, authorized the government to grant an exclusive national guarantee to the foreign bank which would grant loans to agriculture at a rate of interest lower than that of the internal money market. In order to have centralized sugar mills for the improvement of their product, the sugar planters asked that those mills be constructed at the expense of the nation. The coffee planters have made the same kind of demand. The so-called great property has not only requested central sugar mills and money at low interest rates; it has also asked for convenient railroad freight rates, official coffee expositions, exemption from every form of direct taxation, Asian immigrants, and a contract-labor law which turns German, English, or Italian immigrants into white slaves. Even the national population must be subjected to a new agrarian recruitment in order to satisfy various agricultural clubs; [6] and, even worse, the rate of exchange, by an economic fallacy, must be kept as low as possible so that coffee paid for in gold will have greater value in terms of paper money.

Moreover, the terrible usury that victimized agriculture in various provinces, particularly those of the North, is the best evidence of the shoddy system established by slavery, of which the two principal characteristics—extravagance and imperma-nence—are incompatible with the agricultural credit it demands. "The interest rate upon loans to agriculture levied by its com-mercial correspondents," says the official extract of provincial re-ports of 1874, "is set in some provinces from 7 to 12 percent. In others it rises as high as 18 to 24 percent," and "there are ex-amples of interest rates as high as 48 and 72 percent annually!" Since it is not suggested that the yearly profit from agriculture is more than 10 percent, and since the entire agricultural sector is in need of loans, these rates quite simply imply bankruptcy. Cer-tainly this is not a class which can be described as prosperous and flourishing, a class to be called opulent.

In regard to social functions, a landed aristocracy can serve in various ways. It can advance and develop the well-being of the surrounding population and the appearance of the territory where its establishments are found. It can put itself at the fore-front of the nation's progress. It can cultivate and protect the arts and letters. It can serve in the army and in the navy or distinguish itself in the various careers, incarnating what is good in the national character or the superior qualities of the commonwealth, that which deserves to be preserved as tradi-tion. We have already seen what our agriculture accomplished

---

6. For example, the Agricultural and Commercial Club of Taubaté appointed a committee to study the contract-labor law, and the result of this study was a bill whose first article was designed to impose a labor contract upon any Brazilian twelve or older who might be found with no honest occupation. This Brazilian would have the choice of being *recruited* into the army or contracting his labor to a farmer *acceptable to him*. Article 6 resolved: "The worker who complies with his contract for five years will have the right at the end of that time to payment not to exceed 500$000 [$275]. This compensation will be financed by the govern-ment in cash or in bonds guaranteed by the public treasury." Slavery has brought about so much extravagance that I cannot call this the worst example. But just as Valença [a community in Rio de Janeiro province] doggedly regards itself as Sparta, and Rio de Janeiro and Bahia see themselves as Delos and Corinth, it may be said in view of this proposed gift of 500$000 that Taubaté, which J. M. de Machado describes as "ancient, historic, and proud of its past," wishes to become known as the Boeotia of slavery.

in each of these areas when we observed what the institution of slavery, administered by the agricultural sector, has done with our land and population, with the masters and the slaves. Since the only class for whose profit slavery was established and now exists is not an aristocracy of wealth, birth, intellect, patriotism, or race, what permanent role in the state does it perform, this heterogeneous aristocracy which does not even maintain its identity for two generations?

If we turn from the various classes to the social forces, we find that slavery either appropriated them to its own interest when they were willing, or established about them a void when they were slavery's enemies, or impeded their formation when they were incompatible with the institution.

Among those who identified themselves from the beginning with slavery, becoming one of the instruments of its pretensions, is, for example, the Catholic Church. In the regimen of domestic slavery, Christianity mated with fetishism, just as the two races were crossed. Through the influence of the wet nurse and house slaves upon the development of the child, the physical terrors of the converted fetishist—of him, that is, who traded one hell for another—exercise upon the ramparts of the mind and will the worst form of despondency. What emerges as faith and religious system from that crossing of African traditions with the anti-social ideal of the fanatic missionary-priest is a complex of contradictions which only the unprincipled can find any way to reconcile. And, as religion goes, so goes the Church.

Neither bishops, priests, nor confessors denounce the marketing of human beings; the papal bulls which condemned it are today out of date. Two of our prelates were sentenced to prison at hard labor because of the struggle they waged against Freemasonry; yet none of them has acknowledged the duty to reject slavery. It is understandable that examples of the prophets invading the palace of the kings of Judah to reproach them for their crimes, and the ancient martyrs suffering on behalf of moral truth, would seem to those who represent religion among us like forms of behavior quite as ridiculous as Saint Simeon Stylites's residing at the top of a column to bring him nearer to God. But if the present system of priestly allowances and emoluments and of still more important honors and personal benefits does not permit the survival of those traces of religious heroism today suitable only to a Himalayan yogi, despite that glacial chill from a part of a spirit which once glowed, even today slavery and the

Gospel ought to be ashamed to encounter one another in the House of Jesus, succored by the same priesthood.

Not even on behalf of marriage of the slaves or of their moral education has the Church done anything of significance. The monks of St. Benedict emancipated their slaves, and this produced among the panegyrists of the convents an explosion of enthusiasm. When monasteries are the owners of human herds, nobody familar with the origins of monasticism, with the vows of the novices, with the disinterestedness of their intentions, and with their renunciation of the world can be anything but astonished that they expect recognition and gratitude for having ceased to treat men like animals, for having ceased to exploit women as instruments of production.

"If even among free persons one sees neglect," wrote the priest of the district of Sacramento of the Município Neutro to the government in 1864, "indifference to the fate of the slaves reaches a point of scandal. Few masters take care to grant their slaves spiritual support while they are alive; rare are those who comply with the charitable responsibility of granting them the last rites of the Church." [7] Many priests own slave women, and clerical celibacy does not prohibit it. That contact—more accurately, contagion—of slavery lent our religion its materialist tendencies, destroyed its spiritual quality, and denied it every hope of performing the role of an upright force in the social life of the nation.

Patriotism, another element of national conservation, was pilfered in the same manner. The work of slavocrats has always consisted of identifying Brazil with slavery. Whoever attacks slavery is immediately suspected of collusion with foreigners, of being an enemy of the institutions of his own country. On behalf of slavery Antônio Carlos was accused of being un-Brazilian. [8] Though the country is monarchical, to attack the monarchy is acceptable; though it is Catholic, to attack religion is legitimate to any man. But to attack slavery is treason, a felonious act against the nation. In the United States, the "peculiar institution" generated in its own defense so much misunderstanding between itself and the nation that it was able to raise up its own banner against that of the federal government in Washington, was capable during a brief spell of madness—from the moment it felt

---

7. Conference of June 18, 1864, *Consultas do Conselho de Estado sôbre negócios eclesiásticos.*

8. Antônio Carlos was one of the Andrada brothers. See chapter 3, note 5.

itself threatened with destruction—to produce a separatist patriotism, crushing the nation underfoot. As with every other decent
element that it subdued, slavery, while it conquered Brazilian
patriotism, also caused its degeneration.

The Paraguayan War is the best instance of what slavery did
to the patriotism of the classes who practiced it, to the patriotism
of the masters. Few of the latter abandoned their slaves to attend
to the interests of their country, though many freed their "Negroes" for the sake of receiving imperial titles. It was among the
neediest strata of the population that the heartbeat of a new
fatherland was heard most clearly: among descendants of the
slaves for the most part, those whom slavery condemned to dependence and misery, and the illiterate poor whose political
emancipation slavery has indefinitely postponed. It was these
who produced soldiers for the battalions of the Volunteers.

With slavery, José Bonifacio said in 1825, "Brazil will never
create an intrepid army and a flourishing navy, as she urgently
must," since with slavery there is no national patriotism, only
the patriotism of caste or of race. A sentiment which normally
serves to unite society's members is thus exploited for the purpose of dividing them. In order for patriotism to cleanse itself,
the great mass of free population heretofore kept in a state of sub-
servience by slavery must, with a spirit of independence and
knowledge of its own power, bridge the wide gap which separates
the citizen who would become an active and thinking member of
his community from the simple national who, motivated by love,
mutely pledges his life to defense of the material integrity and
external sovereignty of the nation.

The press stands out among the forces of progress and change
around which slavery tried to establish a void because of the
press's opposition to it—not only newspapers, but also books and
everything associated with education. To the honor of our journalism, the press has been the great weapon against slavery and
the instrument for propagating new ideas; the various attempts
to create a "black organ," a journal dedicated wholeheartedly to
the cause of slavery, have always failed. Whether timidly insin-
uated or vigorously affirmed, the dominant thought of all our
journalism from north to south is liberation. However, in order
to create a void around the newspaper and the book, and anything else which might prematurely arouse abolitionist feelings,
slavery instinctively rejected the school, keeping the country in
ignorance and darkness, the environment in which slavery pros-

pers best. The slave hut and the school are opposite poles, mutually repellent.

What national education is in a system which thrives on mass ignorance is well revealed in the following passage from the outstanding report of Mr. Rui Barbosa, head of the Committee on Public Education of the Chamber of Deputies:

> The truth is—and the Committee wants to be most explicit in this respect, regardless of whom we may offend—that public education just teeters on the brink of what is possible for a nation which presumes to be free and civilized. The truth is that there is decadence instead of progress, that we are a nation of illiterates, and that if the actual number of the great illiterate mass is declining, it does so at a desperately slow pace. The truth is that academic education is infinitely remote from the scientific level of this age, that secondary education sends on to higher education a group of young people who are always less and less ready to receive it, and that public education in the capital of the Empire, as in the provinces, is completely inadequate.

Here we find the effect but not the cause, as in all the countless cases in which the effects of slavery are pointed out to us. For example, a planter from the province of Rio de Janeiro, Mr. Pais Leme, was commissioned by our government in 1876 to travel to the United States. He wrote reports about what he saw in North America, and he made speeches in the Provincial Assembly of Rio de Janiero which were also influenced by that journey. But it never occurred to him, when drawing parallels between Brazil and the great Republic, to attribute any part of our backwardness to slavery. The same can be said of all our political literature, Liberal or Republican. The very significant role of the factor of slavery is not recognized.

Among the forces stifled by slavery is public opinion, the awareness of a national destiny. With slavery that powerful force known as public opinion, that force which is the lever and rallying point for those who represent what is most advanced in the nation, does not exist. Just as slavery is incompatible with free immigration, so it prevents an influx of new ideas. Incapable of invention, it is equally averse to progress. We are not referring here to that public opinion, that assemblage of common interests, which supported the slave traders against the Andradas, since this is a rude, unscrupulous force, numbers for the sake of numbers. Two hundred pirates are worth as much as one pirate, and surrounding them with the entire population that they enrich and despoil will not increase their value. The public opinion that I am talking about is strictly the national conscience, enlightened, humanized, honest, and patriotic. The existence of such a force is all but impossible while slavery endures, but if it does begin to appear, slavery moves to destroy it.

It is because that force of social change does not exist among us that politics is the sad and degrading struggle of lackeys we are witnessing. No man has any value, since none enjoys the backing of the nation. The Prime Minister lives at the mercy of the Crown, the source of his power, and only exhibits the appearance of power while in fact viewing himself as the Emperor's lieutenant, knowing full well that the decree of dissolution and the right to select a new Chamber composed of his own supporters are in the Emperor's pocket.[9] The members of the cabinet exist just below this level, at the mercy of the Prime Minister, and the deputies are at a third level, at the mercy of the ministers. Thus the representative system is a grafting of parliamentary forms upon a patriarchal government, and senators and deputies only play out their roles in this parody of democracy for the advantages to be had. Eliminate their salaries and deprive them of the right to exploit their position for their own benefit and that of their kin, and no man who has something important to do will waste his time in such a *skiamaxiai*, in shadow duels, to use an analogy from Cicero.

Ministers without public support, who when dismissed fall into a vacuum; prime ministers who live night and day to sift through the esoteric thought of the Emperor; a Chamber aware of its impotence and demanding nothing but indulgence; a Senate which is reduced to the level of a prytaneum;[10] parties which are nothing more than cooperative agencies for public employment or for security against destitution—all this evidence of a free government is maintained, like the consular dignity of the Roman Empire, to bolster the pride of the citizens. But deep down what we have is a government of primitive simplicity, in which responsibilities are endlessly delegated and power is concentrated in the hands of one man alone, the Chief of State.

---

9. *Translator's note:* Nabuco refers here to the Emperor's power, established by the Constitution of 1824, to choose members of the Imperial Cabinet and to dissolve the Chamber of Deputies.

10. *Translator's note:* A public building in ancient Greece used as a meeting place of the local administrative council.

When someone else seems to have some power of his own, some
effective authority and personal prestige, it is because at that
moment the light of the throne happens to focus upon him.
However, if he takes one step either to the right or left and leaves
that beam of light behind, no one will again discern him in the
darkness.

It was to this that slavery, as an inevitable cause of social corruption, by its terrible contagion reduced our politics: the people enjoying the morbid pleasure of electing the worst candidates
thus demeaning themselves with the knowledge that they are an
unorganized mass, with no discipline to subject themselves to,
with no goals to propose. The town magistrates of the capital, at
the center of the nation's life, were always selected by this principle. Until yesterday the *capangas* and *capoeiras,* hired hench-
men from the backlands and cities, turned our elections into a
jubilee of crime.[11] Except when the bayonet usurped their function, the pocketknife and the razor have always enjoyed a plu-
rality at the polls. With the advent of direct elections, all this
disappeared in the hubbub of the first moment, because there
was a resolute Prime Minister who claimed that he aspired to the
honor of electoral defeat. Mr. Saraiva was canonized, however,
by his own self-denial, and there were already enough minister
martyrs to fill whole books with saintly biographies. Thus it was
seen that not even official candidacy is essential for the election
of chambers dominated by the ministry's party. The electoral
machine functions automatically, and however much the laws
are changed, the result must be the same. The *capoeira* knows his
importance, knows that the day of Claudius does not pass as
fast as once was thought, and soon direct elections will be what
indirect elections were before them: the same unbridled orgy in
which no decent person ought to involve himself.

Among us only one power possesses independence: the power
of the Emperor, responsible to nobody. Only this power can look
forward optimistically to a new day; only it represents the con-
tinuity of the national tradition. The ministers are nothing but
second-class, sometimes grotesque incarnations of this superior

---

11. *Translator's note:* These terms have several meanings. A *capanga* is a
hired killer, but the word also refers to a black person living in a forest. In the
nineteenth century the word *capoeira* referred to a style of fighting brought from
Africa and to the persons who employed that kind of personal combat. Today
capoeira is a graceful dance in which the performers, all male, accompanied by
music played on special instruments, feign attacks upon one another, notably with
their feet.

entity. Looking about him, the Emperor finds not one person to restrain him, not one will—individual or collective—to which he must submit. In this sense he is as absolute as the czar or the sultan, though he stands at the center of a modern government provided with all the higher bodies: Parliament (which neither Russia nor Turkey has), parliamentary supremacy (which Germany does without), and absolute freedom of the press (which very few countries know). This means that, instead of "absolute sovereign," the Emperor should be known as Brazil's permanent Prime Minister. Though he does not appear before the chambers, though he allows the ministry substantial freedom, particularly in financial and legislative matters, not for a day does he lose touch with the activities of the cabinet or cease being master of his ministers.

This so-called *personal government* is sometimes explained away by the ridiculous theory that the Emperor corrupted an entire people, that by means of supreme satanic temptations he undermined the honesty of our politicians, that he deliberately demoralized parties which never had ideas or principles of their own. The truth is that this government is the direct result of the nation's involvement with slavery. A people which accustoms itself to slavery places no value on freedom, nor does it learn to govern itself. From these conditions arise the general neglect of civic functions, the political indifference, the dislike for the obscure and anonymous exercise of personal responsibility without which no nation is free, since a free people can be nothing more than an aggregate of free persons. From all these causes results the supremacy of the permanent and perpetual factor, the monarchy. The Emperor is not to blame (except perhaps for not reacting against this national abdication of responsibility) for being as powerful as he is, so powerful that no delegation of his authority could now create a national force superior to the Crown.

But, for this reason alone, Dom Pedro II will be judged by history as the one man responsible for his long reign. Having been his own favorite for forty-three years, he has never tolerated prime ministers stronger than himself, has never in fact abandoned the Prime Minister's responsibilities.[12] Thus history will view the Emperor not as a constitutional sovereign but as a statesman, a Louis Philippe and not a Queen Victoria. And as

---

12. Concerning certain men who occupied that position, it was perhaps better for them and for the country that they were victims of this *liberum veto*.

a statesman he will be held strictly accountable for the existence of slavery, illegal and criminal, after a reign of almost half a century. Brazil squandered more than 600,000 *contos* [about $330 million] in a politically disastrous war but until today has spent only 9,000 *contos* [about $5 million] to liberate her slaves. She has a budget about one-sixth that of Britain, and of this budget less than 1 percent is used to advance emancipation.

Whatever may be the personal responsibility of the Emperor in regard to slavery, there is no doubt that his increasing powers and prerogatives are the result of that long-lasting institution. In the midst of the dispersion of individual energies and of the rivalries of those who might have served their country, there is raised up the statue of the Emperor, symbol of the only strong and independent national power, overshadowing the shops of the political stock jobbers and the dens of the electoral gladiators which surround our *Forum*.

But in all this social ruin in which the most avid materialism reigns and good and patriotic men are skeptical of everything and everyone, in this situation who does not see the colossal image of the accursed race rattling the chains on their wrists, scattering their blood upon the land? This is the revenge of the black race. It does not matter that so many of their bastard sons have imposed the same yoke upon their brothers, have linked themselves as accomplices to the fortunes of the murderous institution. Slavery in America has always been the crime of the white race, the predominant element of our civilization, and that miserable state to which Brazilian society has been reduced is nothing less than the retinue of the African nemesis which visits at last the graves of uncounted generations.

JOAQUIM NABUCO
Courtesy of Museu Imperial, Petrópolis, Rio de Janeiro

PREPARING MANIOC

Charles Ribeyrolles, *Brazil pittoreso. Album de vistas, panoramas, paisagens, monumentos, costumes, etc., com os retratos de Sua Magestade o Imperador Dom Pedro II e da Familia Imperial, photographiados por Victor Frond* (Paris, 1861). Courtesy of Biblioteca Nacional, Rio de Janeiro. All illustrations following are from the same source.

WEAVERS

GRINDING MANIOC

QUISSAMAN PLANTATION NEAR CAMPOS, PROVINCE OF RIO DE JANEIRO

Packing and Weighing of Sugar

BEFORE THE DEPARTURE FOR THE FIELDS

Sugar Mill at Ubá, Province of Minas Gerais

DEPARTURE FOR THE FIELD

WORKERS IN THE FIELD

PREPARING FOOD IN THE FIELD

LUNCHTIME IN THE FIELD

CHAPTER XVI

The Need for Abolition, The Danger of Delay

> Should (Brazil's) moral and intellectual endow-
> ments grow into harmony with her wonderful
> natural beauty and wealth, the world will not
> have seen a fairer land. At present there are sev-
> eral obstacles to this progress; obstacles which act
> like a moral disease upon the people. Slavery still
> exists among them.
> —PROFESSOR AND MRS. LOUIS AGASSIZ [1]

"BUT," some people will ask, "if slavery, as you say,
is a force which affects every class, the mold in which the entire
population has been formed for centuries, what power exists
outside of slavery which can end it as fast as you desire without
at the same time wrecking society, which, as you insist, is a
blend of several elements for which slavery is the chemical affinity? In the second place," the same persons will wonder, "since
we are dealing here with interests of such magnitude, upon which
so many people and the nation's whole economy depend, interests sustaining the fabric and foundation of the state, however
artificial you may have proved its present proportions to be; and
if you will not and cannot respond to the fact that slavery is
certain to disappear within a period which for our continuing
moral progress cannot exceed twenty years, why do you not hope
that the end of the institution, already existing in our country
for over three hundred years, will not be brought about naturally? Why do you not hope that it will be done without sacrificing public and private fortunes, without racial or class
antagonism, without any of the calamities which in other countries accompanied the forced emancipation of the slaves?"

I leave to the next chapter my response to the first question.
There I will show that, despite the retarding effects of slavery,
there exist in Brazil moral forces capable of eliminating the institution as a possessor of men, just as there are not now forces
capable of eliminating it as a major component of our national
character—though the country's first need is to create such
forces. In this chapter I will answer only the politically formi-

---

1. *Translator's note:* From Professor and Mrs. Louis Agassiz, *A Journey in
Brazil* (Boston, 1868).

dable charge of unreasonable impatience, of blindness to the interests of the slaveholding class, as Brazilian at least as the slaves, of blindness to the economic difficulties involved in an issue—whether slavery ought to continue indefinitely—which from the humanitarian or patriotic point of view has already been solemnly and convincingly resolved.

These accusations are so much more distressing to me because, as seen throughout this book, I do not believe that when the slaves are all freed slavery will cease to have its present effects. The emancipation funds, which accumulate enough money to free a slave, add yet another person to the list of Brazilian citizens. Yet much more than the contributions of the compassionate or the generosity of the master is needed to make this new citizen capable of contributing, even in the smallest degree, to the formation of an American nationality. What is true of the slave is true of the master. He can liberate his slaves (thus sacrificing his material interests while advancing his children's education) and so break the last obvious tie to slavery of which he is aware. But not by this act alone will the spirit of slavery cease to cripple his capacity for citizenship in a free country, his ability to exercise the ideals which turn the most vigorous nations toward individual freedom rather than despotism.

In both cases, more than an end to suffering, more than an end to the infliction of bondage upon others is required to convert the masters and the slaves into persons motivated by tolerance and respect for the principles of justice, even principles contrary to their own interests. Much more is needed to turn them into persons motivated by a desire for progress, willing to submit themselves to the higher interests of the nation, without which no national society can exist except in a spineless form.

Those who look back to the three and one-half centuries of slavery now behind us and who fear the long epoch essential for the elimination of its last traces evidently do not regard the twenty- or thirty-year period still left to them to enjoy the use of their slaves as unbearably long. Setting aside the individual fate of the slaves, they say, and keeping in mind only the general welfare of the community (indeed, we should not even be asked to consider the private interests of a comparatively few slaveholders more than the welfare of the slaves and of the whole nation), is not a period of twenty years, they ask, sufficiently brief to allow us to avoid shortening it even more, thereby endangering what might otherwise be saved?

"You claim that you are politicians," I will add, to sum up the serious and thoughtful arguments of men who oppose slavery as much as I do but balk at seeing it suddenly destroyed, believing that such destruction would be the work of an Erostratus [2] or a brutish Samson. "You say that you do not attack slavery from the point of view of the slaves, though you have made common cause with them to better waken the nation's generosity. Instead, you say, you confront slavery from the standpoint of the patriot, holding the view that the nation owes equal protection to all its sons and can neglect none of them. You are political men, you say, willing to be judged by history and ready to prove that you have no desire to stop the nation's progress or to disorganize labor even for reasons of justice and humanity. If all this is true, do you not think you would better satisfy your debt to the slaves and to the masters (who have a right at least to your indulgence because of the ties between abolitionism and slavery in the common national heritage), would you not in fact do your duty better to the whole country if, instead of proposing laws which annoy the masters and cannot be passed because of their opposition, and instead of seeking to protect the slaves through public justice or by stealing them from their owners, you were to try to find out what the discrete and, politically speaking, reasonable masters would be willing to do to contribute to the work of emancipation, which admittedly is today a national cause? Would you not be wiser, more practical and realistic, and so more useful to the slaves themselves if, instead of being propagandists and agitators running the risk of arousing (which naturally you do not want to do) between masters and slaves, between masters and abolitionists, feelings which undermine the harmony of the various classes—a harmony which even under slavery is one of the country's honorable achievements—if, instead of this, you were to associate yourselves as Brazilians with the peaceful work of liquidating that system?"

I discussed each one of these observations and many similar ones with myself before I burned my ships, and in good faith and against my own will I reached the conclusion that to grant slavery the span of life it theoretically possesses as a result of the law of September 28, 1871, would be to abandon all Brazil to the probability of the worst possible disasters. On the other hand, I

---

2. *Translator's note:* In 353 B.C. Erostratus set fire to the colossal Artemesion in Ephesus, thus destroying one of the seven wonders of the world.

was also convinced that nothing but abolitionist propaganda could significantly shorten that term of slavery, the effort, that is, to focus the country's attention upon all that is horrible, unjust, and economically debilitating about an institution to which the nation has entirely accustomed itself to the point that it is no longer able to look at the subject objectively.

For the last three years the country has been disturbed in the name of abolition as never before in its history, and the results of that active and patriotic propaganda have been such that to-day nobody expects slavery to last as long as it seemed capable of lasting when in 1878 Mr. Cansanção de Sinimbu convoked the Agricultural Congress, that Noah's Ark which was expected to rescue the "great property." [3]

By the law of September 28, 1871, slavery has been limited to the life of the slave born on the eve of the law. But even those waters are not yet stagnant, because the source of the children was not blocked, and each year slave women give thousands of *twenty-one-year slaves* to their masters. By a legal fiction, they are born *free,* but in fact at the age of eight, according to that same law, they are worth 600 *milréis* [about $330] each. The female slave born on September 27, 1871, could in 1911 be a mother of one of these *ingênuos,* who would thus be a provisional slave until 1932. That is the law, and this is the length of time it still grants to slavery.

If he were alive today, Viscount Rio Branco, the illustrious statesman who sponsored the law, would be the first to acknowledge that this prospect of another half century of slavery is an absurdity and was never the lawmaker's personal aim. Before he died he had already received as his reward the best kind of recognition from the slaves: the gratitude of the mothers. National posterity must listen to this hymn to his memory, detaching itself like some sweet and unspoiled note from the delirium of tears and sobs of that vast tragic choir. But merely because Rio Branco authored the law, he would be the first to recognize that, because of the dislocation of social forces brought about thirteen years ago and because of the momentum which the abolitionist idea has recently acquired after the torpor of a decade, the law

3. *Translator's note:* João Lins Vieira Cansanção de Sinimbu was a Liberal party politician who was president of the Council of Ministers (Prime Minister) from January, 1878 until March, 1880. He convoked the famous Agricultural Congress of 1878, intended to explore ways of solving the serious problems of agriculture.

must now be obsolete. What we did in 1871 is what Spain did
the year before. Our Rio Branco Law of that date is equivalent
to the Spanish Moret Law of July 4, 1870. But subsequently
Spain wrote another law, that of February 13, 1880, which nominally ended slavery at once but, since it converted the slaves into
patrocinados [wards], provided in fact for its elimination only
after eight more years.[4] We, on the other hand, have not pro-
gressed beyond that first law.

Through the action of our present legislation, what is lost to
the slave system on the one hand is gained by it on the other. No
one is insane enough to suppose that Brazil can maintain slavery
for another twenty years, whatever the law may say. And the
fact that the *ingênuos* will be slaves for twenty-one years and not
for life does not change the basic problem we face: the need to
rescue one and one-half million persons from bondage.

Commenting this year on the decline of the slave population
since 1873 through death and manumission, the *Jornal do Comércio* stated:

> Since on that date [1873] 1.5 million slaves were registered in the
> entire Empire, a rather questionable total, it can be reasonably
> estimated that the slave population of the Empire, having dimin-
> ished by one-sixth in Rio de Janeiro province, has declined in the
> rest of the Empire by the same rate at least, thus presumably leav-
> ing 1.25 million slaves still in existence. This figure may be sup-
> posed to have declined to as little as 1.2 million slaves, however,
> if we remember that in various parts of the Empire certain factors
> have resulted in a larger number of manumissions.

To these 1.25 million slaves must be added the *ingênuos,*
whose number exceeds 250,000. If 60,000 of the 1.5 million persons who are today subjected to bondage can escape that condition each year—twice the average, that is, of the past ten years
—slavery will have disappeared, admittedly with a large surplus
of *ingênuos* to be freed, within twenty-five years, that is by 1908.
And if the slave population should decline by 75,000 persons per
year—at a rate, that is, of 5 percent, or two and one-half times
as fast as at present—the institution will have been liquidated in
1903, or within twenty years. This calculation is optimistic and
is made without reckoning with the effects of the Rio Branco

4. *Translator's note:* For the terms of these Spanish laws, see Arthur F. Corwin,
Spain and the Abolition of Slavery in Cuba, 1817-1886 (Austin, 1967) , pp. 245-57,
301-2.

Law, but, to the honor of our higher national inclinations, I
accept it as accurate.

"Why then are you not willing to wait for those twenty years?"
is the question which is always put to us.[5]

This entire book is a response to that question. Twenty more
years of slavery will bring the collapse of the nation. Indeed,
this period is a brief one in our national history, just as our
national history is only a brief moment in the life of humanity,
and the life of humanity merely an instant in the life of the
earth, and so on indefinitely. But twenty years of slavery will
mean the ruin of two more generations: that generation which
has just recently reached maturity, and that which will be educated by it. This will mean a delay of half a century in the development of a liberated national conscience.[6]

Twenty more years of slavery will find Brazil celebrating the
fourth centenary of the discovery of America in 1892 with her
flag draped in black crepe! If slavery lasts so long, the whole
younger generation will be condemned to live with slavery, to
serve it during the greater part of their lives. They will be forced
to maintain an army and a body of magistrates responsible for
its enforcement and, perhaps even worse, to see their own children, destined to take their places in twenty years, brought up in
the same school of servility. *Maxima debetur puero reverentia*
is a principle which under slavery would evoke ridicule if it were
applied to the *crias*. But it ought to have some meaning when
applied to the masters' children.

Moreover, twenty more years of slavery would mean a stain
upon Brazil's name during that entire time, its identification

5. Some persons who act in bad faith argue that without any propaganda
whatsoever, by natural processes alone, through death and private generosity,
property which now exceeds 500,000 *contos* [about $275 million] in value will be
removed spontaneously from the national economy without state intervention.
There are also people who possess the ability to re-enact the miracle of the loaves
who hope the slaves will be redeemed in twenty years by the Emancipation Fund,
which in the entire country does not accumulate as much as 2,000 *contos* [about
$1.1 million] annually.

6. An editorial of September 28, 1882, in the *Jornal do Comércio* stated in
regard to the effects of the Rio Branco Law: "The state has been able to emancipate only 11,000 slaves, an annual average about equivalent to 0.7 percent of the
average total slave population existing in the country during the period from
1871 to 1882. Obviously this is a shabby record which does not measure up to
the original goals. Certainly no one thought in 1871 that after such a long time
the state's humanitarian enterprise would have made such a poor showing."

with the name of Turkey.[7] It would mean dragging Brazil's reputation through the mire in Europe and America. It would make our nation the object of derision in ancient and traditional Asia and modern Australia, three centuries younger than Brazil. How can a nation thus lashed to the world's whipping post lend manly military virtues to its army and navy, perhaps to be called upon tomorrow to suppress some slave revolt? How can it inspire them with respect for the nation they serve? How will it be able to compete in equality, at the end of that era of enfeeblement, with the smaller nations developing at its side: the Argentine republic spontaneously attracting immigrants and workers at the rate of 40,000 per year, and Chile with its homogeneous free labor force, with its entire organism healthy and strong? To maintain slavery as a national institution for that entire period would be equivalent to giving it twenty more years to use its influence to reinforce the belief that Brazil needs slavery in order to exist—this when the North, thought of once as the section of the national territory which could not dispense with the slave, is living without him, when slavery flourishes only in São Paulo, which with its climate and prosperity is able to attract the European immigrant and to pay the wages of the workers, national or foreign, whom it employs.

Consider the effects of a power of slavery's extent and universality upon the character and disposition of the people. Observe what government is among us: the collective instrument which represents the interests of only a small minority and so involves itself in everything pertaining to its employment of the private reserve; whereas, on the other hand, it desists from its real responsibilities, such as protecting life and personal security or guaranteeing the freedom of contracts. Finally, by use of the imagination, project over another twenty years the present state of our institutions, undermined by anarchy and sustained by servile habits which slavery implanted, rather than by a spirit of liberty and order. Then tell the Brazilian who loves his country whether we can continue that degrading and destructive system for twenty more years.

If the delay of another twenty years is meant to prepare the way for change through education of the slaves, through develop-

---

7. *Translator's note:* This is probably a reference to the continuing existence of slavery in the Ottoman Empire.

ment of an environment of cooperation, through promotion of industries and improvements in the status of our serflike rural inhabitants; if it is meant to divide among rural inhabitants the land which they cultivate, as the Countess of Rio Novo did in her generous testament; if it is meant to suspend the purchase and sale of human beings, to abolish corporal punishment and private oppression, to encourage development of families, respected despite their condition, honored in their poverty, to import European settlers; if all this were to be done, the interim would certainly be a time of progress. All this, however, is incompatible with slavery in its age of decline, in its bankruptcy, since all these reforms would mean increased expenses, and slavery only seeks to reduce the cost of the human machines which serve it, and to increase their toil.

To give ten, fifteen, or twenty years to the planter to prepare himself for free labor, to burden him, that is, with so much foresight so far in advance, to charge him with accomplishing such a complex change, is to fail to acknowledge the national tendency to do everything tomorrow which should be done today. This scorn for the future will be overcome, not by prolonging the days of slavery, but by destroying it, thereby creating new needs, the real molder of character.

Any other action will have to be seen for what it is: the sacrifice of 1.5 million people to the private interests of their owners, interests we have recognized as murderous, morally and physically, however unconscious of this fact the exploiters of slavery may be. In other words, so that a few thousand individuals will not be ruined, they demand not only a reliable and stable labor force—which they could have by simply paying wages—but also that their human property remain negotiable, that it possess value, that is, in the bank director's office and in the market place. For these reasons, 1.5 million persons must be sacrificed to the Minotaur of slavery, and we must feed it for twenty years longer with the blood of new generations. Even worse, 10 million Brazilians—who perhaps during that time will become 14 million—will continue to endure the real losses and declining profits which slavery causes, will be victims of the same corrosive spirit which impedes the country's development and the uplifting of the various classes and which keeps the free backland population in rags and, sadder still, indifferent to their own social and moral wretchedness. What concern or compassion can the world have for ten million people who confess that they will be left to starve without the forced and unpaid labor of a few hundred thousand field slaves—old men, women, and children among them—despite living in the wealthiest, most fertile, and most beautiful territory ever possessed by any nation? Does not this same underdevelopment of the instinct of self-preservation and this absence of the energy which survival demands demonstrate the compelling need to abolish slavery without the loss of another second?

CHAPTER XVII

Fears and Consequences: Conclusion

> The history of the world, and especially of the States of this Union, shows most conclusively that public prosperity bears an almost mathematical proportion to the degree of freedom enjoyed by all the inhabitants of the State.
> —FREDERICK LAW OLMSTED [1]

THE NEED for rapid abolition is recognized by all who are dissatisfied with the concept of Brazil as a new Java in America. The necessity of this operation has been demonstrated, just as surgical science can prove the need to amputate a gangrenous arm or leg in order to save a human life. With these facts in mind, we must analyze the fears and predictions originating with the opponents of the reform.

First, however, we should try to determine whether forces exist in Brazil which can challenge slavery and overwhelm it. We have seen how slavery controls the land and, as a result, has the interior population at its command, a population made up of impoverished and tolerated squatters. We know that it is master over all available capital, that it has the commerce of the cities at its mercy, all the property of the country behind it, and, finally, a formidable clientele in every profession: lawyers, doctors, engineers, priests, teachers, and public employees. Beyond all this, most of the established social forces, certainly all those that are free and able to resist, support it as much as they can.

Furthermore, it is known that slavery, so well defended with this huge army of followers enlisted under its banner, is not disposed to surrender, is not even besieged except by moral forces which, to be effective, need to find a rallying point within the conscience of slavery itself. On the other hand, it is certain that slavery, determined not to lose an inch of legal ground, will tenaciously resist any attempt on the part of the government to go to the aid of the slaves.

Vague words, deceitful promises, harmless pronouncements—all these are tolerated. However, the moment there is an attempt to pass a law aimed directly at slavery, whether a major or minor

---

1. *Translator's note:* From Frederick Law Olmsted, *A Journey in the Back Country in the Winter of 1853-54* (London, 1860).

assault upon the institution, the jackal bares its fangs at anyone who dares to enter its bone-filled lair.

Unfortunately for slavery, however, as it undermined the entire nation, it weakened itself as well; while corrupting every-thing else, it was also self-corrupting. As a result, this proslavery army is a mixed and undisciplined mob eager to flee the field of combat. The clientele of slavery are ashamed of living upon the scraps they are tossed, of depending upon slavery's indul-gence. The people who survive like vagrants on lands not their own, when given the hope of legitimately possessing those lands where they are now suffered to squat as pariahs, will reject their present serflike status. In regard to the several social forces, slavery has made them so weak, timid, and unreliable that they will be the first to welcome any change which brings their own downfall and reconstructs them with new elements.

Mistress of everyone and everything, slavery could not assemble a band of guerrillas anywhere in the country which a line battal-ion could not disperse with ease. Accustomed to the whip, slavery does not conceive of taking up arms, and so, just as it is determined to use all of the tactics it used in 1871—the agricultural clubs, anonymous letters, defamation through the press, insults in Parliament, personal harassment—which provide a measure of its potential energy, it has also decided beforehand to resign itself to defeat. What is most certain in such a struggle is that, as happened with the campaign of 1871, ten years after it has ended, those who were involved in it as opponents of free-dom will blush at the reputation they acquired, and will be forced to implore the support of those upon whom they wished to inflict the greatest harm which one man can inflict upon another: that of casting him into slavery, him and his children, at a time when a generous hand was fighting to save them.

For all these reasons, the power of slavery, like slavery itself, is a mere shadow. Yet slavery has succeeded in producing an even more powerful shadow in the form of the Imperial Government, the result, as we have seen, of the wholesale abdication of the civic function of defending our people. There is no better and more precise way to characterize this force than with the previ-ously cited phrase, "Power is Power," words fashioned by an eloquent statesman who with his eagle-eye personally surveyed this vast horizon from that same peak of power. From the height of that gigantic phantasmagoria, from that emanation of the weakness and torpor of the nation, from that mirage of slavery itself in the desert it created, the plantation big house is worth as much as the hut of the slave. Unquestionably, with the new electoral processes, the small parliamentary cliques, which are so powerfully influenced by agriculture, are imposing their point of view. Nevertheless, the government still stands above the Chambers, and when it becomes necessary to repeat the phenomenon of 1871, the Chambers will once again bow as they did then.

This is the force emanating from slavery itself which can destroy that system, even if in the end, perhaps, the government and slavery will go down to defeat together. At the moment this force remains the servant of the landlord's power, but it is obvious to everyone that someday it will have to clash with him and that that clash will be a desperate one, whether what is being demanded is immediate abolition or only indirect measures, whether the aim is to end slavery with one blow or to take only a small step such as shutting down the markets where men and women are bought and sold.

Public opinion, as it is now developing, possesses strength and has its effects upon the government. It represents the nation before the world, holds within its grasp the leadership of a huge political complex which would be amenable to emancipation if it were not for the coffee districts in the provinces of São Paulo, Minas Gerais, and Rio de Janeiro, a political mass which is each day more and more impelled by the national conscience to abandon the orbit which slavery marked out for it.

However vast the power of slavery, however impressive the credit it can command in the banks, however huge the value of its mortgaged estates, it stands like a dogmatic aberration in the face of established truth. An ounce of science is worth more, in the final analysis than a ton of faith. Similarly, the smallest particle of high-minded sentiment on behalf of humanity will eventually destroy the largest monopoly erected against humanity's interests. I do not attribute any metaphysical power to principles when there is nobody to impose them, when the human mass to which such principles might be applied is unreceptive to them. Yet, setting private interests aside, I do not elevate too highly the character, tendencies, and aspirations of the Brazilian people when I say that all their sympathies are on the side of freedom and against slavery.

Yet the following truth must also be recognized: the reluctant attitude of the government—the one force capable of destroying slavery—the still inconsequential extent of its response to public opinion, and the slowness of the latter's development do not allow us to hope that the break between the government and slavery will occur soon. If the abolitionist pressure did not exist, the government would delay even more than it does. Consequently, our strength will grow as we are able to arouse such opinion, as we call each class to action based upon its understanding that slavery not only degrades our country but undermines it physically. The instrument of success exists and is known to us; this instrument is power. The way to produce power, which is also known to us, is through public concern. What remains to be done is to endow that public opinion with the needed energy, to draw it out of the lassitude which renders it useless, to prove to it that prolonged inactivity is suicidal.

Let us look now at the fears which the reform inspires. It is claimed that abolition will destroy agriculture. Yet the truth is that there is no other way to revitalize agriculture. Ninety years ago, in a pamphlet about the effects of slavery on morals and industry, Noah Webster wrote the following:

> To a citizen of America it seems strange and even astonishing in the 18th century (and to us Brazilians a hundred years later) that such a question could admit of a doubt in any part of Europe; much more that it should become the subject of grave discussion (The question: "Whether it is most advantageous to the State that the peasant should possess land or only personal effects, and to what point should that property be extended for the good of the public?" placed under discussion by the Economic Society of St. Petersburg). Yet not only in Russia and in great part of Poland, but in Germany and Italy, where the light of science has long since dispelled the night of Gothic ignorance, the barons would be shocked at the idea of giving freedom to their peasants. This repugnance must arise from the supposition that by giving liberty to their peasants, their estates would be materially injured; for their *pride* alone would not withstand a regard to their *interest*. Yet this is a most fatal error, and Americans ought not to be the last to be convinced of it; free men not only produce more, but they squander less than slaves; they are not only more industrious, but more provident; *and there is not an owner of slaves in Europe or America, the value of whose estate might not be doubled in a*

few years, by giving liberty to his slaves and assisting them in the management of their farms." [2]

The final words, which I have emphasized, are as true today as they were when written; as true then as they were essentially when Roman Sicily was covered with *prisons* and the slaves there survived only by stealing and begging.

In this respect, the greatest possible proof is the physical and economic transformation in the southern states of North America after the war. Agriculture there is today many times richer than at the time when the cotton crop signified tears, deprivation, and wages stolen from the black race, more prosperous and flourishing than when that barbarous system was thought to be essential to the cultivation of that product. The states of the South are not only richer because they produce a larger crop and yield a greater income; they are also richer because they enjoy a new stability, because industries are multiplying abundantly, machines are accumulating, and the population is growing in a state of unhampered moral, intellectual, and social development.

On September 1, 1882, the correspondent of the *London Times* in Philadelphia wrote:

A Southern delegate stated impressively at the recent Bankers' Convention at Saratoga: "At the close of the war only lands and debts were left to the South." Yet her people ultimately went to work to develop the one and get rid of the other, and after several years of intelligent devotion to these great duties they have achieved results which are as surprising to themselves as to the rest of the world. Thus has the abolition of slavery, with the downfall of the systems of agriculture which it nurtured, been of the greatest advantage to the South. No country on the globe has undergone a more complete yet comparatively peaceful and almost unnoticed revolution in social affairs than the Southern states since 1865. The close of the Rebellion found the South stripped of everything but its land, and owing a vast individual indebtedness—besides that of the States—which private debts had mainly been incurred upon the credit based upon the property value of the slaves. In the largest Southern state—Georgia—this value reached $30,000,000. The abolition of slavery wiped out the security, but left the debts, and the cessation of hostilities found the

---

2. Noah Webster, *Effects of Slavery on Morals and Industry* (Hartford, 1793), pp. 40-41.

South exhausted, half starved, and bankrupt, nationally and individually, with the freedmen practically the masters and led into all sorts of political excesses by the unscrupulous whites who assumed their leadership. . . .

After the restoration of peace, the high price of cotton induced the planters to cultivate as much of it as they could, and as the negro's new condition put the control of his labour out of the power of his former master, it became the almost invariable custom at first to rent the plantations to the freedmen and try to get, if possible, as large a revenue as anterior to the Rebellion, and without personal labour. Many of the planters removed to the cities, leaving the entire management of their lands to the freedmen, and so long as the cotton rent was paid, they cared little for the methods pursued in farming. The negroes, free of all control, worked immense tracts of land, scratching it over with the smallest ploughs, using little or no fertilizers, never resting the soil, and following in the easiest ways such methods of farming as they had learnt while slaves. In this way the plantation soon became exhausted on the surface of the soil, and they were unable to raise enough crops either to pay rent or provide their own living. The owners, living in idleness, soon found their revenues cut off and their lands worn out, while the country being full of plantations in similarly reduced conditions, their sale was almost impossible at any price. Necessity then forced them to return to their plantations, so that by personal supervision they could be brought back to their former productive power; but these evil and improvident processes had in the meantime kept the South for several years in an extremely depressed condition. . . .

During the last decade the planters became gradually convinced that this sort of process would not do to go on indefinitely; that the style of farming was impairing their lands; that the factors and bankers with their high interest, enormous profits and undisputed control of the crops were reaping all the benefits; and that for want of enough capital to conduct business on a cash basis, they were kept poor and were working their farms at great and increasing disadvantage. This led to changes that have been for the lasting welfare of the South. Plantations are being cut up into smaller farms, and the more intelligent class are now working fewer acres, rotating crops, resting the land, adopting a better and deeper system of ploughing, and more extensively using fertilizers. They now get, in many instances, where this better policy has been followed for several years, a bale of cotton to the acre where it used to require five or six acres to produce a bale of poorer quality. They are also planting more corn and oats, raising more meat for the labourers and more grain and forage of different kinds for the animals. Cotton is still raised as the great crop—a much better yield generally for the surface planted than in years gone by—but cotton is not such an absolute king as heretofore. The South has become self-supporting in almost every part, as to food supplies. The North and West now find that section a rather poor provision and breadstuffs market. By going to work upon sensible systems, the planters are achieving far better results, have generally cleared off their debts, and are feeling in more improved condition, while the Southern labour is so contented that nothing has been heard from it this summer. This is the great peaceful, social, and industrial revolution that has been going on during the decade, yet so quietly as to cause surprise where the census publications disclosed it.

On April 1, 1880, the same correspondent had transmitted some observations of Jefferson Davis, ex-president of the Confederacy, about the results of the emancipation measure:

In regard to the growing of cotton and sugar, he confessed, his opinions had changed completely. These principal commodities of the South can be produced more cheaply and in the greatest abundance by paying the wages of workers rather than the price of slaves. This, he said, has been proved, and serves to demonstrate how advantageous the abolition of slavery was for the whites. The South is less dependent upon the North than before the war. While it continues to export its major products (cotton and sugar) the people are producing a greater variety of crops for their own use, and will eventually compete with the North in manufacturing and in the mechanical arts.[3]

---

3. In 1861 (before the war) the cotton crop was 3,650,000 bales; in 1871 it was 4,340,000 bales and in 1881 6,589,000. In two years the South produced 12,000,000 bales. "The South is also making progress in the production of agricultural instruments, hides, wagons, furniture, soap, starch, etc.," says the *Times*, "and these products, with the growth of the production of cotton, sugar, tobacco, rice, wheat, and naval supplies, will materially increase the wealth of the several states. As a natural corollary of this surprising progress, the farmers are growing richer and more independent, and in some of the southern states a great effort is being made to prevent the absorption of the small farms by the large." Furthermore, Professor E. W. Gilliam believes that the black race has increased in the last ten years at the rate of 34 percent, whereas the white increased by about 29 percent. He estimates that within a century there will be 192 million persons of color in the southern states.

Possessing the authority of experience and elaborated under our very noses, both of these quotations contain important suggestions for our planters and also provide great encouragement for our country. There is no doubt that free labor is more economical, more reasonable, more beneficial to the soil, more profitable to the district where it is located, more suitable to the development of industries, to the civilization of the country, and to the development of the population. For agriculture, free labor means a new existence, fruitful, stable, and lasting. Buarque de Macedo envisioned the present slaves as owners of small farms surrounding central sugar mills, and called this concept to our attention in order to awaken private initiative. In every respect, free labor is more advantageous than slave labor. There is no agriculture in existence which would suffer as a result of this reform.

Would the present owners suffer, however; and if they did, would they have the right to turn to the government for redress? We have just read that the American Civil War left only land and debts in the hands of the former masters. But what transpired in the United States will not happen in Brazil. There emancipation came after an incomparable rebellion, after a ruinous blockade, and far sooner than the most optimistic abolitionists of Boston and New York could have dreamed. In Brazil a law was passed twelve years ago which for the present slaveholders could only be seen as a signal that the nation was eager to put an end to slavery, was ashamed of remaining a nation of bondsmen, and had only refused to free the slaves themselves, instead of their newborn babies, because they desired to avoid damaging the interests of the masters. In other words, so as not to strike a careless blow at the property rights of a class, many of whom are citizens of countries where slavery is nonexistent and where prohibitions against slavery must by now constitute a personal code of nationality, Brazil agreed to remain accountable for the crime.

The slaveholders' argument, in effect, is this: "My slave is worth a *conto,* invested in him in good faith, or is legally possessed in accordance with the principle that the offspring belongs to the owner. If you have a *conto* to give me in exchange for him, you have the right to free him. However, if you do not have that amount, he will remain my slave." For the moment I will yield to this argument, which means that once a generation has decided to tolerate any crime whatever, whether it be piracy

or slavery, no other generation will have the right to suppress
that crime without first indemnifying those who would cease
to profit by it. As long as the capital which that crime represents
is not available, no matter how much the conscience may rebel
or strive toward decent behavior, the existing generation will
lack the power to free itself from its commitment to back that
crime with its sovereign power or to defend it with its armed
forces if that need should arise. In the light of this theory, no
country can rise in the scale of civilization and moral rectitude
if it does not have the means to pay the price of its backwardness
and misdeeds. For the moment I will accept this point of view
in order to simplify the question. I will concede for a moment
the principle that the state should agree to indemnify slave
property legally possessed.

In 1871, however, the Brazilian nation first informed slaveholders that its conscience was troubled and that it was eager
to eliminate its unfortunate past and start a new life. Can anyone
who has acquired slaves since that date complain that he was
not informed that pride and shame had begun to make the
nation blush? Since the result of each humanitarian law restrict-
ing human property is to increase that property's value like that
of any other merchandise whose production declines while
demand continues strong, the price of slaves rose after passage
of the law, as it did after suppression of the traffic; and in São
Paulo the price of a slave reached three *contos de réis* [about
$1,650]. But must the state respond to these increased slave
values, this bitter parody of every step toward social improvement which shows how the business in human beings hurls
everything beyond the reach of patriotic feelings? The citizen
concerned for his country's good name should not only con-
sciously avoid doing what the law prohibits, he should also
abstain from acts which he knows the law fails to prohibit only
because it lacks the power to do so. He should avoid doing everything which puts the law to shame, especially after the nation
has made it known to him that the abuse of slavery must be
ended as soon as possible with the help of every Brazilian. Is
there anyone among us who does not know that those who wrote
the Constitution were ashamed to mention slavery or that the
law of September 28 was a solemn national declaration, a plea
to the nation's patriotism?

For fifty years the greater part of slave property has been
illegally possessed. Nothing would be more difficult for the

masters, taken collectively, than to justify before an honest court the legality of that property, also taken as a whole. On the other hand, twelve years after passage of the law of September 28, upon what grounds could those same masters accuse the government of bad faith, of spoliation of property, or of any other unfair dealings in regard to their slaves?

Unfortunately, nobody believes that slavery will end completely before 1890. There is no power now known which allows us to anticipate a shorter duration, and a law which would today impose that deadline would calm at once the agitated waters. And yet there is not one slave who could not indemnify his value within five years if his services were intelligently employed. Let our agriculture reflect on this. Let each planter make an accounting of his slaves, of what they really cost him and the profits he earned from them, of the *crias* they have produced for him—discounting Africans imported after 1831 and their known offspring, for whom it would be an outrage to demand public indemnification—and let him then decide whether, after great and solemn warnings to stop this cruel business, the nation does not have the right to abolish it with one blow, without being accused of sacrificing the interests of the planter class.

If they cannot now redeem their mortgages or pay their debts, they should not blame the poor slaves, who help as much as they can. They cannot make the slaves answerable for those features of slavery which are harmful and against the planters' own interests. Let each master issue a certificate to each of his slaves, inscribing on the first page not his original cost, which alone would eliminate half of the *legal* slavery, but his present market value, and then let him credit the slave with all the services he performs. In a short time the debt would be redeemed. And if something still remained for the slave to pay, he would do honor to his master's signature, serving him after his liberation. Anything else is the worst kind of usury, that of a Shylock, inflicted on human flesh; or, worse yet than that of a Shylock, initiated and enforced by the moneylender himself.

If agriculture today does not yield enough income for the reduction of mortgage debts, and if there is no likelihood that under the present system agriculture will ever free its slaves without harm to itself, there is no advantage to the state for landed property to remain in the hands of those who cannot make it profitable—and this aided by the retention under law of a discredited system of personal sequestration. In this regard, emancipation would have the advantage of introducing new blood into agriculture, of promoting the liquidation of the present system. Agriculture, whether producing sugar or coffee, has nothing to fear from free labor. If today labor is scarce, if a proficient but unemployed free population now estimated to number some three million workers in six provinces alone remains inactive,[4] if the freedman himself refuses employment on the plantation where he grew up, all this is the result of slavery, which made working alongside slaves seem a disgrace to the free Brazilian. And though the freedman recognizes that the European worker feels no such dishonor, he lacks the ability to overcome deeply ingrained attitudes.

The outcome of the entire abolitionist process, so easy if there is understanding between agriculture and the nation, so difficult if the former rejects the inevitable, will depend upon our planters. If slavery had not, so to speak, exhausted our credit; if the Paraguayan War, whose distant origins are still so well known to us, had not blocked the door to the future for an entire generation, nothing would be more profitable to the government than to lend its capital to the rapid rebuilding of our agricultural system. But to help the planters for a purpose other than emancipation—to cause slave property, for example, to circulate in Europe in the form of mortgage bonds, as the law of November 6, 1875, was intended to do—would be more than an unjust scheme for aiding the most favored class at the cost of all the others. It would also involve the government in agriculture's mistake and would drag them down together to the same ruin. In a democratized country like ours, moreover, which needs a land tax to open up territory to our rural population, "aid to agriculture" cannot be taken to mean a subsidy to the large estates without regard for the small farmers who aspire to ownership of the land they cultivate as tenants. But, on the other hand, in no way could the state make better use of its credit in an emergency than by helping agriculture to achieve the transition from the Roman regime of captive workers to the modern system of the salary and the free contract.

There is nothing in the entire abolitionist movement or in

---

4. *Tentativas centralizadoras do governo liberal* by Senator Joaquim Floriano de Godoy. In this pamphlet there is the following estimate of workers employed in the agriculture of the provinces of Minas Gerais, Ceará, São Paulo, Bahia, Pernambuco and Rio de Janeiro: free, 1,434,170; slaves, 650,540; able-bodied but unemployed free workers between thirteen and forty-five years of age, 2,822,583.

the future which it is preparing except benefits for agriculture as a national industry, for the solvent farmers as a class, or for those who will know how to take advantage of the country's transformed conditions. The example of the United States ought to serve them as a beacon; each of the reefs on which the ship might wreck itself has been carefully lit up. What must be avoided in light of the North American experience is rebellion against a higher national conscience, distrust of the former slaves, complete abandonment of estates to the freedman, *absenteeism,* the routine of the old agriculture, discouragement. What farmers should do in light of that experience is to recognize the consummated fact as progress for the entire country and even for themselves, who are and will remain the most powerful national class, to create new ties of gratitude and friendship between themselves and those who served them as slaves and are prisoners on their lands, to lift this class to freedom, to improve the education of their children, to foment industry and scientific agriculture, to persevere.

We are not struggling with agriculture against its own interests. Not only will the political influence of our farmers increase when those walls of prejudice and suspicion which surround the coffee and sugar estates come tumbling down, but their personal security will have increased as well, and their resources will expand along with the prosperity, dignity, and individual worth of the neighboring population. Free labor, by dispersing the last vestiges of slavery, will open our country to European immigration. It will signify the onset of a manly transformation and will allow us to take the road toward organic and therefore harmonious development. The latent antagonism between the races—for which slavery is a constant provocation and which it does not let die whatever advantages might ensue—would entirely disappear. All this will serve to reconstruct upon solid foundations the social power of the large estates, to open up high and patriotic ambitions to that power, to infuse it with a spirit of freedom which never disgraced a people or a class. Let our agriculture resolutely turn its back on slavery as it did upon the traffic, and after twenty years of free labor the Brazilian landed proprietors will form a class in every way richer, more useful, more powerful, and more respected in their communities than they are today.

If agriculture and slavery are synonymous, whoever speaks such language with sincerity must be regarded as an enemy of agriculture. If, however, agriculture is slavery's victim, if while humiliating the bondsman slavery accomplishes nothing but the ruin of the master, nothing except to deliver his lands to the moneylender after two generations and to throw his descendants upon the welfare of the state, whoever sincerely condemns slavery does not denounce agriculture but tries to divorce it from the influence which cripples it; even if in order to rescue agriculture it becomes necessary to demonstrate candidly what slavery has done to it.

It was always the fate of those who opposed the madness of a class or of a nation, who tried to convince them that they were sacrificing themselves by persevering in an error or a crime, to be taken as enemies of one or the other. Cobden was considered an enemy of English agriculture because he asked that the poor be given the right to buy cheap bread; and Thiers was accused of being a traitor to France because he hoped to deter her on the road to Sedan.[5] Let our own farmers, however, look to the future.

Two babies were born on the same night, the 27th of September, 1871, on that plantation whose present labor system some people would like to save. One is the owner of the other. Today each is about twelve years old. The master is now receiving a distinguished education; the slave is being brought up in his mother's hut. Who can have so little faith in Brazil as to suppose that in 1903, when they have both reached thirty-two years of age, the relationship between these two men will be that of master and slave? Who will deny that these two children, one educated for great things, the other brutalized by slavery, represent two social currents which follow different courses— and that there is a third, that of the *ingênuos,* born after that night—and that these currents are nevertheless moving toward a fixed point in our history where they must certainly meet and blend?

What abolitionism desires is that these two currents should not converge mechanically because the slope of the land happens to bring them together, but that they should meet spontaneously, the result of a conscious national affinity. We want to see the illumination of that part of the master's person which lies in

---

5. *Translator's note:* Richard Cobden, a radical member of the British Parliament, in the 1830s and 1840s championed repeal of the Corn Laws. Louis Adolphe Thiers was a French statesman and historian who opposed French imperialism in the Chamber of Deputies in the years before the Franco-Prussian War.

shadow, to see him recognize that the man he knows as a *slave* is a person as free as he is in accordance with the law of our century; that he who calls the other *master,* brought up below the level of human dignity, will be lifted up and instilled with the thoughtful outlook of the citizen he will become; and that both should be wrested from the grip of that Brazilian tragedy of slavery which morally destroys them.

. . .

I can now regard the task that I undertook at the beginning of this volume of propaganda as completed, since I do not intend to discuss the various measures which have been proposed to improve the law of September 28, 1871, such as the plans to localize slavery or to convert the slaves and the *ingênuos* into serfs or to expand the Emancipation Fund. All these suggestions are the work of individuals who do not recognize slavery as a social factor, as a barrier placed in the path of the entire nation, an impediment to the development and well-being of every class, to the education of the new generations. None of their authors would understand the political, moral, and economic meaning a testament like that delivered by President James Garfield in his 1881 State of the Union Message, about the effects of emancipation in the United States, would have for any nation immersed in slavery:

> The will of the nation, speaking with the voice of battle and through the amended Constitution, has fulfilled the great promise of 1776 by proclaiming "liberty throughout the land to all the inhabitants thereof."
> The elevation of the negro race from slavery to the full rights of citizenship is the most important political change we have known since the adoption of the Constitution of 1787. No thoughtful man can fail to appreciate its beneficent effect upon our institutions and people. It has freed us from the perpetual danger of war and dissolution. It has added immensely to the moral and industrial forces of our people. It has liberated the master as well as the slave from a relation which wronged and enfeebled both. It has surrendered to their own guardianship the manhood of more than 5,000,000 people, and has opened to each one of them a career of freedom and usefulness. It has given new inspiration to the power of self-help in both races by making labor more honorable to the one and more necessary to the other. The influence of

this force will grow greater and bear richer fruit with the coming years.

Convinced that this same language, creditable to ex-slaves and ex-masters alike, could well be employed a few years after the abolition of Brazilian slavery, we cannot resign ourselves to the sacrifice of great national interests to those of a backward class, a class which has never been inclined to join the march of the century and of the nation, despite legal promptings and pleas from Brazilian patriots—so much less so since such a sacrifice would mean an extraordinary loss.

> Our policy is to look to Brazil as the next great slave power . . . (a newspaper of the American South declared in 1854). A treaty of commerce and alliance with Brazil will give us the control over the Gulf of Mexico and its border countries, together with the islands; and the consequence of this will place African slavery beyond the reach of fanaticism at home or abroad. These two great slave powers . . . ought to guard and strengthen their mutual interests. . . . We can not only preserve domestic servitude, but we can defy the power of the world.[6]

That dream of a slaveholding union and alliance was thwarted by successive struggles which forestalled formation of a vast and powerful American state intended to perpetuate throughout all America the bondage of the African race. Brazil, however, remains in the eyes of the hemisphere the symbol of a slave nation, the representative of a primitive, oppressive, and outdated social form. How much longer must we keep this reputation? How much longer will there exist in our maritime cities that mark of pestilence which drives immigrants to countries competing with us for their presence?

Our land has been visited and studied by men of science. The greatest of them all, Charles Darwin (I have used this example more than once), could find no other words than these with which to take leave of a country whose admirable nature ought to have had the greatest possible effect upon his creative mentality: "On the 19th of August we finally left the shores of Brazil. I thank God, I shall never again visit a slave-country." The spectacle of slavery in America—in the kingdom of Nature itself, in the midst of the most beautiful, most varied, and mightiest forms

---

6. The *Southern Standard,* cited by Theodore Parker in "An Anti-Slavery Address Delivered before the New York Anti-Slavery Society, 1854."

which life assumes on our planet—could not, in fact, arouse other sentiments among men of science than those expressed by Darwin, Agassiz, and before them by Humboldt and José Bonifacio.

It is not, however, the disinterested and unquestioned disgust of those who love and admire our nature which cause us the greatest harm. It is the reputation we have throughout South America as a *country of slaves,* of being a hardened, disreputable nation insensitive to the human side of things. Even more, it is that reputation—unjust because the Brazilian *people* do not practice slavery but are victims of it—broadcast to the whole world and drilled into the consciousness of civilized humanity. Brazil and slavery have thus become synonymous. From this fact arose the cynicism with which the myth was generally received that we had gone to Paraguay to establish freedom; from this results the channeling of immigration toward the Rio de la Plata, which, if it followed a Machiavellian and selfish policy inspired by envy, would wish Brazil the thirty additional years of slavery which the advocates of that system demand.[7]

If Brazil could not survive except with slavery, it would be better that she not survive. Yet this view of the matter is no longer reasonable. Alongside a population which, including

7. The following is an excerpt from a news item in the *Jornal do Comércio* in which an informant describes a reception given to Dr. Avellaneda, former president of the Argentine Republic, by one of our principal planters, a leader of his class and one of its most enlightened men, the Baron Rio Bonito: "Upon entering, he encountered a veritable forest of Venetian lanterns and allegorical coats of arms upon which one could read, for example, *Greetings to the promoters of industry!* or *The brotherhood of nations is a smile from God*, etc. A quadrille was then formed inside a gigantic circle formed by the 400 slaves of the plantation, who cried out enthusiastic salutes to their affectionate owners."

With this recent Brazilian celebration and the contrast of human *brotherhood* with slavery in mind, Dr. Avellaneda will have read with the immense pride of an Argentine citizen the following excerpts from the last message of his successor: "In 1881 32,817 immigrants arrived, and in 1882 51,503 entered our ports. . . . This progressive growth of immigration is entirely spontaneous. Once funds have been voted for this purpose, once the propaganda campaigns which you sanctioned last year are accomplished, as they soon will be, and as soon as we are better known among those great pools of human resources in Europe, with land being offered under favorable conditions and with the continuation of peace amongst us, immigrants will favor our country in compact masses which, no matter how large, will find ample space and generous compensation for their labor." *Mensaje* of May, 1883, pp. 31-32.

If we maintain slavery and if the Argentine republic remains at peace, within twenty years the latter will be a stronger, more advanced, and more prosperous nation than Brazil, and its growth and the nature of its progress and its institutions will exercise upon our southernmost provinces the effect of a separatist attraction which will perhaps be irresistible.

slaves and *ingênuos,* does not amount to more than 1.5 million persons, we have a free population six times that large. If the result of emancipation were—and it could not possibly be—to destroy our huge production of export commodities, and if the country were to pass through a crisis involving its sources of national income, even this would be a minor problem compared to the present situation which, if it does not already constitute insolvency masked or postponed by loans, borders on insolvency and will undoubtedly lead to bankruptcy if slavery endures. Slavery deprived us of the habit of working to feed ourselves, but it did not deprive us of the instinct or the need to preserve ourselves, and this will drive us toward a reassertion of our diminished vitality.

If, on the other hand, slavery should be unavoidably prolonged for the entire time left to it under present law, Brazilians educated in the liberal principles of this century ought then to seek another homeland. For slavery (and this is the firm belief of all those who fight against it), instead of moving us forward, holds us back. Instead of bringing progress and expansion, it impedes the spontaneous development of the country. To allow it to dissolve itself and to disappear bit by bit, as its supporters intend, is to retain a seed of permanent moral rot in the heart of the society for two more generations, making servility and the exploitation of man by man endemic in the entire country for a long time to come.

What this system represents we already know. Morally it is the destruction of every basis and principle of religious or positive decency—the family, property, social harmony, humanitarian aspirations. Politically it is slavishness, the degradation of the people, the disease of bureaucratism, the languishing of patriotism, the division of the countryside into feudal domains, each with its own penal system, its own seat of judgment, beyond the reach of police and courts. Economically and socially it is the temporary prosperity of one class alone, and this class decadent and constantly in a state of renewal. It is the elimination of accumulated capital through the purchase of slaves, the paralyzation of each potential separate unit of national labor, the closing of our ports to immigrants who look to South America, the exaggeration of the social importance of money however acquired, contempt for all those whose scruples make them unfit to engage in our materialistic competition or cause them to fall behind in that competition. It is the sale of noble titles, the demoralization of authority from the highest to the lowest level, the inability of persons worthy of leading their country toward a higher destiny to rise to authority because of the people's reluctance to support their defenders, their disloyalty to those who sacrifice themselves on their behalf. And the nation, in the midst of all this demeaning of character, of honest labor, of quiet virtues, of poverty which would rise above its condition with clean hands, is, as was said of the southern states, "enamoured of her shame." [8]

Not everything, certainly, in this sad business of slavery is entirely discouraging. Today, fortunately, everywhere we turn we see signs that manumission of slaves has become associated with Brazilian patriotism and constitutes the main event in family and public celebrations. From 1873 until today, 87,005 manumissions have been inscribed in our official records, and though it is impossible to estimate the capital represented by this figure, not knowing the condition or ages of the freedmen, it is a lofty token of the generous character of the Brazilian people. This is especially so since it is the cities, where slave property is very much divided up among many poor families, which stand out prominently in the emancipation lists, and not the countryside, where the great rural factories exist. In the capital of the Empire, for example, with a slave population of 54,167 in this decade, while death eliminated 8,000, public and private liberality freed 10,000; whereas in the province of Rio de Janeiro, with a slave population of 332,949 during the same period, death lowered the registration figures by 51,269, while only 12,849 were freed. In other words, in the nation's capital Brazilian generosity keeps up with death, but in the province of Rio de Janeiro death reaps four times faster than generosity.

However proud we may be of having registered 87,005 manumissions in ten years, we should not forget that in that same period in the province of Rio de Janeiro alone 124,000 slaves were shifted in and out of the various counties. This means that transactions involving the purchase and sale of human property overshadow the value of the liberations granted. Furthermore, in the entire country, whereas 70,183 slaves were liberated between 1873 and 1882, 132,777, or nearly twice that many, died in bondage. But when death, which is an inert and unthinking force, eliminates two while the nation eliminates one, the latter accomplishes ten or twenty times less than the former, which lacks

---

8. *Times,* London, January 7, 1861.

interest in the problem being resolved, which owes no debt of honor.

Above all, let Brazilians consider that immense slave population which exceeds 1.2 million, and let them think of the *owners* of those people. Let them think of those who die and those who are born either to be reared as slaves or to be educated as *masters;* then let them decide whether these 2 million individual Brazilians ought to be delivered over to slavery at this late date so it can torture some until they die and corrupt others from their infancy. And let them decide whether the remaining Brazilian millions should continue to be the clients or servants of an interest which repels them, whether they should be made to live under a universal and compulsory system of slavery which has become an *imperium in imperio.*

Thus it has always been everywhere. "As rivers glisten in different colors, but a common sewer everywhere looks like itself," writes Mommsen, studying the unchangeable picture of ancient slavery, "so the Italy of the Ciceronian epoch resembles substantially the Hellas of Polybius and still more decidedly the Carthage of Hannibal's time, where in exactly similar fashion the all-powerful rule of capital ruined the middle class, raised trade and estate-farming to the highest prosperity, and ultimately led to a hypocritically whitewashed moral and political corruption of the nation." It is this very same institution, burdened with all of History's sins, now eliminated from Asia and Europe, stamped out in North America, banned by the human conscience and about to be looked upon as piracy, which now seeks in Brazil a haven and implores us to permit it to die a natural death, that is, by nourishing itself on the last 1.5 million victims still remaining to it in the civilized world.

What are we then to do? What do those who have acquired the right to counsel suggest to the country, which until today has been manservant of that diabolical spirit, but which now begins to repudiate that dishonorable tutelage? What is the advice of the Church, whose bishops are silent while witnessing the open slave markets? What is the advice of the press, the academies, the men of letters, the professors of law, the educators of youth, all the caretakers of the people's moral health? What are the views of the poets, to whom Castro Alves clearly demonstrated that in a slave country the mission of the poets is to combat slavery? What is the advice of youth, for whom Ferreira de Meneses and Manuel Pedro—to speak of the dead alone—may be singled out as examples of how fruitful talent can be when fertilized by freedom?

What is the advice, finally, of two men, each of whom has the duty to lead the people? One of these, Mr. Saraiva, wrote in 1868: "With human slavery and expansion of the right to vote we will remain what we are today, scorned by a civilized world which cannot understand how Brazil can progress so slowly with a nature so rich," and declared in 1873: "The great injustice of the law is that it did not attend to the present generations." The other is the heir to the name and blood of José Bonifacio, in whose mind must resound the last words of the *Memoir Addressed to the Constituent Assembly* as an irresistible call from beyond the grave, whose political career will be judged by history as that of an eloquent sophist if he does not put the sentiments of justice, liberty, and equality, which he tried to awaken in us, above the interests of the owners of human beings in São Paulo.[9]

Considering all the influences which are hastening slavery's end, it is my firm conviction that if we do not recommit ourselves each day to ever greater efforts toward the total liberation of our land, if we do not constantly keep before us the thought that slavery is the principal cause of all our vices, defects, dangers, and national weaknesses, its remaining period of legality will be characterized by growing symptoms of social dissolution. Who can say that the historian of the future will not see fit to apply to us one of the following statements: first, that of Ewald concerning Judea, "The total overthrow of the ancient kingdom was necessary before an end could be put to a slavery which no one was able to take any further steps to banish"; [10] or, even worse, that of Goldwin Smith about the United States, "The Christian States of North America have tampered with Slavery for Empire and for the pride of a great Confederacy; and they have paid the penalty, first, in the poison which the domination of the slave-owner has spread through their political and social system, and, secondly, in this dreadful and disastrous war." [11]

---

9. *Translator's note:* José Bonifacio de Andrada e Silva the Younger was the great-grandson and namesake of the patriarch of Brazilian independence. As a professor at the Law Academy of São Paulo, he took an antislavery stand in the years prior to passage of the Rio Branco Law and greatly influenced such young liberal students as Antônio de Castro Alves, Rui Barbosa, and Nabuco himself.

10. Heinrich Ewald, *The Antiquities of Israel* (London, 1876), p. 215.

11. Goldwin Smith, *Does the Bible Sanction American Slavery?* (Cambridge, 1863), pp. 106-107.

With her banner still stained by slavery, any war that Brazil might wage against a free people would instinctively set the world's liberal sympathies against her. Thus, because of the existence of slave markets which no one has the courage to close, a nation of great native intelligence, free of the plague of political militarism and of the South American wars, gentle and soft of heart, peaceful and generous, would be considered more reactionary and backward than other countries which do not possess the same intellectual and cultural development, the same selflessness, or the same spirit of democracy and equality.

I wrote this book thinking of Brazil, and only of Brazil, without hatred or resentment, and without detecting in myself a conscious speck of that envy toward anyone which, according to Antônio Carlos, is "the main ingredient of our souls." I attacked abuses, vices, and practices. I denounced an entire system, and for this I have offended those who identify themselves with it. One cannot, however, struggle against an interest of the magnitude and character of slavery without defining what it is. The masters are the first to recognize, as I do, the nature of the institution with whose destiny their fortunes are entangled. The difference between them and myself is that I believe that a national system thus unanimously condemned must not be allowed to survive any longer, since it is leading the country further and further toward ruin; and they, on the other hand, call for a permanent legal respect for this institution.

End slavery, have the courage to eliminate it, and it will be seen that the abolitionists are struggling on behalf of agriculture itself, on behalf of the solvent farmers, it being recognized that even slavery will not rescue the bankrupt except at the cost of transferring their lands and slaves to others, of eliminating themselves, that is, as farmers. If, on the other hand, instead of being heroically, patriotically, and gallantly suppressed with the help of many enlightened proprietors who, recognizing the rights of human nature, dare to renounce, in the words of Victor Schoelcher, "their intelligent property," the present system should continue to weaken and corrupt the country, bringing it to the edge of social dissolution, the future unfortunately will justify our despair, our patriotic anxiety, the humiliation and pain which the postponement of abolition arouses in us.

I analyzed with care some of the many effects which slavery exercises in opposition to the physical development of our country. No sincere person will question the cause of those effects or the vital importance of the diagnosis. Slavery sought in every way to identify itself with the nation, and in the minds of many people it succeeded. To attack the black flag is to outrage the country. To denounce the regimen of the slave huts is to disgrace all Brazil. By a curious theory, every Brazilian is responsible for slavery, and there is no way for us to wash our hands of the slaves' blood. Not to be the owners of slaves does not by itself make us innocent of the crime. Whoever was born with this original sin finds no cleansing baptism.

All Brazilians are responsible for slavery, according to that theory, because they have all consented to it. It is not explained, however, how the Brazilian who personally rejects it can destroy it, or how the victims of a system which insults them for not reacting against it can be blamed for the moral paralysis which has struck them. The Neapolitans were thus responsible for Bourbonism, the Romans for the temporal power, the Polish for the reign of the czars, and the New Christians for the Inquisition. But supported by fact or not, this is the opinion of many. And, therefore, when slavery comes under attack in the most respected havens where it has sought refuge, in its intermingling with everything the nation holds most dear—when it is wounded, so to speak, in the arms of Mother Brazil herself—then the cry of *Treason* is loudly raised against the abolitionist movement!

"I do not know what a public writer can accomplish which is better than to point out the faults of his fellow countrymen. If to do this is to be considered anti-national, I do not wish to avoid the accusation." [12] For my part, I echo these words of Stuart Mill. The contrary, perhaps, would be a safer road to follow because of our national inclination, which demands indulgence and sympathy from others just as our virgin forests require humidity. But no writer of conscience who hopes to serve his country, to arouse its better instincts, would take that humiliating path of adulation. The superstition of the people's infallibility and the belief that all history is a contradiction are not needed to establish democracy's law, which amounts to the following: Nobody has the right to decide for the people or to impose standards upon them.

Concerning the motherland, which we are accused of mutilating, it is difficult to define exactly what it is. The motherland

---

12. *Translator's note:* The original English source for this quotation could not be located. The quotation as it appears here is a retranslation made from Nabuco's Portuguese translation.

is different for every man. For the Alsatian it is to be found in the soil, in the *montes patrios et incunabula nostra.* For the Jew it is fundamentally the race, for the Moslem the religion, for the Pole his nationality, for the immigrant prosperity and freedom, as for the Confederate soldier it was the right to possess his own institutions. "Brazil" does not signify this generation alone, nor can it hope to deify itself, to become the motherland of us all, who envision another ideal. Antônio Carlos was accused of having turned his back upon his country when he advised Britain to cover our coasts with ships in order to blockade the pirates' nests of Rio de Janeiro and Bahia,[13] but who is unaware today that he, according to his own phrase, *passed on to posterity as the avenger of Brazil's honor and dignity?*

Rather than harming the country by demonstrating that everything about her which is vicious, weak, indecisive, and primitive springs from slavery, it might appear that in this way I hoped to convert this isolated, all-absorbing institution into a scapecoat, to load slavery down with all the people's sins and suffer it to escape with those sins into the wilderness. National pride always tries to keep at hand such expiatory victims. It is better if they are individuals, but repentance is regarded as more complete if they are families or classes or even an entire government.

My conscience, nevertheless, does not accuse me of having promised the millennium on the day when Brazil celebrates her Hebraic jubilee, liberating all her slaves. Slavery is an evil which no longer requires new sources in order to poison our blood, which today can dispense with the relationship between master and slave, since it has already injected itself into the national bloodstream. It is not, therefore, by the simple emancipation of the slaves and *ingênuos* that this infection, for which the national organism acquired such an affinity, will be destroyed.

In my view—and this can be repeated, since it is the fundamental point of this book—the emancipation of the slaves and the *ingênuos* is only the beginning of our work. When there are no more slaves, all of us who today find ourselves divided into different camps can begin to fight slavery together, united by pervasive material concerns.

Only after the slaves and the *masters* are liberated from the yoke which makes them equally incapable of a free existence can we undertake that serious program of reforms among which

---

13. A. C. Tavares Bastos, *Cartas do solitario,* Letter IX.

those that can be established through legislation, despite their immense importance, are insignificant alongside those which must be accomplished by the people, by means of education, fellowship, the newspapers, voluntary immigration, an improved religious life, a new vision of the state; reforms which cannot be achieved all at once, in the public plaza, to the cheers of the crowd, but which if a strong, intelligent, patriotic, and free people is to result from them will have to be executed day by day and night by night, without fanfare, anonymously, in the secret daily routine of our lives, in the privacy of the family, with no other acclaim or compensation but those of a strengthened, moralized, and disciplined conscience, at once virile and humane.

This personal reform, this reform of ourselves, of our character, of our patriotism, of our attitudes toward civic responsibilities, is the only way slavery can be effectively dislodged from our social constitution. The emancipation of the slaves is therefore only the beginning of a Brazilian *Rinnovamento,* for which we still lack our Gioberti, and, after him, our Cavour.[14]

Compare the Brazil of today and its slavery with the ideal of a motherland which we, the abolitionists, uphold. The latter is a country where all are free, where European immigration, attracted by the openness of our institutions and by the freedom of our system, will endlessly send to the tropics a current of lively, energetic, and healthy Caucasian blood which we can absorb without danger, instead of that Chinese wave with which the large landholders hope to contaminate and corrupt our race even further. What we wish is a country which may work in her own unique way for the good of humanity and the development of South America.

This is the justification of the abolitionist movement. Among those who have contributed to it, it is still too early to pass out laurels, and the wish of us all should be that at the eleventh hour the mass of contributors will be so great that later it will not be possible to distinguish one from another. In order to fight the new idea, our opponents need to take aim at individuals whose personalities have nothing to do with the problem they are debating. For this reason alone, we should everywhere

---

14. *Translator's note:* Nabuco refers to Vincenzo Gioberti, an Italian political philosopher, and Cammillo Benso Cavour, an Italian statesman, and their roles in the struggle for Italian independence and unification.

struggle with principles, and not names, inscribed upon our banner. None of us can aspire to personal glory, because at the end of the nineteenth century there is no glory for men educated in the ideas and the intellectual culture of an epoch as advanced as ours in requesting the emancipation of the slaves. If some among us should have the power to touch the people's sentiments and imagination enough to arouse them from their lethargy, they should remember that they did not rise to their present prominence except on a ladder held erect by the support of youth, by the workers in our cause, and by the slaves themselves, and that the nation's shame motivated them to stand out as speechmakers or as journalists or as liberators above the dark abyss of their country immersed in slavery. For this reason they should hope for the disappearance of this distinction as quickly as possible. What makes us conspicuous today is the nation's grief. Whatever the present talent, dedication, enthusiasm, and sacrifices of the abolitionists, our most ardent desire should be to cease being symbols, that the effects of time may even erase the memory of the struggle in which we are now engaged.

Forgetfulness of the past, the eradication of slavery from the human memory, the reconciliation of every class, the moralization of every interest, an assurance of free contracts, order emanating from the voluntary cooperation of all members of Brazilian society—these are the necessary conditions for reforms which will elevate the political ground on which that society has existed until today. The moral stratum that we represent is the residue of a time long gone. The Brazilian people need a new environment, an entirely different atmosphere in which to develop and grow.

None of the great national causes which produced as their heroes the greatest spirits of humanity ever had better reason to exist than ours. Let every true Brazilian become the instrument of that cause. Let the young people, from the moment when they accept the responsibilities of citizenship, swear to abstain from the purchase of human flesh. Let them prefer an obscure career of honest labor to amassing wealth by means of the inexpressible suffering of other human beings. Let them educate their children —indeed, let them educate themselves—to enjoy the freedom of others without which their own liberty will be a chance gift of destiny. Let them acquire the knowledge that freedom is worth possessing, and let them attain the courage to defend it.

The positions, the sinecures open to men in our society have fallen beneath our dignity, and thus the greatest usefulness that the Brazilian of intellectual and moral value can have is to expound opinion (pleased that he has acquired the strength to do so) , providing an example of indifference to honors, distinctions, and debased titles, to positions without real power. Those who regard themselves as sufficiently strong, intelligent, and honorable to serve their country in the most useful way, let them forsake that self-seeking path of political ambition. Let them give themselves body and soul to the work of popularizing the principles which make modern nations strong, happy, and respected, through the press, the book, the public meeting, the word, the school. Let them spread the news seeds of freedom across an entire land now covered by *dragonseeds* (Mommsen) . And then that past whose collapse we are now witnessing will give way to an order of things founded upon an entirely different concept of our duties toward life, property, the individual, the family, personal rights, honor, and individual integrity. That past will make way for a society in which there is a new regard for our fellowman, for the individual before the nation, for personal freedom, for civilization, for equal legal protection, for established social achievements, for humanity itself, which inspires us with the will to participate in this immense heritage of our species, which in fact tacitly delivers this heritage over to the protection of each one of us.

The abolitionists include all those who believe in a Brazil without slaves, all those who anticipate the miracles of free labor, all those who suffer *slavery* as a detested vassalage imposed upon the entire nation by some and in the interests of some. They include those who now gasp in the foul air which slaves and masters freely breathe—those who do not believe that Brazil, with slavery gone, will lie down to die, as did the Roman in the age of the Caesars because he had lost his liberty.

This means that we are seeking our country's highest interests, her civilization, the future rightfully hers, the mission to which her place in America calls her. But, between us and those who are blocking the path, who will win? This, indeed, is the very enigma of Brazil's national destiny. Slavery injected fanaticism into her bloodstream, and she is now doing nothing to grasp control of her fate from those blind and indifferent forces which now silently lead her on.

SUGGESTIONS FOR FURTHER READING

FOR THE READER generally unfamiliar with modern Brazil, Charles Wagley's *An Introduction to Brazil,* rev. ed. (New York: Columbia University Press, 1971), is a good beginning. Two good single-volume histories of Brazil are Rollie E. Poppino's *Brazil, the Land and People* (New York: Oxford University Press, 1968) and E. Bradford Burns's *A History of Brazil* (New York: Columbia University Press, 1970). An outstanding study of colonial Brazil with brilliant insights into slavery and other social and economic issues is Caio Prado, Jr., *The Colonial Background of Modern Brazil* (Berkeley: University of California Press, 1967). Also of great value are C. R. Boxer's studies of colonial Brazil: *The Golden Age of Brazil, 1695-1750* (Berkeley: University of California Press, 1964), *Salvador de Sá and the Struggle for Brazil and Angola, 1602-1686* (London: Athlone Press, 1952), and *The Dutch in Brazil, 1624-1654* (Oxford: Clarendon Press, 1957). Useful studies of colonial Brazil which deal with aspects of slavery are Kenneth R. Maxwell, *Conflicts and Conspiracies: Brazil and Portugal, 1750-1808* (Cambridge: Cambridge University Press, 1973) and A. J. R. Russell-Wood, *Fidalgos and Philanthropists: The Santa Casa da Misericordia of Bahia, 1550-1775* (Berkeley: University of California Press, 1968). A valuable account of the sixteenth-century enslavement of Indians in Brazil by the Portuguese is Alexander Marchant's *From Barter to Slavery* (Baltimore: Johns Hopkins University Press, 1942).

Basic studies bearing on nineteenth-century Brazil with some references to slavery and the slave trade include Alan K. Manchester, *British Preeminence in Brazil, Its Rise and Decline* (Chapel Hill: University of North Carolina Press, 1933); Mary Wilhelmine Williams, *Dom Pedro the Magnanimous* (Chapel Hill: University of North Carolina Press, 1937); C. H. Haring,

Empire in Brazil (Cambridge: Harvard University Press, 1958) ;
Gilberto Freyre, *The Mansions and the Shanties* (New York:
Alfred A. Knopf, 1968) ; Richard Graham, *Britain and the Onset
of Modernization in Brazil, 1850-1914* (Cambridge: Cambridge
University Press, 1968) ; and Peter L. Eisenberg's excellent *The
Sugar Industry of Pernambuco: Modernization without Change,
1840-1910* (Berkeley: University of California Press, 1973) .

Many studies of Brazilian slavery exist. Among the best of the
early ones is Agostinho Marques Perdigão Malheiro's massive
and brilliant *A escravidão no Brasil: ensaio histórico-juridico-
social*, 3 vols. (Rio de Janeiro, 1866-67) ; reprint ed., 2 vols. (São
Paulo: Edições Cultura, 1944) . An early attack on slavery often
referred to by Nabuco in this book is José Bonifacio de Andrada
e Silva's *Memoir Addressed to the General Constituent and
Legislative Assembly of the Empire of Brazil, on Slavery* (London, 1826) . Later nineteenth-century works of value are Frederico L. C. Burlamaque's *Analytica acerca do commercio
d'escravos e acerca dos malles da escravidão domestica* (Rio de
Janeiro, 1837) ; A. C. Tavares Bastos's *Cartas do solitario* (1862;
reprint ed., São Paulo: Companhia Editora Nacional, 1938) ;
*Agricultura nacional. Estudos economicos. Propaganda aboli-
cionista e democratica*, by Nabuco's friend and fellow abolitionist, André Rebouças; and L. Anselmo da Fonseca's *A escravidão,
o clero e o abolicionismo* (Bahia, 1887) .

European and North American travelers in Brazil were in-
trigued by slavery and rarely resisted writing about what they
saw. Among the best accounts by such nineteenth-century visitors
are Henry Koster's *Travels in Brazil* (London, 1816) ; John
Luccock's *Notes on Rio de Janeiro and the Southern Parts of
Brazil Taken During a Residence of Ten Years in that Country
from 1808 to 1818* (London, 1820) ; Maria Graham's *Journal of
a Voyage to Brazil and Residence There During Part of the
Years 1821, 1822, 1823* (London, 1824) ; Robert Walsh's *Notices
of Brazil in 1828 and 1829*, 2 vols. (London, 1830) ; Jean Baptiste
Debret's magnificently illustrated *Voyage pittoresque et his-
torique au Brésil*, 3 vols. (Paris, 1834-39) ; Thomas Nelson's
Remarks on Slavery and Slave Trade of the Brazils (London,
1846) ; Thomas Ewbank's *Life in Brazil* (New York, 1856) ;
J. C. Fletcher and Daniel P. Kidder's *Brazil and the Brazilians*
(Philadelphia, 1857) ; William D. Christie's *Notes on Brazilian
Questions* (London, 1865) ; and *Recollections of My Life*, 3

vols. (London, 1868) by the Emperor of Mexico, Maximilian I.
Many twentieth-century studies of slavery and race relations
exist. Among these are Evaristo de Moraes's *A escravidão afri-
cana no Brasil* (São Paulo: Companhia Editora Nacional, 1933) ;
João Dornas Filho's *A escravidão no Brasil* (Rio de Janeiro:
Civilização Brasileira, 1939) ; Gilberto Freyre's *The Masters and
the Slaves* (New York: Alfred A. Knopf, 1946) ; Maurilio de
Gouveia's *História da escravidão* (Rio de Janeiro: Gráfica Tupy,
1955) ; Raymond S. Sayers's *The Negro in Brazilian Literature*
(New York: Hispanic Institute in the United States, 1956) ; and
Stanley J. Stein's classic *Vassouras, A Brazilian Coffee County,
1850-1900* (Cambridge: Harvard University Press, 1957). Other
useful studies are Roger Bastide and Florestan Fernandes,
Brancos e negros em São Paulo, 2d ed. (São Paulo: Companhia
Editora Nacional, 1959) ; Fernando Henrique Cardoso and Oc-
tavio Ianni, *Côr e mobilidade social em Florianópolis* (São
Paulo: Companhia Editora Nacional, 1960); Fernando Henrique
Cardoso, *Capitalismo e escravidão no Brasil meridional* (São
Paulo: Difusão Européia do Livro, 1962) ; Gilberto Freyre, *O
escravo nos anúncios de jornais brasileiros no século xix* (Recife:
Imprensa Universitaria, 1963) ; Marvin Harris, *Patterns of Race
in the Americas* (New York: Walker, 1964) ; Edison Carneiro,
Ladinos e crioulos: Estudos sôbre o negro no Brasil (Rio de
Janeiro: Civilização Brasileira, 1964) ; José Honório Rodrigues,
Brazil and Africa (Berkeley: University of California Press,
1965) ; Thomas E. Skidmore, *Black into White: Race and Nationality in Brazilian Thought* (New York: Oxford University
Press, 1974) ; Warren Dean, *Rio Claro: A Brazilian Plantation
System, 1820-1920* (Stanford: Stanford University Press, 1976) ;
and Florestan Fernandes, *The Negro in Brazilian Society* (New
York: Columbia University Press, 1969), a major contribution
to our understanding of modern Brazilian race relations. Two
recent studies of Brazilian slavery are Vincente Salles, *O negro
no Pará* (Rio de Janeiro: Fundação Getúlio Vargas, 1971) ; and
José Alipio Goulart, *Da palmatória ao patíbulo: Castigos de
escravos no Brasil* (Rio de Janeiro: Conquista, 1971). A particularly valuable synthesis of present knowledge of Brazilian slavery
and race relations is Carl N. Degler's *Neither Black nor White*
(New York: Macmillan, 1971). For a comprehensive bibliography of slavery and abolition, see Robert Conrad, *Brazilian
Slavery: An Annotated Research Bibliography* (Boston: G. K.
Hall, 1977).

The slave trade to Brazil and its abolition have been dealt with in Mauricio Goulart, *Escravidão africana no Brasil* (São Paulo: Livraria Martins, 1949) ; Leslie Bethell, *The Abolition of the Brazilian Slave Trade* (Cambridge: At the University Press, 1970) ; Pierre Verger, *Flux et reflux de la traite des nègres entre le Golfe de Bénin et Bahia de Todos os Santos* (Paris: Mouton, 1968) ; and Philip D. Curtin, *The Atlantic Slave Trade: A Census* (Madison: University of Wisconsin Press, 1969). Some basic works on the abolitionist struggle include Evaristo de Moraes's pioneering *A campanha abolicionista (1879-1888)* (Rio de Janeiro: Livraria Editora Leite Ribeiro, 1924) ; Raimundo Girão's study of the movement in the province of Ceará, *A abolição no Ceará* (Fortaleza: Editora A. Batista Fontenele, 1956) ; Octavio Ianni's analysis of the conversion to free labor in the southern province of Paraná, *As metamorfoses do escravo: Apogeu e crise da escravatura no Brasil meridional* (São Paulo: Difusão Européia do Livro, 1962) ; Emília Viotti da Costa's admirable *Da senzala à colônia* (São Paulo: Difusão Européia do Livro, 1966) ; and two recent works, Robert Brent Toplin's *The Abolition of Slavery in Brazil* (New York: Atheneum, 1972) and Robert Conrad's *The Destruction of Brazilian Slavery, 1850-1888* (Berkeley: University of California Press, 1972).

Valuable books on slavery and race relations in other countries of the Americas include Frederick P. Bowser, *The African Slave in Colonial Peru, 1524-1650* (Stanford: Stanford University Press, 1974) ; David Brion Davis, *The Problem of Slavery in Western Culture* (Ithaca: Cornell University Press, 1966) ; Gwendolyn Midlo Hall, *Social Control in Slave Plantation Societies: A Comparison of St. Domingue and Cuba* (Baltimore: Johns Hopkins University Press, 1971) ; H. Hoetink, *The Two Variants in Caribbean Race Relations* (London: Oxford University Press, 1967) ; Franklin W. Knight, *Slave Society in Cuba during the Nineteenth Century* (Madison: University of Wisconsin Press, 1970) ; and John V. Lombardi, *The Decline and Abolition of Negro Slavery in Venezuela, 1820-1854* (Westport, Conn.: Greenwood Press, 1971).

Four recent and well-selected collections of articles on slavery in Latin Ameria are: David W. Cohen and Jack P. Green, *Neither Slave Nor Free: The Freedmen of African Descent in the Slave Societies of the New World* (Baltimore: Johns Hopkins University Press, 1972) ; Laura Foner and Eugene D. Genovese, *Slavery in the New World* (Englewood Cliffs, N.J.:

Prentice-Hall, 1969) ; Robert Brent Toplin, *Slavery and Race Relations in Latin America* (Westport, Conn.: Greenwood Press, 1974) ; and Ann M. Pescatello, *The African in Latin America* (New York: Alfred A. Knopf, 1975).

The study of Joaquim Nabuco's abundant writings has been facilitated by Osvaldo Melo Braga's *Bibliografia de Joaquim Nabuco* (Rio de Janeiro: Imprensa Nacional, 1952), which lists both published and unpublished works as well as speeches, articles, letters, and sources useful for the study of his political, reformist, literary, and diplomatic activities. The best biography of Nabuco is *The Life of Joaquim Nabuco* by Carolina Nabuco, his talented daughter, trans. and ed. Ronald Hilton (Stanford: Stanford University Press, 1950). A brief survey of Nabuco's life and career is contained in Ronald Hilton's *Joaquim Nabuco e a civilização anglo-americana* (Rio de Janeiro: Instituto Brasil-Estados Unidos, 1949). Another useful study is Olimpio de Souza Andrade's *Joaquim Nabuco e o Pan-Americanismo* (São Paulo: Companhia Editora Nacional, 1950).

Among Nabuco's most significant writings on slavery, aside from the present work, are: *Manifesto da Sociedade Brasileira contra a Escravidão* (Rio de Janeiro, 1880) ; *Campanha abolicionista no Recife (Eleições de 1884): Discursos de Joaquim Nabuco* (Rio de Janeiro, 1885) ; *O eclypse do abolicionismo* (Rio de Janeiro, 1886) ; and "A escravidão," a work written in 1870 and published at last in 1949 in *Revista do Instituto Histórico e Geográfico Brasileiro* 204. Many of Nabuco's other works have been assembled in his *Obras completas,* published by the Instituto Progresso Editorial (São Paulo, 1947-49). These include the following works, all published in 1949: the political biography of his father, *Um estadista do Império, Nabuco de Araújo,* 4 vols.; his equally important autobiography, *Minha formação; Escritos e discursos literarios; Discursos parlamentares, 1879-1889; Pensamentos soltos: Camões e assuntos americanos; Campanhas de imprensa, 1884-1887;* and his revealing *Cartas a amigos,* 2 vols.